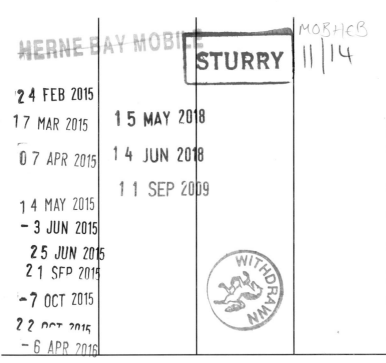
Please return on or before the latest date above.
You can renew online at *www.kent.gov.uk/libs*
or by telephone 08458 247 200

636.300

CUSTOMER SERVICE EXCELLENCE

Libraries & Archives

00884\DTP\RN\07.07   LIB 7

THE YORKSHIRE SHEPHERDESS

Amanda Owen has been seen by millions on ITV's *The Dales*, living a life that has almost gone in today's modern world, a life ruled by the seasons and her animals. She is a farmer's wife and shepherdess living alongside her husband Clive and seven children at Ravenseat, a 2000-acre sheep hill farm at the head of Swaledale in North Yorkshire. It's a challenging life but one she loves.

THE YORKSHIRE
SHEPHERDESS

THE YORKSHIRE SHEPHERDESS

by

Amanda Owen

Magna Large Print Books
Long Preston, North Yorkshire,
BD23 4ND, England.

British Library Cataloguing in Publication Data.

Owen, Amanda
 The Yorkshire shepherdess.

 A catalogue record of this book is
 available from the British Library

 ISBN   978-0-7505-4010-0

First published in Great Britain in 2014 by Sidgwick & Jackson
an imprint of Pan Macmillan,
a division of Macmillan Publishers Limited

Cover illustration by arrangement with Macmillan Publishers Ltd.

Picture credits: all photographs courtesy of Amanda Owen
except for cream teas illustration © Stuart Howart.

Published in Large Print 2014 by arrangement with
Macmillan Publishers, trading as Pan Macmillan Publishers Ltd.

Magna Large Print is an imprint of Library Magna Books Ltd.

Printed and bound in Great Britain by
T.J. (International) Ltd., Cornwall, PL28 8RW

To my family

Contents

Introduction

Introduction

'Will you take the trailer and fetch a tup from a mate of mine? He's a right good Swaledale breeder, and he lends me a tup every year.'

It was a normal enough request from the farmer I was working for. A tup is a ram, and he needed to put one in with his sheep, for obvious reasons. He helped me hitch an old trailer on to the back of his pickup, and off I went, with only minimal directions, and worried about whether the pickup and trailer would make it.

It was October 1996, chilly and dark as I drove along the road from Kirkby Stephen, heading across the border of Cumbria and Yorkshire into Swaledale, peering through the murk to spot a sign to the farm where his friend lived. I was used to farm signs that are nothing more than a piece of wood someone has scrawled the name on, so as the road unwound and switchbacked through the dark hills, I began to think I must have missed it. But I hadn't passed any turnings: this was as remote as you could get.

Then there it was, a good clear road sign picked up in the truck headlights, RAVENSEAT ONLY, 1¼ MILES. I turned up the narrow road, the rickety wooden trailer bouncing behind, the headlights occasionally picking up sheep staring fixedly towards me. *Better not run over one of his sheep before I get there*, I thought.

At last, after what seemed like an age, I came to a dead stop. With no warning, I had reached a ford. I wasn't risking driving the low-slung pickup with its rusty doors through the stream, but a quick paddle in my wellies showed the water was only up to my ankles. The pickup plunged through the ford and up into a muddy farmyard, with a farmhouse to my right and some ancient stone barns ahead of me. In the dim light over a stable door I could see a cow chewing her cud, and within a second of me arriving a barking sheepdog emerged from the darkness. Experience has taught me to be wary of territorial farm dogs, so I was relieved when a pool of light spilled from the front door and the farmer came out.

'Ga an' lie down.'

I assumed the command was not for me and, sure enough, the dog slunk away back into the shadows.

'Away in, mi lass, and I'll get t'kettle on.'

There was no great feeling that I'd met my destiny; no instant romantic attraction. I was just relieved to have made it, in need of a cup of tea, and anxious to get on with the hair-raising return journey.

But looking back, with a marriage and seven children to our credit, I can see that this was the defining moment in my life. This was when I met two of the things I love most: Clive Owen, my husband, and Ravenseat Farm, the most beautiful place on earth.

I really mean it when I say it is beautiful. Yes, it's bleak, it's remote, the wind howls round it, driving rain into the very fabric of the building.

The snow piles up in winter and when the electricity and the water are off we live like those farmers who built the place, all those centuries ago, carrying water from the river and cooking over an open fire. But it's the best place in the world to rear children and animals, and I wouldn't swap it for anything. Even now, after years of living here, there are moments when I catch my breath at the splendour of the place.

But life here is no idyll. We work hard to keep our animals and our children safe and healthy in this challenging environment.

For most hill farmers, it's a traditional way of life, one they were born into. But me? I'm a townie. An 'offcumden', or incomer. When I talked to the careers teachers at the large comprehensive in Huddersfield where I went to school, 'shepherdess' and 'farmer' were not options that came up.

So how did I find my way here, to the highest, most remote farm in Swaledale, the most northerly of the Yorkshire dales?

This is the story of me, my family and, in a starring role, Ravenseat itself.

1

A Normal Childhood

If I had to choose one word to describe my childhood, it would be 'normal'. I was born in Huddersfield, in September 1974, the first child of Joyce and Maurice Livingstone. Huddersfield grew big around the wool-weaving mills that sprang up during the industrial revolution. A small woollen industry survives but, like so many northern towns, the main focus has gone. Still, it is a thriving, busy place.

They were happy days. Our semi-detached house had been built at the turn of the century. It had a substantial garage, a front and back garden and a steep driveway leading down onto a busy road. One of my earliest memories is of pedalling up and down the drive on my three-wheeler bike, which became unstable when cornering at speed. I crashed into one of the big stone pillars at the gateway and knocked four front teeth out. Luckily, they were my first teeth, so no lasting damage. On several occasions I was precipitated into the laurel bushes, and once I remember being skewered by the thorns of a vicious rose. I also had a succession of roller skates, go-karts and scooters, but the downside of living at the top of quite a steep hill meant that outings would often end in tumbles and tears. To a small child there seemed to be lots of places to play, although, of course, when I've been back it all seems much smaller than it is in my memories.

My first school was Stile Common Infants, an old Victorian building a short walk from home. It was a multiracial school, and I grew up with Asian, black and white friends. At seven I transferred into the more modern Stile Common Juniors, but kept my same circle of friends.

When I was six my sister Katie was born, an event I can only vaguely remember. I do recall my secret trick to pacify her when she was fractious. I would reach through the bars of the cot and pluck Katie's dummy from her, then nip downstairs to the kitchen. By standing on a lidded yellow bucket in which her nappies were soaking, I could reach a jar of honey and dip the dummy into it, scooping up a big sticky blob. Then I'd pop the honeyed dummy back into Katie's mouth. Mother thought that I had some kind of magic touch. But it was only a matter of time before I was found out: the lid of the bucket caved in one day, the contents sloshed across the kitchen floor and the smell of bleach pervaded the house.

Father was an engineer, working at the famous David Brown factory which made tractors and tanks. He spent as much of his spare time as he could in our garage at home, repairing motorbikes, which was his passion. However, he had the ability and knowhow to be able to fix anything, whether it was a sausage machine from a factory or a refrigeration unit at a local supermarket.

Father's family had all had motorbikes when they were young, and he had won many trophies for road racing and trialling. He had a number of bikes, some entire, others in pieces. His pride and joy was his blue metallic Honda, but his Norton road bike with its wide square seat was my favourite, not least because I felt more secure when riding pillion. I would cling on to him, my arms wrapped round his greasy Belstaff coat while he drove rather cautiously – I suspect on instruction from my mother, who was understandably worried for my safety. Sooner or later it was bound to happen: I was eight or nine when I took a backwards tumble off a trials bike at Post Hill, near Leeds, an area of rough land with woods, stream and quarries where bikers try their skills. Trials bikes are not designed for two and while negotiating a steep, rocky incline my father perhaps forgot I was there, perched up on the rear mudguard. It was only when he cleared the section that he looked back and saw a small figure wearing an oversized crash helmet, waving frantically from below. My dignity was more hurt than my body.

If you wanted to find my father then you just had to look to the garage. He would have lived in there if he had a choice, and Mother had an intercom from the house installed so she could summon him. Me and Katie would earn pocket money sweeping up metal turnings from under the lathes and reborers. He was *the* man to see if you needed precision work doing; he had incredible patience and would help anyone who had any kind of mechanical problem. Sometimes you'd open the front door in the morning and find an exhaust or a big greasy crankshaft lying on the doorstep and shortly afterwards you'd see

Mother scrubbing the step for all she was worth to clean off the oil stains. I soon learned to distinguish my con rods from my carburettors and my pistons from my crankshafts.

He had a colourful clientele for his services as a bike mechanic: we had a procession of leather-clad Hell's Angels who would roar up on their Harleys for help customizing and tweaking their machines. I particularly remember a striking, pink-haired young biker girl called Toyah. Mother wasn't as fond of her as Father was. It was Toyah who gave me a black ripped T-shirt with the slogan THE PISTON BROKE CLUB that I wore with pride until Mother realized what it said. It was swiftly consigned to the pile of oily rags for the garage. The only problem Father had was that he was far too kind-hearted for his own good: some people paid him, others were less forthcoming. He would often take on jobs that others had turned down, just for the challenge.

Mother, in contrast to all this, was very elegant. She met Father when she worked in the typing pool at David Brown, but she also had a part-time career as a model and beauty queen, winning prizes and titles at beauty pageants before she married and had children. It was the age of Twiggy then, and Mother was tall and willowy with the gamine looks that were so fashionable. She had wonderful clothes, some of which were gathering dust in the attic while others were offloaded into a dressing-up box full of ponchos, flares and a glamorous velvet cape, all worn by Katie and me during our games. I remember a pair of thigh-high silver boots that she had for a photo shoot: these were a particular favourite and Katie and I would fight over who was to wear them. I wish Mother had kept more of her clothes. Many of them would be valuable now and, apart from that, it would be fun to see them.

Both my parents were tall: Father was six foot nine inches and Mother is six foot, so it's no wonder that Katie and I are both tall. I'm six foot two inches, and was always the tallest and, unfortunately, also the biggest-footed girl in the class from infants' school onwards.

All four grandparents lived nearby, within half a mile. Father's parents, Grandma and Granddad, were huge fans of James Herriot, the vet who wrote *All Creatures Great and Small*. I watched all the TV programmes as a small child, and they had a shelf full of all the books, which eventually I read. (In so many ways, things come full circle. Now at Ravenseat we host visits from the James Herriot fans who travel from America, Canada and Japan to see the places featured in the books and to visit a working farm that is much as it was in the days that James Herriot was writing about, the 1940s and 1950s.)

Father's parents were a bit more well-heeled than Mother's, who were known more informally as Nana and Ganda. Both granddads had practical jobs: Mother's father worked for a coach-building firm and later drove lorries while my other grandfather had a good job with Philips, the electrical company.

When I was eleven I went to Newsome High, a large comprehensive with more than a thousand pupils, including a special disabled and deaf unit. It was a very mixed school racially and in terms of social background. I remember the police coming into the school and arresting a boy during an art lesson: apparently he had spent his dinner time stealing car radios. I wasn't one of the really cool girls, out there rocking it; I didn't have the most fashionable clothes and shoes. Money was tight and was not going to stretch to buying me the latest trainers. I wasn't bullied, but tried to make myself as unobtrusive as possible. I didn't want to be noticed, for good reasons or bad. I had plenty of friends, and we shared passions for A-Ha and Madonna; also, though I'm ashamed to admit it now, I was a Brosette, a fan of the spooky-looking Goss twins whose band was Bros. There were certain fashion statements that didn't cost much: net tops, the sort worn by Madonna, which we called 'teabag tops', could be bought cheaply from the market, and many a happy hour was spent rifling through a skip at the back of the Fountain pub looking for Grolsch beer-bottle tops to attach to our lace-up shoes. If we weren't at the forefront of fashion, then we weren't too far behind. As for schoolwork, I wasn't a slacker by any means, but I didn't feel massively inspired by school and coasted along, keeping myself to myself.

As soon as I was old enough to go out on my own, I took our West Highland terrier, a soppy little dog with the unlikely name of Fiona, for long walks. The alternative, hanging out in bus shelters with other kids, didn't appeal and, any-way, Fiona was not the right 'status' dog for this. Newsome, the area where we lived, sits poised in

20

perfect equilibrium: if you walk thirty minutes in one direction you are in the middle of the town, and thirty minutes in the other direction has you up on the moors, away from the buildings and traffic. That's the way I always chose. Some find the moors desolate and foreboding, but I loved the openness of the skies, the imposing shapes of the hills and the granite outcrops.

When I was about eleven or twelve I got a mountain bike which was great, and served me well for many years to come, right through school and way beyond. It was massively too big for me when I first got it, but I quickly grew into it and it gave me the freedom to cycle out on my own. I'd often say I was going collecting bilberries, which I did, but not because I had a particular addiction to the little purple berries: I simply wanted an excuse to cycle up onto the moors. I can't explain it, I just felt happy when I was up there. I didn't inherit my love of the outdoors from Mother and Father because, although they didn't hate the countryside, they weren't country people, and they certainly weren't farming folk. Nobody in my family had ever skinned a rabbit or ploughed a field – at least, not for generations.

Once, when I was around thirteen, I cycled up to Meltham and then out onto Saddleworth Moor to find the place swarming with police, road blocks, and helicopters whirring overhead. It was like all hell had been let loose, and I had to turn back. I later heard that this was one of the days when either Ian Brady or Myra Hindley was taken up there by the police to try to find the missing grave of the last of their victims.

Apart from Fiona, my contact with animals was limited until I started riding lessons. To pay for them, I had to get a weekend job, and I couldn't do that until I was legally old enough, at fourteen. For some odd reason there was a riding stables on a council estate very close to where I lived, in amongst all the pebble-dash houses. I use the word 'stables' very loosely, as it consisted of a disparate collection of tin sheds and leans-tos, an 'arena' made from recycled motorway crash barriers and a string of the world's most ramshackle horses. Lessons cost £10 an hour, and I paid for Katie to have a lesson too, so I could only afford it every two weeks.

To earn the money, I worked in Barratts shoe shop in the centre of town each Saturday. It was bad enough having to dress smart in a pencil skirt and a white blouse, but I was also expected to wear a pair of Barratts court shoes, the opposite of cool. For the first time ever, having big feet helped me out: it was difficult to find a suitable pair that fitted me, so I had to wear a pair of my own. I would watch through the shop window and duck into the stockroom if any of my classmates came in – or, should I say, were forced in by their mothers. No savvy teen would ever have come in willingly.

Because of my height, when we went riding I always got a large horse – usually Drake, a one-eyed cobby type, heavily feathered with huge hooves, a brush-like mane that stood on end, a black coat with a propensity of scurf, and an unwillingness to go anywhere faster than an ambling gait. I loved the feeling of being on the back of a

horse. We didn't go anywhere particularly interesting, just onto a scabby stretch of waste ground
at the back of some industrial units, where
everyone else could canter while I brought up the
rear at an uncomfortably quick trot, and we also
patrolled the maze of streets on the estate. These
horses were bombproof, nothing fazed them.
Abandoned bicycles, loose dogs, police sirens and
shop alarms: they had seen it, heard it and were
oblivious to it all. I think that I was too. For a little
while I was in a world of my own. It was always the
most fantastic hour, and there was a feeling of
disappointment when it was over, knowing I
wouldn't be back for another fortnight.

As a teenager I was very tall and skinny. I remember clearly a comment made to my mother by
another mother sitting behind us on the bus with
her own pudgy daughter:
  'Your daughter can't wear jeans, she's got nothing to put in them.'
  But that was the physique you needed to be a
model, and Mother had plans for me to be the
next Jerry Hall. When I was about fourteen or
fifteen she saw an advert in the local paper that
said 'Models Wanted' so she got on the phone
and arranged an appointment to have some
pictures taken at the photographer's studio. I was
reluctant, but then I was reluctant about most
things in those days. It was a kind of automatic
reluctance: Mother likes it, so I don't.
  She came with me on the bus, me dressed up to
the nines and feeling quite uncomfortable about
the amount of turquoise eyeshadow and frosted

pink lipstick that had been applied. We should have been alerted by the grotty place we went to, on the outskirts of Huddersfield, but the chap seemed OK, and behind the doors of the shabby-looking lock-up there was a studio, set up with various backdrops and lights. I suppose that I had a rose-tinted view of how modelling worked and thought that it would be *Vogue* or *Cosmopolitan* but the 'work' he showed us was knitting patterns and catalogues. Still, I figured, everyone starts some-where, and he said I definitely had potential...

He told me to go into the changing room and put on the clothes that were in there, a truly awful 1980s dress in lemon complete with shoulder pads, teamed with a particularly dated matching cardigan. I reasoned that it would have been more worrying if he'd wanted me in a bikini or under-wear, so I was lulled into a false sense of security. All I had to do was sit on one of those huge wicker peacock chairs that you found in conservatories in those days, and pretend to be on the telephone.

He took pictures to see 'if the camera loved me', then said he would put together a portfolio and that he'd be back in touch.

We didn't hear anything until a few weeks later when his picture was in the local newspaper. Apparently it was all an elaborate con: he had a camera hidden in the changing room and he was filming girls as they got undressed. I discovered that lots of girls from my school had been to have their pictures taken to see if they too had model potential... That was the beginning and end of my modelling career, and thankfully Mother never mentioned it again.

I've always loved books. From early on, I consumed books avidly, much preferring factual ones to fiction. I had a bookcase in my bedroom, and I'd spend my pocket money on second-hand books from the dusty old shops in the town, where pennies could buy battered, well-thumbed tomes. I loved anything about vets, farming or animals. I'd been glued to the television every Saturday evening watching *All Creatures Great and Small*, and this had somehow fired my imagination, although watching them on the television screen was as near as I ever got to sheep and cows. I found a roll of old Anaglypta wallpaper, and drew a picture of a cow, a sheep and a horse, using an out-of-date copy of *Black's Veterinary Dictionary* to label them with all their possible ailments. My Madonna, Bros and A-Ha posters came off the bedroom wall to make room for them. I dreamed of being a vet. Not one of the clean, sterile variety that I would meet when Fiona had something wrong with her; I had no wish to be gelding cats all day. What I wanted was to be a farm vet just like James Herriot.

When I was sixteen and about to take my GCSEs I had the standard interview with the careers teacher at school. What was I planning to do with my life? One of my friends was already pregnant, another had a job lined up in a factory making bed headboards. Mother was keen that I should go to work at Marks and Spencer, but at that age wearing a striped blouse and selling clothes all day didn't appeal.

I didn't even dare to mention the vet dream: it

all seemed such a far cry from Newsome High. I was handed a careers guidance booklet which told you what grades you needed to follow your chosen career path and I was very intimidated by it. I would have to put in some serious academic work to become the new James Herriot. But I did well enough in my exams to qualify for a place at college to do my A levels, which bought me a bit more time to decide the direction my life was going. I always had to work hard to pass exams, and I wasn't sure I could dedicate so many years to struggling with an enormous amount of studying at veterinary college.

In the end I opted to do A levels at Greenhead College, taking English Language, Biology, Geography and General Studies. Again, like at school, I was coasting, not putting in 100 per cent effort, with no clear idea where it was leading. The college staff were keen that as many of us as possible should go to university, and I vaguely considered doing a business degree, but not with any enthusiasm.

It was at college that I met my first proper boyfriend, Jason. He was doing a computer course. We really had nothing in common other than our dress sense and our shared love of black eyeliner. We were both Goths, although maybe not as committed as some were: I didn't dye my hair black, and neither did he. We *did* wear black from head to foot and sported sunglasses at all times, whatever the weather. We would trawl record shops looking for anything by The Mission, me wearing paratrooper boots, ripped tights, net petticoats and a blanket with knots in it, Jason in the same leather trousers and ripped T-shirt he always wore. I suppose it was a form of rebellion, and Mother was not very happy about it, but she got nowhere telling me what she thought. In fairness to her, she wasn't heavy about it, but when I look back I can see it must have been a blow for this elegant woman to have a daughter wandering around looking like that!

Whatever we thought at the time, Jason and I weren't really that alternative: we got engaged! How conventional is that? He bought me a ring with a microscopic diamond from H. Samuel which cost him £90. I was very impressed, it was such a lot of money to me at that time. I flashed it around college, thinking it was wonderful. It seems funny now but I can't even remember why we split up. However, I do remember that I threw the ring back at him. We were never really that serious, and never for one moment did I think, even then, that we would get married. I've no idea what happened to Jason. I never saw him again after we left college. In a big town you can stay quite anonymous and keep yourself to yourself even though you are in a crowd. Lots of people like to keep in touch with friends from their past, but I never have, mainly because I've moved on and away.

As part of my Biology course I could opt to do different modules, and there was one in Dairy Microbiology, which was run by the University of Liverpool. The majority of the work was written and done in college, but a site visit to a working dairy got me thinking about farms and cows and the possibilities of working with them. I realized there were other ways of working with farm animals which didn't involve qualifying as a vet, and that perhaps my dream was not over...

I started thinking that maybe I could work in farming.

So I got on my bike, literally – it was the same mountain bike I'd had since I was about twelve – and I cycled round the farms near the edge of the town, offering my services free to anyone who could use me. Now, there's nothing a farmer likes more than free labour, especially from someone who is prepared to work their guts out and doesn't mind getting stuck in and mucky. I think one or two were a bit cynical about me when I showed up, as they were definitely more used to lads than lasses. But I showed willing, worked hard and, most important, I was free.

After A levels (I didn't do great...) I still didn't see how I was ever going to get the kind of job I wanted. I was used basically for shovelling the proverbial; there was never any talk of payment or even a job. I needed to find a way in, so I headed for the technical college in Huddersfield and enrolled on an NVQ course in veterinary nursing. It felt like a backwards step going from A levels to an NVQ, but I figured it could help me get work on farms if I had some basic practical qualifications.

It was at this time I discovered a book that played such an important role in my life. I was always in and out of Huddersfield Library, borrowing books about animals and farming, when on one visit I found *Hill Shepherd,* by John and Eliza Forder. You can usually tell pretty quickly whether a book is going to 'grab you' and this one certainly did. Even at first glance, flicking through the pages, it captivated me: beautiful, evocative photographs of shepherds and their flocks, and a narrative that told of the seasons of their lives. I borrowed it three times in succession, then received a letter from the library informing me that I couldn't keep renewing it any longer, and I would be fined if I didn't return it. I couldn't afford to buy it back then, so reluctantly I took it back. I loved every detail of it: the photo of a farmer skinning a dead lamb; the flock of sheep being walked on the road, closely followed by a couple of sheepdogs; a shepherd gathering the sheep down from the fells of the Lake District, the sheep trickling down through the bracken, making for home. (Another example of how my life comes full circle: recently I bought a second-hand copy of this wonderful book, and in one of the photographs, of a sheep sale at Hawes auction, there is Clive, who is now my husband. Little did I know...)

As part of my college work experience I landed a fortnight's lambing work on a farm. It was a baptism of fire. If I hadn't have been as enthusiastic as I was, then this job would almost certainly have sent me scurrying to Marks and Spencer for an application form. It was just me and another girl, who was a vet student, and an awfully large modern shed packed to the rafters with heavily expectant yows. Although we were both full of theory, we had no practical experience whatsoever. We made it up as we went along. It was an incredibly steep learning curve.

This was a commercial flock and all the lambing was inside, not, as I had imagined, out in the fields. It was very hard work, and we were left to get on with it. My companion was a good workmate, and we pulled together well. The farmer, however, was foul-tempered and incredibly miserly. He did not have any of the equipment required at lambing time, no dried colostrum, the vital fluid that new mothers produce before their milk comes in, and which babies of all species need. We did the best we could, pinching a bit here and there from sheep who had plenty for the ones who didn't. But his attitude was that small lambs should simply be put down. Worse, he didn't put them down humanely. He hit them over the head and concussed them, then flung them into a big, blue forty-five-gallon drum. I felt sick when he whacked them, and even more sick when I looked over the top and saw some of them still moving. Nowadays I like to think that I would hit *him* over the head but back then I was very young and less sure of myself.

It was bad farming. One thing I learned, very early on, is that there are good farmers and bad farmers; just, I suppose, like every other walk of life. Working for bad farmers may not have been a great experience, but it shaped me, taught me how things should not be done, and gave me a clearer idea of the sort of farming I wanted to do. I certainly didn't have any romantic notions about the job. After my fortnight the farmer was supposed to pay me £20 and, true to form, he didn't turn up that day.

I did more casual work in a livery yard which involved lots of grooming and mucking out.

Much as I loved the horses, I knew I didn't want to spend the rest of my life working exclusively with them. Another job taught me how to run a small milking parlour, and there was an enjoyable spell on a small farm which had cows, sheep, horses and pigs. By the time my NVQ course was over I had sorted it out in my head: shepherding was what I wanted to do.

I got a lucky break. My course was in veterinary nursing, but there was an agricultural element, learning how to assist vets who worked with farm animals. One of my tutors had some farming contacts, and he happened to know someone who was looking for a farmhand – or, possibly, just a mug...

2

Wild Oats and Wool Sacks

My first full-time farming job was milking cows on a family farm at Wakefield, and I soon realized I had to navigate a difficult path between two bosses who had different ideas about what I should be doing. There were actually two farms, and on one the old father ruled, and on the other his son, freshly back from agricultural college, was in charge. Or that was the theory: the old farmer would turn up and tell me to do things completely differently from the way his son had, only minutes before, told me to do them. The old fella wanted everything done the traditional way, like it always had been, and the young lad had lots of new ideas, which his father thought were plain daft. They disagreed over the simplest things.

For example: there were 130 cows to milk and usually about 25 calves to feed, and the son wanted me to wash the buckets, sterilize them and stand them in a line as he reckoned there was a danger that dirt could be transferred from one to another if they were stacked. Then the old chap would appear and ask what on earth I was doing with all the buckets spread out as they would get dirty, and were in the way and they should be stacked together. I was forever being lambasted by one of them because of something the other had told me to do. You could never do things right: one of them was always on your case. There were two YTS (the government's Youth Training Scheme) lads working there as well, and we were all permanently in the dog-house with one of our bosses. There was another old farmhand who had been there since the dawn of time, and it was a bit of a blokes' paradise: they'd never had a girl working there.

When I got the job I was told, 'Make sure thi brings thi bait box.'

I thought, *Bait? What's fishing got to do with it?*

I soon found out it meant 'lunch box'. We'd sit outside to eat if it was fine, but if it was raining – and it usually was – we'd sit inside a shed on plastic milk crates and tea chests. The tea chests were full of porn magazines. It was a bit off-putting trying to eat your sandwich with three chaps studying *Playboy*, but it never *really* bothered me. If you want to work in a world that has for centuries been traditionally male, you can't be indignant and feminist when you get a bit of banter or hear some crude talk.

It was hard work. I left home on my bike at 6 a.m. every morning to be there by 7 a.m., an hour's ride up and down hills. If I didn't take the bike, I had to travel on two buses, which took much longer. There was one thing for sure after I'd been on the farm all day: I could literally clear the bus, I smelt so bad, usually of silage – a smell that really sticks in your throat.

The job was seven days a week, but every third weekend I got what the farmer called my 'weekend off'. This was the worst time of all: I was still expected to do the morning and evening milking, so the only time I got off was a few hours in the middle. And it meant doing the journey twice a day, instead of once. I seemed to be on that bicycle saddle pedalling all day. No wonder I had no time for socializing with friends or going out on dates. By this time my school and college friends had gone their different ways. One was at Oxford, studying hard, and another was a trainee cashier at Lloyds Bank; others, too, had sensible, normal jobs. I didn't feel that I wasn't as good as them, but I was still a bit confused about everything. I liked the farm work, but the hours were crucifying, and I felt I hadn't quite got my life right yet.

The farm was part arable, which was something completely new to me. I spent hours shovelling grain into silos and grain lofts, then filling sacks with barley. I also had a combine harvester to grease up, 130 grease nipples to do every morning during the harvest. It was the old fellow's pride and joy, an ancient belt-driven piece of machinery, and he'd do spot checks to see that I'd greased it properly.

I was sent out with a hessian sack tied across my back to carefully pick the wild oats that were growing amongst the barley, and told to take my bait with me. Looking across the fields of golden, ripening barley, I could see the wild oats, their green panicles standing head and shoulders above the barley ears. At first glance it seemed there was only a handful of the weeds, but when I was crouching down in the field I could see the extent of their spread. No wonder he told me to take my bait. The upside of these long days in the fields was that I developed a golden tan like nothing you can buy in a tanning salon. The downside: it stopped at my welly tops.

Harvest time was very intensive: when the moisture meter registered the required grain dryness it was all hands on deck. Floodlights were rigged up in the fields and nobody stopped until all was safely gathered in. Although it was very hard work I felt that at least I was getting good practical experience. I learned how to set up an umbilical spreader, which is a long pipe to spread slurry on the fields using a tractor or a metal pulley contraption; how to use a power harrow to break up clods of soil to prepare the ground for planting; how to dehorn a calf and how to drive a tractor. I already knew how to drive a car, because Father had patiently taken me out to show me the ropes. Then I had one lesson with an instructor, just to refine the bits you need for the test, and I passed first time.

I think Mother and Father did wonder 'What on earth is she doing?', especially when I came home filthy and stinking. The truth is, I was right at the bottom of the food chain, the dogsbody who was expected to do anything, but I was happy to be working, and I was learning all the time. You had to start somewhere and, besides, there were other things going on at home that were more important than my career.

It was at this time, when I was eighteen, that my father died. For years he thought he had a stomach ulcer, and he'd been prescribed Gaviscon, an antacid used for indigestion. Eventually, when the pain got worse, his doctor sent him for tests and they discovered he had stomach cancer. He was quite ill by this stage and had to give up work. Eventually, he could no longer even tinker with his beloved motorbikes. That was the worst bit for him. It was heartbreaking to see him clearing out all the bikes and cataloguing the parts and spares that filled the garage, cellar and loft. I might have known my crankshafts from my con rods but there was a whole lot more stuff that he had accumulated over the years, and he was adamant that after he died we should not be hoodwinked by any unscrupulous buyers. Other than making us promise to never sell his compressor, he made every effort to get as much of his collection as possible sold to enthusiasts before he died. Mother had been working as a school dinner lady, and she had to give up work to look after him. Katie was twelve at the time, so it was a difficult period for all of us.

I was with Father when he died. He was at home and had been on a morphine drip for days. I am still haunted by it. It was such a strange experience, it felt like it wasn't really happening to me: dealing with the practicalities involved, ringing a doctor and a funeral director and, worst of all, having to go to Grandma's house and tell her that her son had died. I didn't want to go to the funeral, but Mother insisted. I had another argument with her:

'You're not going dressed as a Goth.'

'He wouldn't know me any other way. Anyway, the theme is black, I can't see your problem.'

I've hated funerals ever since, and I rarely go to them.

As far as my job went, I was just trying not to upset the apple cart, keeping any worries about my future to myself because Mother had enough on her plate.

I realized that if I was to stay in farming I needed to leave Huddersfield. I didn't want to work on such commercial, industrial-type farms. I can sum it up by saying I wanted more fields and fewer sheds. You might say that I had a romantic view of where I wanted to be, but I was sure there still existed places where dog and stick were the name of the game, instead of plate meters and dry-matter levels. But it wasn't the right time to leave home, so soon after Father's death.

One dismal, slate-grey, wet, back-end kind of a day, after coming home on the bus, humming as usual, I was walking through the centre of Huddersfield. As I trailed up the main street, being given a wide berth by shoppers, I passed a shop called Strawberry Fair, a three-storey china and gift shop on the corner of Byram Arcade. I had walked past this place on many occasions, on my way to the upper level of the arcade where there was a grunge-style 'vintage' shop run by two punk girls who would buy clothes from the many charity shops dotted around Huddersfield and then rework them. It was my favourite place to buy clothes during my Goth days, and next door was Dead Wax records, where many a wet afternoon was wasted flicking through dog-eared albums in plastic boxes. Strawberry Fair was a high-class shop not previously on my radar. There were polished silver and glass displays full of delicate ornaments in the window, and a glistening crystal chandelier in the sales foyer, with well-presented sales assistants gliding between the displays and customers. A sign hung on the door: SALES ASSISTANT WANTED. APPLY WITHIN.

A thought flashed through my mind: *Should I have a go at doing something else?* I think it was fuelled by a combination of the onset of winter, the relentless grind of the farm and, I suppose, a feeling that, after Father's death, perhaps I should be more responsible and do something more conventional.

Before I'd even had a chance to fully formulate my thoughts, a woman poked her head out of the door and said, 'Are you interested in the job? Because if you are, Philip, the boss, is in the stockroom at the moment and he could interview you now.'

Caught off guard, I let her usher me in, me

pointing towards my muddy wellies. I was conscious of the beige thick-pile carpet, but all my offers to leave them in the doorway fell on deaf ears. Irene, the shop assistant, took me to the back of the sales area and downstairs. I felt like the proverbial bull in a china shop – I certainly smelt bovine as I picked my way between glass shelves loaded with Lladro ornaments and bone china tea services. Philip quizzed me and I told him quite honestly that I only wanted the job for a time and didn't see it as a career. I think he thought I was a bit odd, but he seemed to pick up that I was a hard worker, and the bottom line was that he must have been desperate because he said, 'If you want the job, it's yours.'

The next day I broke it to the farmer that I wasn't coming again. He wasn't that bothered: there is a limitless supply of young folk wanting jobs and I was entirely expendable. I ceremonially burned the smelly jodhpurs and morphed into the epitome of refinement, in a pencil skirt, a crisp white shirt and the dreaded Barratts court shoes: they finally got me.

I actually liked the job. My new colleagues were a friendly but formidable bunch who stood for no nonsense, and I soon learned the patter and became a real expert in the art of selling to customers. I was constantly baffled by the goods I was selling. I was in the cookware department, and well-heeled gentry types would come in to discuss their wedding lists, agonizing about which design of cutlery, and which egg cups they wanted, and whether or not they needed a fish kettle or a fondue set. I'd be nodding in agreement while debating the merits of nine-inch plates over eleven-inch plates and thinking *How bloody pointless is this?*

I'd look at the prices: hundreds of pounds for the cast-iron cookware, thousands for some of the beautiful wooden presentation boxes filled with shining, polished cutlery. There were many variations of forks, spoons and knives, and I hadn't a clue what you'd use some of them for. Apostle, salt and caddy spoons! I actually had a lesson in how to set up a formal table from one of the cutlery manufacturers, so that I could look like I was an expert. Ridiculous sums were paid for some of the vases and ornaments. I was mystified by it all but I did learn one thing that stood me in good stead. There was a huge, lidded, black cast-iron pot that sat in the corner of the cookware department; it weighed an absolute ton and was called a 'goose pot'. I was pretty much resigned to the fact that I was going to dust it, occasionally stand on it to reach a pan stand, but never sell it. For once I was right: nobody seemed to want it. But then on Boxing Day we had a massive one-day sale, and a Jamaican lady came in and bought it at a greatly reduced price. She told me that she had a big family and could easily cook more than two chickens in it.

I've now bought one myself to use on the big open fire range at Ravenseat. I like to use the black range during the wintertime as it is economical, warming the house, drying the washing, heating the water and cooking the dinner. We also rely on it when the electricity is off. The only problem is that the smell of food pervades the whole house, whets the children's appetites and makes them so hungry that they all eat far more than they normally would.

But back at Strawberry Fair, I was always honest about my intention to get back into farming. I enjoyed my brief stay in the normal, civilized world, and I was around for my mother and Katie after Father's death, but farming was my true love. I bought the *Farmers Guardian* and *Farmers Weekly* and pored over the job ads. With spring approaching there were plenty of lambing-time jobs, some indoor, some outdoor. Most of the outdoor lambing jobs required a shepherdess and sheepdog. I didn't have one of those so I was more limited, but eventually I found a job that fitted my criteria:

**WANTED for immediate start.
Enthusiastic young person required for shepherding and lambing on Salisbury Plain. No dog needed. Just a willingness to work and use initiative. Accommodation provided. Please ring.**

I had by this time bought myself a car, a Mini Metro, with £900 that I'd carefully saved. So one Sunday I drove down to Wiltshire for an interview. I had never driven so far before. I left very early in the morning, straight down the motorway, negotiating Birmingham and Bristol, and eventually arriving at Warminster at lunchtime. I was feeling sick with nerves by now. This was the first time I had really broken free and left the safety of home, but I knew it was time to stand on my own two feet.

I drove up the long gravelled farm driveway to a large modern house, not the kind of farmhouse I had imagined. I was met by a man who I assumed to be the farmer, but it was difficult to tell, really. You can usually spot a farmer a mile off, but this guy was slick, certainly not what I'd expected. I introduced myself to him, took a deep breath and, trying to give off an air of confidence, spouted as many technical farming terms as I could think of, doing my best to impress with my outstanding knowledge of sheep and lambs (more practical theory from the vet books than actual hands-on, but he wasn't to know that). Without more ado he showed me a small room at the rear of the house that would be mine and said I could have the job. I could have sworn he wasn't really listening to anything I said, but it didn't matter. I was ecstatic. Once again, it wasn't exactly the farm I dreamed about, but it was sheep, and that was a good start.

When I gave my notice in at Strawberry Fair, Philip told me I could always have my job back if ever I wanted it, which was very reassuring, but I knew I wouldn't be taking up the offer. They gave me a lovely leaving present. One of the expensive dinner services that we sold was decorated with sheep and shepherds, and the manufacturer supplied some small china sheep ornaments to go on display with the samples. I liked these twee little sheep and so did many of the customers, who asked if they were for sale, but they were for display only. I was presented with two of these, and I have them still, in a corner cupboard at Ravenseat, high up out of reach of little hands.

I loaded up my car with all that mattered to me and off I went, feeling more confident than I had done previously. When I arrived the farmer wasn't there. I was told he'd gone on a water-skiing holiday in America. I instantly thought this was odd: I was counting on him showing me the ropes and telling me what was expected of me.

I found out later at the pub that the locals nick-named the farm Waco, after the place in Texas where eighty cult members died in a siege the year before. They saw a procession of young workers coming and going from the farm and had decided they were all followers of a cult, and they also knew how badly the farm was run. I had no idea of any of this when I first arrived.

Living in the farmhouse with me were two other young workers who had been hired to look after the cows, and an older man who was sup-posed to oversee everything. Needless to say, he didn't: he just watched the television or disap-peared altogether. Nobody was in charge, it was left entirely up to us.

That first morning the cowman and cow-woman told me they were going to check on their beasts and they took me along so I could look at the sheep and sort out the electric fences. The land was all Ministry of Defence land and it was not divided up with walls or fences, but was one giant expanse of rough grazing, completely flat with occasional copses of trees. There were unin-habited villages used by the army for training and you had to be careful where you walked as there were dummy incendiaries and hidden pits in which tanks covered with camouflage netting would be concealed. While I was there some unfortunate person was riding out on the plain when their horse stepped on a dummy mine, which exploded with a loud bang and a puff of smoke. The rider was thrown, and the horse galloped off into the sunset, not to be seen for a whole week, other than the occasional sighting of it with its saddle under its belly and its reins still dangling. On the plus side, the aluminium mine tops made brilliant dog bowls, so there was some recompense for being 'blown up'.

Another notable find was an army sweater decorated with the Bomb Disposal Team cipher. It was not in perfect condition but was very wearable (I still have it). I wondered if the previous owner had actually been blown up for real, and his jumper was all that remained... As you can imagine, it was a pretty surreal place to farm.

The way my absent boss made money was by wintering hoggs. That's when farmers in tougher climes, up in the wilds (like the Yorkshire Dales and Lake District), send their young female breeding sheep (hoggs) to kinder climes for the winter. They usually send them away at the beginning of November and get them back at the beginning of April. We do it now at Ravenseat – it's normal practice for hill farmers. The farm where the sheep are wintered gets paid so much per head, and this farm had hoggs wintering from several farms in the Lake District.

But although he had a lot of sheep, it was halfway through February and there had, I learned, been no shepherd there since Christmas. What I met with out on the plain was horrific. The sheep were all there, surrounded by electric fencing, but the ground was bare. They had not been moved to fresh grazing for some time and were literally starving to death. Some of the sheep had tried to escape and had become entangled in the electric wire. They may have been frightened, probably by the low-flying military helicopters or by deer, and some were hung up on the wires by their horns. Quite a few were dead, others I rescued, but they were very weak through lack of food and water. The ones that were not on the wires were all skin and bones. Nobody had been feeding them. My two fellow workers were shocked at the state of affairs, and had been oblivious to what had been going on. Cows were their responsibility and the cattle were elsewhere on the plains, and looked very well.

I didn't know what to do. I knew the theories about shepherding but had limited hands-on experience. With the help of the other two workers and a YTS lad who came in every day, I took up the electric fence and moved the sheep that could still walk onto some fresh grazing. The weaker ones were trailered back to the farm and into a barn for some intensive nursing. The farmer had not left a contact phone number, but there was a number for his ex-wife. I rang and told her the situation, and she let the owners of the hoggs know, and also must have informed the authorities. Reading between the lines, it became apparent that he and his ex-wife had not parted on good terms, and it came as no surprise when the RSPCA and Trading Standards came knocking as a result of her intervention. (Farms, like all

44

other businesses, are now inspected periodically by Trading Standards, just to make sure we're doing what we say we're doing.)

The owners of the sheep were clearly devastated by what had happened. They had been down to visit their sheep at Christmas to give them a wormer dose and everything had been fine then, but because they were so far away they had not been back since and had no idea about what had gone on. The sheep could not be taken on the long journey back to the Lake District, as a movement restriction order was issued, banning movement until an inspection visit assessed them as in better health and able to withstand the journey. I looked after them, moving them regularly to different pastures, checking on them every day. The sick ones had hay and cake and were eventually let out around the gardens.

It was an eye-opener to actually see behind the facade of the spotless new farm buildings. No expense had been spared. There was a brand-new indoor sheep-handling system with races, shedders, guillotine gates, every mod con to make life easy. Turn-over crates, weighers, even a super-size round dipping tub, filled with what I assume was old dip, complete with the floating corpses of two sheep. The only thing this farmer didn't have was either the knowledge or inclination to do the work. The memory of this horrible breach of trust with the farmers, whose animals he had agreed to care for, means that we always visit our hoggs regularly when they go away for the winter, just to make sure everything is OK. It's certainly not a case of out of sight, out of mind. Of course, over the years

45

we have found good places to winter them, and we tend to stick to the same farms.

It took a few weeks for the sheep to recover and for Trading Standards to remove the movement restriction. They still weren't in the greatest shape, and it had taken a lot of hard work to get them to that point. Moving the electric fence was a time-consuming job in itself. A contraption that attached to the wheel of a quad-bike trailer was supposed to make it a simple task by unwinding the tape, but it invariably ended up in a knot, and by the time you had jumped off and put another electric fence post in the ground it was easier to do it by hand. To my astonishment, it turned out there was another flock of sheep that actually belonged to the farmer, and they were away on a different farm being looked after by another farmer. Unbelievable! Even now, I look back and think: *how could that happen?* I never saw the farmer again, and the man who was supposed to be in charge disappeared completely. It was the ex-wife who paid me for my efforts: she said that she was very pleased with how things had worked out, and I had the feeling that it had been payback time as far as she was concerned.

For me personally, there was a new plan: I had talked to the Lake District farmers when they came down to collect their sheep on the lorry and one of them said to me, 'You're in the wrang spot. If thoo wants ta see how proper shepherding is done then yer need to be heading up into our country.'

They were relieved to be going home with at least some of their stock. It had been a nightmare for everyone involved and, obviously, I didn't have a job any more. So there wasn't much to consider really and when the sheep went, I followed them.

I loaded up my car again and set off in a northerly direction. I didn't get very far. I had decided to take a more scenic route rather than the motorway, a decision which, in hindsight, probably saved my life. I was driving out of Bath when I spectacularly crashed the car. I wasn't travelling at any great speed, but as I met a sharpish corner, I braked – and nothing happened. I pumped the brake pedal frantically, and the wheels locked up. I could hear the tyres screeching as the car careered on in a straight line towards a low wall. I hit it, then time seemed to stand still as the car flipped over it and tumbled twenty feet or so, landing on its roof in a field. I was still sitting in the driver's seat but hanging upside down, held by my seat belt, a little dazed but quite unhurt. I had been wearing a Puffa jacket and the padding had cushioned me. Even more useful was the fact that I had my penknife in the pocket, as I had to cut the seat belt to free myself and then wriggle out through the car window. My beloved Metro was completely wrecked and all my belongings were scattered across the field. There were bras, knickers, books, CDs, everything, strewn about. I was mortified.

I scrambled my way up the steep bank back to the road. I had no mobile phone in those days, but someone must have either seen me become airborne, or noticed the skid marks followed by the gap in the wall, and had alerted the police. A police motorcyclist appeared and insisted (much

47

to my embarrassment) on helping me gather up my possessions. It was while I was telling him what had happened that I realized, now my little car was belly up, that the wires in the tyres were sticking out and had clearly played a large part in my inability to slow down. The policeman gave me a ticking-off and then took me back into Bath to ring the AA. Eventually a tow truck came, loaded me and my wrecked car up, and took me all the way back to Huddersfield, dumping the car in a scrapyard en route.

I stayed with Mother for a week until I got myself organized, buying a second-hand VW Polo. The Lake District farmers had given me the telephone number of a man named Bob who ran a farming recruitment agency and was on the lookout for keen young people to lamb sheep. Just talking to him on the phone I knew that I was heading in the right direction. He told me that if I loved sheep, dog or no dog, he could fit me up with a job.

It was a lovely afternoon as I left the motorway at Shap. Away in the distance I could see the mountains of the Lake District with a mantle of snow still visible on the peaks. My spirits were high as I wound my way along the quiet roads, a weak spring sun shining down, and in the fields a few lambs taking their first tentative steps under the watchful eyes of their mothers. I had been given directions to a village called Crosby Ravensworth, where I was to be lambing for a farmer called John Wood. All I knew was that I was to get to the village, turn right and follow the road until I saw a sign for Crosby Lodge. This wasn't a live-in job, because they had two sons and the farmhouse was already full to capacity, so I was to be living in a caravan in the farmyard. I was nervous, not knowing what to expect, but as I pulled into the yard I was greeted by a ruddy-faced, smiling man.

'You must be Amanda, we've bin expecting you. Come in an' get a cup of tea an' then I'll show yer around.'

We talked for a little while and then I was taken on a guided tour of the farm, ending at the door of a caravan in the corner of the yard.

It was an old van, probably dating back to the 1950s, and the overall impression of it was ... brown. It was chocolate brown outside and caramel brown inside, with a decent-sized bed. There was a gas cooker, but as I didn't feel confident with the gas-and-matches aspect, I only really used the electric kettle. There was no water supply, but the farm had an old dairy which was no longer in use, where there was a cold-water tap over a big plastic sink, so I could keep some basic standards of cleanliness.

The worst thing was that I couldn't wash my hair. I tried to wash it in the dairy sink but it was unbelievably cold. I've always had long hair, and I really didn't want to cut it off. Shortly after starting work at Crosby I discovered Kendal, the nearest town of any size. On a mad impulse I visited a tattoo parlour there, had my hair plaited into dreadlocks and, just to complete the look, had two studs put in my nose. Remember, I was only twenty. The nose studs lasted until clipping time, in July: I kept getting the wool caught in them.

Once you've accidentally got your nose caught up in wool that is still attached to a sheep, you know you've made a mistake, and I decided to take them out before a sheep did it for me. The dreadlocks were a good solution to the hair-washing problem though, as they meant I didn't need to wash it at all – I would just sprinkle some talcum powder over the roots when it got a bit rank.

In hindsight, I must have looked like Swampy, the eco-warrior, but this new look just washed over Johnny, the farmer. He was a grand fellow. He knew that although I was keen I was a bit green and he took time to show me round and explain how everything worked. He had Swaledale sheep, the horned black-faced sheep with the white noses and white around the eyes, and Cheviots, the ones with sticky-up ears and white faces and compact, round little bodies. The lambing was mainly done outside, in large undulating pastures with shelter afforded by a band of trees, perfect for the yows, with plenty of places for them to sneak off and lamb away from prying eyes. Any sheep having problems were brought back to the farm to be monitored. On one of the cold, clear nights I remember lying on a bed of straw in a Dutch barn and looking out at a starry sky, watching the shooting stars and feeling a contentment that I had never experienced before.

Everyone was friendly, it was a lovely family atmosphere. I am so glad I met them as my previous experiences had nearly been enough to put me off forever, to completely lose heart. So they came into my life at the right moment. I had lots of theories and ideas about sheep in my mind, and I was so enthusiastic about it; Johnny Wood, known to all as Woody, added the practical stuff and showed me how it was done right. It was a farm that operated on teamwork, with everyone pulling together. I absolutely loved it, and for the first time in my life I remember thinking: *Thank goodness I've got to where I want to be.*

Out of my caravan window I could see across a little valley and one morning, early, I watched two foxes playing in the sunshine. They weren't doing anything wrong, just frolicking like little children. But it wasn't an entirely idyllic scene: on a few occasions a lamb would be carried off by a fox. Worse still were the crows, who would pick the eyes out of a recumbent lamb or yow if given the chance. Nature can be cruel sometimes.

As the lambing slowed down, I was starting to feel a little anxious. I didn't know where or what was to come next. One day while doing the rounds Johnny casually said, 'It can't be much fun living in that shed of a caravan.'

I think he and his wife were concerned about me, living in such a basic way, but they may also have wanted the unsightly caravan and the unsightly dreadlocked Swampy out of the farmyard.

'I've gotten an empty cottage down in t'village, I wondered if yer were interested?' he went on.

This was right out of the blue, but there was one major thing that concerned me.

'How much will it cost?' I asked.

'Sixty quid,' he said.

I was busy working out in my head that I wouldn't be able to afford £60 a week, especially now that I was effectively jobless once again and not sure where my next work would come from. I shook my head.

'I can't afford that every week.'

'No, yer daft beggar, it's sixty pounds a month.'

Well, I couldn't believe my luck. I reckoned I could manage that, if I was careful. I'd no idea how I was going to earn a crust but as I'd worked for him for six weeks without a break I had enough money put by to keep me going until something came up.

When I saw the cottage I was thrilled. There was a row of three whitewashed cottages, two of them normal sized, and a tiny one on the end which was to be mine. It was just one room downstairs with a minute annex kitchen, and one room upstairs with a bathroom. But it was a lot bigger than the caravan and, best of all, it had a lovely long garden with a kennel and a small outhouse. Immediately next door was a Methodist chapel. The village consisted of a line of houses on one side of the road; directly opposite ran the River Lyvennet and beyond that were fields of horses, cows and sheep. There was a school, church and a pub, the Butcher's Arms, which was the centre of village life. It was idyllic and I could not have dreamed of anywhere better. People were friendly and I was made very welcome.

As far as work went, I had to broaden my horizons and take on any job I could get. Farming has its own calendar, and there are certain points of the year – lambing, clipping, dipping – when you know you will get work, but the rest of the time I had to do anything that came along. I worked on a saw bench, chopping logs and filling up pickups, cutting Christmas trees, house-sitting and even walking dogs. Anything to earn a few quid.

I had never clipped and I desperately wanted to learn so I decided to give Bob a ring to see whether he had any work. He had brought a shearing gang over from New Zealand, and he needed people to woolwrap, so I joined the gang wrapping the fleeces they'd sheared off. We went all over the place, all around the Lake District wherever there were sheep to be sheared. The New Zealand lads were a motley crew, heavily tattooed and hard drinking. They clipped all year round, moving from country to country. All the time I was clearing the trailer boards of wool I would watch them closely, study their techniques; they made it look so easy. Whenever they stopped for their dinner I got the chance to have a go. They would sit amongst the wool eating their sandwiches and drinking small bottles of beer, shouting words of encouragement – or otherwise, because I was very slow to start with.

They showed me how important it is to move the sheep around with your legs. You'd naturally think that the sheep should be kept immobile but they get more stressed and struggle if they are still, so learning to hold them and move them with your legs is as important as the actual clipping. You can't do it without practice. If you are not careful you can cut the sheep, which happens if you go over a wrinkle in the skin or if the wool is being pulled away from the body and into the blades of the clipper. There's a very fine line between the skin and the fleece, called the rise, and it is the new growth of wool through which the clippers run easily. Invariably you do end up with a few nicks which will heal very quickly after a squirt of antiseptic spray.

So I provided the lunchtime amusement, the lads teased me mercilessly and, of course, they didn't give me great sheep to shear. The worst sheep is always the last, the one that limps, looks a bit decrepit, so they were happy to let me learn on that one. They told me that in New Zealand, where the sheep farms have many thousands of sheep, the last broken down one would be the one they would feed to the dogs. It sounds a bit harsh, but on those huge sheep stations, by the time you've done the muster and got all the sheep in, the last one is probably at death's door anyway. Gradually, over time, I improved and clipping is now one of my favourite jobs.

Although sheep were my passion, I had another string to my bow: I could milk, which I did on a temporary basis when someone was ill, or to cover for holidays. In those days quite a few farms still had small herds of thirty or so cows to milk, while nowadays most milking has to be done on a much bigger scale to be economic. The worst thing about relief milking was that everyone's milking parlour was different. I would just get the measure of one system then I'd be off to another farm with a completely different set-up.

I did quite a bit of relief milking, I enjoyed it. Clive tells me he never liked it, but I think that's because at one time he was doing it twice a day, every day, whereas I didn't do enough to get bored with the monotony. Clive says that women are good with cows, they're gentle and have more patience. I would quite like to have a house cow to provide fresh milk for us every day at Ravenseat but Clive says it would be too tying, having to milk her twice a day. Mind you, his friend Bill, who had a house cow himself, would say, 'It weren't much of a cow that couldnae hold two days' milk.' So watch this space.

I never advertised my services. I wouldn't have dared: I still felt I was bluffing, just learning. But I got jobs by word of mouth. A shepherd in the village retired, so I got a bit of work doing day-to-day shepherding, and it wasn't long before other farmers were ringing me up. I had an answering-machine message that had the sound of a lamb bleating, the pre-recorded message being, 'Say summat – or the lamb gets it.'

There were about five farms in the village, and sometimes I'd get someone hammering on my door and end up chasing sheep or cows up and down the street. I was willing to do anything. I worked chopping logs on the saw bench at a saw mill, where I spent all day pushing logs through the saw, and I was terrified of chopping my arm off. It didn't instil me with confidence that one of the men in the yard had only one hand. I never asked him what had happened. I didn't really want to know... When I wasn't on the saw bench I was bagging dusty sawdust, substituting fear of amputation with an inability to breathe. I wore a face mask but it was so hot that it was difficult to catch your breath.

In Cumbria you are never short of work if you can repair drystone walls. Drystone walls differ from area to area depending upon the stone in that locality. A walling or gapping job in Eden could be relatively easy due to the lovely big red sandstone blocks that fitted together beautifully. At the other end of the scale I could end up with horribly misshapen crumbling limestone which took incredible patience to cobble together, like the walling I did on Orton Scar, where the stones were small and sharp, and it took ages to wall a gap. Even today, when I drive to Penrith, I see stretches of wall beside the road and think: 'I did that.'

I recorded everything I did in my diary, with the number of hours I worked. Some weeks I did not earn very much, but I needed very little to live on. My average earnings would be about £100 a week, and if I had good weeks I'd put a bit aside, knowing that bad weeks could be round the corner. But even being careful, there were times of the year when I was much more flush than others. I knew I'd be flat out at lambing, clipping or dipping times, so at the end of the week I'd have a full pay packet. But other times I wouldn't get more than ten to twenty hours work in a week. It was famine or feast, and I coped with the famine well enough.

I was very independent, so when I spoke on the phone to Mother I never let her know it was a struggle, but she must have realized I was up against it because occasionally parcels of pasta, rice and biscuits would arrive.

Some jobs I did just required strength and willingness, not too much skill. Sheep dipping is one of those. Every farmer needs to dip his sheep in autumn to protect them from sheep scab and lice, and some farms also dip in summer to protect them from flies (we don't at Ravenseat because the high altitude makes us less susceptible to flies). Dipping is also done at sale time to give the sheep a lovely lustrous colour. I was in big demand at dipping time. The phone would ring and it would be: 'Would ta give us a hand getting some sheep through t'tub?'

I did so much splashing about around dip, sniffing it up, that I actually ended up in hospital. Most farmers were using organophosphate dips, some of which have since been banned. The link with neurological damage is still unproven, but it certainly wasn't great to inhale as much as I did.

I was hallucinating, talking a load of gibberish. For a few days I'd been seeing things, thinking there was a tractor in front of me on the road when there was nothing there. Then, in the end, I lost my balance, I couldn't stand up, couldn't focus my eyes. It was so bad that one of the other workers called an ambulance, and I spent a week in hospital.

I was shipped to a psychiatric hospital called Garlands, near Carlisle. It was one of those huge Victorian asylums, now knocked down and the site of a new housing development. The psychiatrists were very interested in the effects of organophosphates, and I had to wear a cap on my head, a bit like a shower cap with electrodes attached, so they could monitor my brain activity. Medical students came to look at me. Apparently there was a research project in Edinburgh that was looking for an antidote, but there still isn't one. I just had to wait until the effects wore off, but in the

57

meantime I was on a ward with a lot of depressed and troubled people. It was surreal, and I was very worried because they were threatening to take my driving licence away, which would have been a big problem: I wouldn't have been able to work. I still do the dipping here at Ravenseat. It's only once a year, and now it's only our own flock, but I am well aware of the hidden dangers and skedaddle any child who ventures anywhere near.

That whole episode was the downside of contract work. But on the whole, almost everything else was great, and I never felt I'd made the wrong choice in life, not for a minute. Even when the snow was thick on the ground, and when I had very little money to live on, I never wanted to go back to Huddersfield and a 'normal' life.

3

One Woman and Her Dog

I loved my little cottage, really loved it. I didn't have any furniture, but people helped me out with bits and pieces. The villagers accepted me: I wasn't a typical townie, or 'offcumden' as they call them. They could see I was trying to fit in with their way of life. At the other side of the chapel lived a lovely old couple, Ruth and Keith Robinson, splendid people who took me under their wing. They lent me things, and gave me advice whenever I asked for it. One day when I was at work they planted up the whole of the front garden with flowers for me.

I never had a bed in all the time I was there. I did once make a valiant attempt at buying myself one with £30 that I had put aside. There was a second-hand furniture shop at Appleby and I spotted a bed in there. Unfortunately, when I looked around the shop I noticed a dusty, unkempt stuffed goat in the corner priced up at £30. I decided in my wisdom that chances to own stuffed goats were few and far between, so I bought it instead. There would be ample opportunities to buy a bed, and in the meantime I slept in front of the fire on a pile of cushions I'd brought from the caravan. There was no point going up to the bedroom to sleep when I'd got the living room warm and there was no heating upstairs, so I used what should have been the bedroom for storage.

There's a second-hand electrical shop in Penrith where I bought a fridge, cooker and a washing machine. A friend gave me a vacuum cleaner, a vital piece of kit when you come in from work covered in straw and hay. I didn't have a television.

I was clueless about cooking, so I lived on pasta and noodles. If I had a little bit more money, it would be mixed with a tin of condensed soup, the height of luxury living. Sometimes farmers feed their stock with turnips and mangolds, and some drop off the trailers and are left in the gutter at the side of the road. I'd pick them up and cook them long and slow. Roadkill also featured on the menu: there was a stretch of road nearby that bordered the woods and was famous for pheasants. I would simply cut the breast off and fry the meat. It's amazing how you can feed yourself for very little if you set your mind to it.

There was a small tiled fireplace in the cottage and so I was constantly foraging for firewood. If there was any windy weather it meant rich pickings in fallen sticks and branches. For a short time I did some work foot trimming and bathing sheep on one of the farms at Greystoke Castle, a beautiful estate near Penrith. One evening as I left work and was driving away from the castle I noticed something at the side of road. I stopped to investigate and found some enormous pieces of coal – the coal man must have delivered some top-grade coal to the castle and lost a sack from the back of the wagon. This kept my home fire burning for a few days.

The wonderful thing about the fire was that it heated the hot water. There was an immersion heater, but I prided myself on never having to use it – I'm the same at Ravenseat now. After trying to keep clean at a cold-water tap in an old dairy, I could luxuriate in a lovely hot shower, and I could wash my hair.

Removing the dreadlocks took a lot of time and patience, and a gallon of coconut oil. I worked away at the knots for literally a couple of weeks, and any matts that were too difficult I snipped off. I was surprised at how much straw and hay had accumulated in it, enough to feed a small calf for a week.

Despite the fact that I had very little money, and certainly wasn't spending my days off window shopping, I still took a pride in my appearance. I might have dressed for farm work much of the time, but I liked to retain my femininity and I enjoyed getting dressed up when I had the chance. I didn't buy new clothes: charity shops were where I did my shopping.

It was getting glammed up for a night out that cost me my back door – or half of it. It was really stupid. I had just put a giant unsplittable hunk of wood onto the fire when a friend rang asking me to go out for the evening. I had a shower, got myself ready, then realized that I couldn't leave the giant log on the fire in case it fell out of the grate. I very carefully managed to manoeuvre it off the fire and onto a shovel, and then deposited it, blackened and glowing, in the back garden. When I got home in the wee small hours I had half a back door: some of the hot ashes must have dropped off as I was carrying it out, and they had fallen onto the stormtrapper, the rubber draught excluder at the bottom of the door. The draught had fanned the embers, and they had slowly smouldered through the varnished door from the bottom upwards, leaving me with only the top half and a pile of ashes underneath. It was like having half a stable door, and my farmer landlord, Woody, had to get it replaced. I had a lucky escape: the whole cottage could have gone up in flames. Woody never asked me too much about what happened and I didn't volunteer the information. I think he suspected foul play because at the time I was being bothered by an unwanted suitor, a local idiot who wouldn't take no for an answer, and Woody had previously chased him off when he'd been hanging around the cottage.

I used to work for one old farmer who lived alone on his farm near Salkeld, where he kept a herd of suckler cows. Mike was a bachelor who had lived in the same house all his life with his sister who had recently died. He was a man of few words who lived frugally but contentedly amongst his cattle. He rarely ventured from his farm, didn't possess a driving licence and relied on a weekly visit from a housekeeper who would bring him basic supplies. Every Monday she would cook a stew, and this would last him all week. The flavour of stew is said to improve with keeping, but by the time it had been reheated for the fourth or fifth time I'd be beginning to worry about food poisoning. He must have had the constitution of an ox: he never seemed to ail or indeed tire of the same meal day in day out.

His farm was a ramshackle place. Everything was held together by baler twine, bedsteads were used for gates, and his cattle sheds were so full of muck that the cattle would escape over the doors: every single five-bar gate had a squashed top bar where cows had crushed them making their escape. Once a year he had a big sale of stirks (year-old cows), and I would help him get the paperwork and ear tags in order and load them onto a lorry. This was no mean feat, as the cows were so used to Mike doing their day-to-day care that they tended to misbehave when the routine varied. Mike would always make himself scarce at the crucial moment of loading up the cows. He couldn't bear to see them go.

Although the buildings and fences were a mess, he looked after his stock properly, almost too well.

He loved them. He would hand-rear many of the calves by bottle-feeding them. Their mothers were so old that they often didn't have enough milk to rear a calf, but he was loathe to get rid of them and consequently had some pretty geriatric cows in his herd. The calves would be overly friendly, because they were very used to human beings. This could create problems, as anybody who ventured into the field would be greeted by the unnerving sight of a half-grown bovine coming towards them at full pelt.

Trying to round up his cows and get them into a wagon for the sale was a nightmare. Their ear tags had invariably fallen out, and legally every cow needs a legible ear tag before it can be sold. The old cows needed to have their numbers read in order to record the calves' details, but their tags were illegible and so old they had probably been written in hieroglyphics. Mike just didn't 'get' the paperwork side of things at all: although he could read and write he flatly refused to fill in any forms or deal with any kind of officialdom. He had an agent who would call regularly and pick up all correspondence. He just couldn't understand why everything had to be so complicated, and I can sympathize, as I tackle the mountain of paperwork that Ravenseat generates.

One of my other regular jobs was working for a lady called Pat Bentley, who lived at Newby. She's a strikingly beautiful, glamorous woman who has travelled the world and was one of the first people to breed alpacas in Britain. She started quite a trend for them, and was a founder member of the

British Alpaca Society. So it's not only sheep that I can clip: I learned to clip alpacas too. And not a lot of people can say that...

She employed me to look after her small farm when she went away on business or, on one occasion, to South America to buy more stock. Most of the time I did a few hours a day for her, but when she was abroad I would stay on her farm looking after the alpacas, her hunter, Scattercash, and her dogs.

I loved working for her; she was a perfectionist and everything on her farm had to be just so. It made a refreshing change from some of the places where I had worked. The alpacas were naturally inquisitive and gentle animals. They seemed to cope with the British weather admirably and, although every paddock had a shelter, they spent most of their time quietly grazing or nibbling at the hay nets. Their general day-to-day care was quite simple. They did not suffer from foot rot as they had padded feet, they only calved during the day, only ever had one cria (baby alpaca), and they did all their poops in one big, communal pile. Brilliant!

Pat sold the alpacas to people all over the country and formed a cooperative so the fibre that was produced could be sold at a premium to buyers in the textile industry. They are difficult to clip, and different to sheep, because they don't have a single fleece, they have a fibre coat which comes off more like cutting hair. There is very little natural grease in it, unlike sheep wool, so you have to keep oiling the clippers as they have a tendency to overheat. The fibre does not need scouring and can be spun directly. It's graded as it's shorn and must be carefully sorted, as there are many different shades.

Now, an alpaca is quite tall, about the same height as me, and getting them clipped required them to be restrained by the legs and stretched over a clipping table, then clipped down one side, turned over and then clipped down the other. They looked very comical when done, with a small furry head that looked a bit like a crash helmet on top of such a long thin neck. It goes without saying that they didn't like it, but with an assistant to hold their head still they were pretty much incapacitated and, other than them spitting an occasional smattering of semi-digested grass and giving some ear-splitting squeals, it would go without a hitch. Well, I say without a hitch, but this is not accounting for a certain alpaca who went by the name of 'The Black Bastard'. Once again the curse of the hand-reared pet animal raises its ugly head. He had been bought from a zoo after being reared on a bottle and, I daresay, petted and cosseted by many children. This meant that he had developed a serious attitude problem. He had his own private paddock which he patrolled methodically, keeping his beady eye out for any person or other alpaca who dared venture near. He would lunge at any unfortunate in the vicinity, rearing up onto his back legs in an attempt to get his front legs over your shoulders so he could down you and … well, I'm not sure what his aim was, and nobody ever volunteered to find out.

One Sunday afternoon after a relaxed pub lunch, Pat's husband, Bill, returned home and, hearing the shrieks of the Black Bastard as he attacked yet another innocent alpaca which had strayed too near, had a sudden rush of bravado.

'That's it, I am going to sort out the Black Bastard once and for all!' he announced.

He nipped to the tack room and returned brandishing a lunge whip and, after much encouragement from Pat and other onlookers, set off to teach the Black Bastard a lesson he would never forget. It took all of ten minutes. Bill returned a broken man: the Black Bastard had claimed another victim. Bill's sadly inadequate attempt to tame him only exacerbated the problem and the embittered alpaca became Bill's nemesis thereafter.

Early one morning I arrived at Syke House to find Pat distraught. One of her best young alpacas had died in the night. This one was particularly special, recently imported from Peru, and Pat had hoped to breed from her, so her death was a big blow.

'Let's turn it into a positive,' I said.

'How can we? She's dead.'

'Let's get her stuffed.'

At the time, Pat was setting up an Alpaca Visitor Centre, a place where people could learn about the animals, buy some yarn and other products made using the fibre.

'I'll find someone to stuff her for you, and she can go on display. The visitors will love to be able to see an alpaca up close and to touch her coat.'

'Really? Can we find someone to do it?'

I knew that we didn't have long to decide what to do with the corpse, and having the vet out to look was not going to make any difference, so we made a few calls. By chance I had picked up a card from a taxidermist at a country show. I rang him, but he only did small birds and squirrels. However, he had a friend in the Scottish borders who, he said, loved a challenge.

'Bring me the body right away,' said the friend when I rang him.

Pat and I used a horse rug to make an improvised stretcher to get her into the back of the open pickup. We hastily wrapped her in a shroud fashioned from a bed sheet and I set off on the long journey with my very precious, very dead cargo. The address I had was a house on an ordinary suburban street in Hawick. I guess the neighbours were either completely oblivious, or entirely used to seeing two people carrying what looked suspiciously like a stiff, outstretched body wrapped in a shroud up the garden path and into the living room.

'Not a problem,' the man said, 'I'll get started now.'

This was a cue for me to leave.

'All I need is some photographs of a living alpaca so I can get the stance right.'

Pat found photographs to send to him, but it was a while before he needed them: he had a lot to do before raising the alpaca to a vertical position.

It cost Pat £3,000 to get her alpaca stuffed but she was mightily pleased with the end result. The stuffed alpaca took pride of place at the Alpaca Visitor Centre, so something good came out of her sad, inexplicable demise.

After I met Clive I introduced him and his

friend Alec to Pat, because what she really needed at certain times of the year was a couple of good strong stockmen, as her alpaca herd had increased considerably due to a new breeding programme. Clive and Alec enjoyed alpaca wrestling, it made a refreshing change from sheep, and they became dab hands in the art of camelid restraint and proficient in the use of an improvised angle grinder to keep their teeth right. Clive at one point went down to a quarantine centre in the south of England to check on a batch of newly imported animals, and I even went to Twycross Zoo, in the Midlands, to clip a couple of the zoo's alpacas. It was all quite funny really, especially when you consider that I didn't even know what an alpaca was until I met Pat.

My first contact with Pat had been through another contract shepherd, Bob, who was very well established in the area and often got offered more work than he could handle. He was happy to pass it on to me, and sometimes I would go out working with him. Gradually, as time went on, my name became known, and the phone rang regularly with work.

One of my great companions entered my life while I was living in the cottage at Crosby. I was clipping at a farm at Melmerby, and we had to gather the woolled sheep down from the fell. As usual I had been taken on the outward journey on a quad bike, and then walked and ran back, zig-zagging the fell, yelling, whistling and hollering to move the sheep – and at the same time being yelled, whistled and hollered at by the other shepherds and farmers. I sometimes felt like I was a poor substitute for a sheepdog but at least it kept me fit. It was after we had finished clipping and were packing up ready for home that night that I was taken to look at a litter of pups in a stable. I had previously seen sheep-dogs of many types and hues, from the traditional ubiquitous Border Collie to the lolloping great New Zealand Huntaways and smaller, finer Kelpies, but there was one type of work dog I had really admired, and that was the Bearded Collies. I had seen them gathering flocks on the steep slopes of the Lakes, moving the sheep through areas of deep bracken with their incessant barking. I liked their more relaxed attitude towards work – they didn't seem quite as 'hot' as the Border Collies.

I looked over the stable door and there in a corner sat the hairiest blue Bearded Collie bitch I had ever seen. Her coat was thick and matted and a pair of dark eyes peeped from behind a fringe of blue tangles. With her were half a dozen pups of the same mould, woolly and fat; she'd milked them well. But amongst the clutter of buckets and bowls and loose straw was another pup, not at all like the others. White and wiry-coated, it seemed to have the look of a terrier about it, perhaps a throwback from previous generations, because it was definitely from the same litter.

'They're all spoken for,' said the farmer.

I said nothing: decent pups off a good working strain are expensive to buy and working Beardies are especially sought after.

'Apart fro' that un.'

He gestured towards the mismatched pup.

'There's no one for that un.'

I looked at the small pup. 'What is't?' I enquired.

'A bitch an' thoo can 'ave it if yer want.'

This was unexpected, and certainly I wasn't going to give him time to reconsider. I put her in the footwell of the car and when I got back to the cottage I made a nest for her from a freshly shorn fleece, and she slept in front of the fire with me. She settled happily.

I called her Deefa, a stupid name, but I knew no better. D is for Dog, but also D for Different, because she was. I also figured that giving her one of the classic sheepdog names such as Fly, Nip or Floss would give her something to live up to and, frankly, I really wasn't sure how to train a sheepdog. I had been working alongside shepherds and farmers who had their own dogs, and I'd watched them work, but how to actually run a dog or, more to the point, make one run for me, was a mystery. I was offered plenty of work and some of it was do-able *sans* dog, but I knew in my heart of hearts that in order to be taken seriously, I needed a dog. The pup and me, we were literally as green as the hills, and sometimes – just sometimes – that works. We both learned together. I didn't know the correct way to train her, but I knew what I wanted her to do. I made up my own signals for her, and we persevered.

I practically begged her to work for me. If I could get her to be a good sheepdog, it would open up a whole new chapter for me. There's a saying among farmers: 'There's nowt worse than a running shepherd.' Meaning that if a shepherd

70

is legging it after sheep, then something has likely gone very wrong.

When someone says they want a shepherd, what they mean is a shepherd and a dog. The two go together. You can get sheep in by cunning and stealth without a dog, and in many places you can use a quad bike, but the dog is still the best method. I remember being on foot coming down Little Mell Fell near Penruddock, an exposed moor between Penrith and Keswick, on a grey, misty day with Deefa. The sheep I was driving towards home kept breaking back and, to add to my problems, I was carrying a lamb, so things were not going to plan. As usual, Deefa, who was now a lanky young dog, was heeling me. She was devoted to me and was as loyal as you could ever wish a dog to be, but she had never actually graduated to helping me other than with the occasional bark here and there.

'Please, please, Deefa. I'm so sick of running after sheep, can't you just get back?'

I'm ashamed to say it now but I actually sat down, using the recumbent lamb as a pillow, and wept. I like to think that at this juncture there was a great moment of clear understanding between woman and dog, because Deefa set off at lightning speed in the direction of the errant flock.

I could hardly believe it. I'd had no lessons; she'd had no proper lessons. I assume that a natural inbred trait to chase sheep must have surfaced. I simply used the commands that I'd seen others use, amalgamated with my own interpretations, which involved a lot of arm waving and gesticulation, and that was it. Deefa became a sheepdog because she *had* to, because I needed her. We weren't *One Man and His Dog* material because my commands were not exactly conventional and she ran with no style or panache, but she was my great mate – she stuck by me and I stuck by her. She had learned, somehow, to work.

With my erratic employment, I had to take the rough with the smooth, and when money was really short I lived on 29p packets of noodles, while Deefa was fed on bags of mixed cereal (an animal mix of corn, maize and peas) made into a hot mash with water and an Oxo cube to make it taste meaty. She ate it. Like me, she didn't have much choice, but we were both as fit as fiddles.

A few months later I acquired a friend for Deefa, a handsome, red and white bearded collie dog given to me by a farmer called Geordie. Geordie and Connie farmed in a picturesque little Lakeland village, the kind of place that attracted sightseers and visitors. The dog was just too territorial: if anyone strayed into the farmyard he would go for them. He could sink his teeth into a shin and disappear so quickly the victim would not see who had inflicted the wound. He was a fine dog, and never developed that same territorial issue with me, probably because we moved from farm to farm. There was one small snag: he was called Roger... Roger was such a ridiculous name for a sheepdog. I found it just too embarrassing to stand in a field yelling for 'Roger', so I changed it, first to 'Roger Red', because of his colour, and eventually just 'Red'.

He was a funny dog, already a considerable age when I got him, and in his prime he had been a brilliant cow dog. For many years he had fetched Geordie's small herd of milk cows in and, although capable among sheep, old age had made him slightly cantankerous and prone to moments of petulance. But with my two sheepdogs I could now get a job done, and I looked quite the part.

I started to gather my own little menagerie. I picked up a few pet lambs on my travels, all given to me by farmers who thought they were too weak to survive. I didn't win with them all, but the majority of them made it, and I then hand-reared them. My garden was plenty big enough for them and alpaca Pat also let me graze them in some of her fields. Eventually I would sell them, taking them to market when they were ready, but I had to be encouraged. The farmers who gave them to me used to get cross: 'We gave 'em to yer so you could mak a bit o' money, not so that yer can keep 'em an spend all yer brass on 'em.'

I was also given a Toggenburg goat called Flymo. She was a very pretty brown and white creature and quite a character. Her name tells you what she was good at. There was a wide verge on the other side of the road from my cottage and I'd tether her there. She ate all the weeds, including the nettles. I had people knocking on my door asking if I could tether her outside their homes: she moved up and down the village clearing the weeds. She came with me to Ravenseat, which Clive wasn't thrilled about, as he's not a big fan of goats. I have to admit, he was right to have his doubts about her, but we'll come to that later...

I increased my menagerie with a horse called Bruno. I had befriended a retired farmer called

73

Colin who still had a few sheep and would, on occasion, need a bit of a hand with them. In return for this he let me have a stable and I, of course, needed something to go in it. I bought a foal at the Cowper Day sale, which is a very big horse sale held every autumn in Kirkby Stephen. I paid the princely sum of twenty guineas and got a friend with a trailer to bring him home. He wasn't anything special to look at – he was a small, forlorn, raggedy piebald pony – but he was mine. My first ever horse.

The VW Polo had served me well but eventually driving the bumpy, potholed farm tracks caught up with us, and proved fatal for the car. It was never the right vehicle for farm work, completely wrecked inside from carrying lambs, dogs and other farming accoutrements. It was in a disgusting state but I managed to sell it for a few quid. The chap who took it said he'd never seen a car in such a mess. I was just amazed it was worth anything at all.

My next vehicle was a four-wheel-drive pickup, a Hilux, which was much better suited to the needs of a freelance shepherdess. Or so I thought. It was advertised in the local newspaper at £1,000 which, although a lot of money to me, seemed a bargain for what it was. It was exactly what I was looking for and within my price range. It was only after I bought it that I found out why it was so cheap: it ran on petrol, not diesel. I couldn't afford to fill the tank and I quickly found out how much each petrol station's minimum delivery was. I would put in two or three pounds' worth at a time, as that would be all the money I had. I got to know certain quieter, steeper roads where I would freewheel in order to save on fuel. That's how tight my budget was.

One farm I worked at, the wife was not into farming at all, and she was very suspicious of her husband hiring a woman. He took me aside and told me, 'Whatever yer do, I want yer to look miserable at all times. I dunt want 'er indoors to look out that window and see yer with a smile on yer face.'

Another farmer who I worked for would occasionally ring me on a Sunday morning asking me to work later that same day. I was surprised the first time, as he came from a devoutly religious family where Sunday was reserved for chapel, quiet contemplation and essential work only. The rest of the family would assume he was feeding the cows and sheep and doing all the necessary farm work, when the reality was that I was doing it and he was sneaking off to a neighbour's to watch the football.

I didn't have any serious romantic relationships during the two years I lived at Crosby. Although I made many friends and was invited to a few parties, I sometimes felt incredibly lonely and, although I enjoyed my work very much, it could seem relentless, getting up at 5 a.m. to milk cows, working day in day out without a break. It wasn't always easy – the times with no work and no money would play heavily on my mind – but there was never a moment when I regretted my career choice. I learned a lot about life, and self-preservation, and realized that a great deal of determination is needed to make your dreams come true.

I also learned that you never know what is round the next corner.

4

Ravenseat Only

My life was certainly busy. I had my regular customers, one of them being Martin Dent. Martin wasn't the typical farming type I was used to meeting. The number of farmers I knew who played bass guitar in a rock'n'roll band and drove around their fields in an old Jaguar were few and far between. I was used to being summoned to milk the cows at short notice on account of Martin being missing in action, or at least missing at milking time. There were many occasions when I'd be summoned by a slurred message on the answerphone with the sounds of 'Born to be Wild' pounding in the background. Martin also ran a livestock haulage business and at certain times of the year would be away for long spells, and then I would take full charge of his small dairy herd and flock of sheep. It isn't uncommon for farmers to have a sideline to help them through the vagaries of farming and, quite honestly, I loved being left to my own devices, pretending that it was my own farm and animals.

His sheep were mainly Rough Fell, which is a hardy breed found only in South Cumbria and around the Lake District: they are a breed which seems to have fallen out of fashion. He also had a small flock of Swaledales, an altogether more popular and profitable breed. Sensibly, Martin saw Swaledales as the way forward and was keen to improve and increase his flock, so once a year he would borrow a Swaledale tup to louse (put in) with his yows, and that's when he would call on his old chum Clive. They had known each other since they were sixteen, both keen farmers and both keen partygoers (it never really left Martin).

It was late October, and with tupping time approaching I was to be sent on a mission.

'Will you take the trailer and fetch a tup from a mate of mine? He's a right good Swaledale breeder, and he lends me a tup every year.'

Darkness was falling by the time I'd finished milking and foddering the cows. I hitched the rickety wooden trailer to the back of Martin's pickup and connected up the lightboard (it didn't work – they never do, not even after a squirt of WD40 into the socket). Mart's directions were basic: go to Kirkby, turn right to Nateby, then turn at the sign for Swaledale and just drive until you see a sign for Ravenseat.

I have now driven this route many, many times and know it like the back of my hand, but this was the first time. I'd travelled plenty of back roads and country lanes in my time, but this was something else. When I left Ash Fell at darkening it was starting to rain, and there was a real nip in the air. It wasn't long before I was in the small village of Nateby, driving slowly, uncertain where I was going. Then my headlights picked up a sign: YOU HAVE JUST PASSED THE LAST PUMPS FOR 22 MILES. I checked the gauge. Yes, Martin had given me a good tank of diesel.

In daylight there are wonderful views from the road, rugged hills and imposing rocky outcrops, and when you cross the border from Cumbria into Yorkshire you see the mysterious Nine Standards Rigg, a line of massive drystone cairns which dominate the skyline. Nobody knows their history: they could have been a lookout post, a warning to the marauding tribes from the north to keep away from the sheep and the women of Swaledale, or perhaps they are more recent, a boundary marker between Westmoreland and Yorkshire erected hundreds of years ago.

I didn't see any of this in the dark. All my headlights picked up was the narrow single-track road ahead of me, with the glint of metal barriers along the side which told me there were steep drops, and snow posts, tall wooden pillars that mark the road when the snow lies deep across it, their height an indicator of just how bad this route is in winter. The road twisted and turned and pitched up and down like a fairground ride. Martin had not told me how far I had to drive: I kept wondering if I had missed the farm, knowing that many farmers rely on a handwritten sign on cardboard or spray painted on a large stone. But I had passed nothing. Occasionally there was a broken-down stone barn that gave me hope I was near habitation, but then the road would carry on unwinding ahead of me, snaking round tight bends, the wooden trailer rattling behind. My lights reflected back the glinting silver eyes of sheep, and I'd have to slow down as they stood, rooted to the spot, before scurrying away into the blackness.

Eventually, after what seemed like hours of nervous driving, I saw it. A large, proper road sign which read RAVENSEAT ONLY, 1¼ MILES. Relief flooded through me: I wasn't going to have to retrace my tracks looking for it. Every time the trailer clattered across a cattle grid I felt it would shake itself to pieces, but it was still there. I couldn't see the fields and ghylls, the stone barns, the imposing hills ahead of me: all I had was the view in my headlights which was the uneven track and more sheep to scare from my path.

I passed a neat farmhouse, but I knew this wasn't the one, as it was only a few yards from the road, and too orderly to be a working farm. Another cattle grid, and then my headlights picked up the humped shape of a small, very narrow stone bridge. I looked at it apprehensively: was I going to have to get the pickup and trailer across it? At the last moment the road swung to the left of it and I realized thankfully that I wasn't going across the bridge. No, I was going through a river instead.

In the muddy farmyard I was greeted by the noisy dog, and then the farmer emerged from the doorway of the ancient stone farmhouse.

This was my first sight of Clive.

'Away in, mi lass, I'll get t'kettle on.'

I was relieved to have reached my destination with the pickup and trailer in one piece, and I didn't particularly want to hang about for too long but I liked the sound of a cup of tea, before getting my arse back to civilization. I followed

Clive into the farmhouse, cracking my head on the lintel above the door. These doorways were designed in days when everyone was smaller. I've learned when to duck and I'm proficient at it now, but I still occasionally get caught out by them. So that wasn't exactly a great start.

The house didn't impress: you can't ever say I went after Clive for his beautiful home, because back then, it wasn't. He had been married before, and his wife had left about a year previously. The carpets still showed the imprints of the furniture she had taken, the walls had green wallpaper tinged with yellow because of Clive's smoking, and the lovely big room where we now have an old-fashioned range had a wooden partition shutting it off from the front door. I imagine that years ago some old farmer said, 'I's sick o' tha' bloody draught, it's bloody freezing.' So with a hammer and nails they cobbled together a tongue-and-groove partition. There was nothing fancy about it, it just cut the room in half.

There was a bare light bulb hanging in the middle of the room, and apart from a well-worn sofa there was just a collection of flock books and shepherd's guides scattered about the floor. Flock books are a sheep farmer's most prized possession: they tell the history of his flock. I now think if Clive had to choose between me and his flock books, it would be a close-run thing...

The sitting room had a green carpet that felt like walking on moss: it was so damp it squelched under foot. The radiators were not attached to the walls, just leaning against them. It was used as a provender store, for animal feed. The place was, in a word, a wreck. Clive was farming all day and just sleeping and eating – and smoking – in the house. But I couldn't be critical, could I? That was more or less what I was doing in my cottage, minus the smoking.

He made tea, and we chatted, but I can't remember any of the conversation. No doubt the weather was the main topic: weather and sheep are what people talk about. Sheep are the main preoccupation. They say round here that if your fella goes missing it's not because he's off with another woman or gambling or drinking, it's because he's studying sheep somewhere.

We headed back outside and Clive took me to a dingy-looking loose box in the farm buildings behind Ravenseat, where he had corralled the tup. He strode in confidently to catch it, but the tup had other ideas. Clive now says that he was trying to impress me, but the tup was distinctly *un*impressed. It evaded him and began to run round and round the edge of the box, Clive trying to grab hold of it. The tup built up speed and in the end was doing a wall of death, like display motorcyclists do: going so fast it was nearly running up the walls. I couldn't stop laughing, while Clive was cursing, getting hot and bothered, and looking quite amateurish. Eventually he managed to get hold of the creature via a double folding body press culminating in an unscheduled parachute roll by the two of them. Then he manhandled it out of the box, we dragged it between us across the bridge, back to the farmyard and with a struggle got it into the trailer. There was a chorus of heavy breathing when it was over, Clive lighting up a fag and the tup staring malevolently from the trailer.

Before I set off back to Martin's, Clive asked for my phone number. I happily gave it: I gave my phone number to any farmer who might put some work my way and I didn't think any more of it, although I knew I liked him. I was intrigued by this wild place that I'd briefly glimpsed through the darkness, and the easygoing, funny man who lived there. Still, at the time I was more concerned about getting the belligerent tup back to Ash Fell along that twisting road, which at least seemed easier now I knew where I was heading.

Clive tells me that from the moment he saw me he was quite taken with me and that his intentions weren't exactly honourable. 'I wooed thi so subtlely yer di'n't even notice,' he says. 'What I saw when thi came was a striking blonde lady wit' lovely long legs, an' it di'n't take me long to make up my mind about thi. 'Twas just a case of hooking yer up an' reeling yer in.'

In his dreams.

He rang the next day, leaving a message on my answering machine.

'Clive here, yer know, thi came to borrow a tup.'

I didn't return his call. In fact, I ignored all of his calls, partly because I guessed he fancied me and I was playing hard to get, but also because I wasn't looking for love right then. But he persisted, and after about a week he left a message that guaranteed I would reply.

'I've had a disaster, we've bin gathering, one of

mi favourite yows 'as broken her leg. I cannae set it on mi own. Can you come and hod her for mi?'

He went on to say that when they bring the sheep down from the moor they have to negotiate a steep ravine with a beck in the bottom, crossing by a makeshift bridge made of railway sleepers. Somehow this unfortunate yow had slipped her foot through a gap in the rotting sleepers and managed to break her leg.

He knew how to pull at my heart strings. I went up there straight away, and between us we struggled to set her leg. It was broken high up, and it was difficult to set as there wasn't much leg above the break to anchor the cast, but somehow, with her sitting on her bum and Clive supporting her, we managed to get a cast on her outstretched leg. She eventually recovered, but forever after had one leg sticking out at an angle: she tripped me up a few times. It certainly didn't hinder her, she'd shoot past you and the leg would take you out. We kept her for many years, until she died at the age of ten, and we'd forever be having walkers stopping to tell us, 'Do you know, there's a sheep up there with a wonky leg.'

I would explain to them that this yow was special, and she had a lot to answer for as she was the reason that I ended up at Ravenseat.

It was a fine autumn day when we set the leg, and I saw the farm and Clive properly for the first time.

'There's plenty that yer haven't seen. You'll have to come back,' he said.

Lo and behold, I did. I went back to help him out whenever he needed it, and he'd send me home with a bale of hay for my sheep. It was a friendship, not a romance, but we were both finding more and more reasons for me to come up to Ravenseat. Gradually, the relationship deepened. Again, I can't look back and pinpoint a moment when I knew he was the right man for me: it was a slow awareness.

So I was spending a growing amount of time at Ravenseat, which was the cause of great gossip down the dale. You may think life up here is remote, so far from our neighbours, and with the population so sparse. But, believe me, you have a lot more privacy in a big city. Up here, the jungle drums start beating when anything unusual happens, and the word was soon out that Clive had a young lady going up and down to see him.

For me to get to Ravenseat I had to travel the same route I did on that first night, crossing over the border from Cumbria, where my cottage was twenty-five miles away, into Yorkshire. In the winter, that road is no-man's land, the snow-ploughs and snow-clearing gangs don't touch it. North Yorkshire council aren't interested in clearing a road that leads to Cumbria: they clear as far as the end of the Ravenseat road, because we are the last habitation. And vice versa: Cumbria doesn't clear their stretch, after the last houses on their side. So there's a seven- or eight-mile stretch that is always blocked with snow in winter. The sparse open moorland means that the snow is whipped up by the westerly winds, making it feel almost arctic. I travelled this road often, and one afternoon a farmer on a tractor flagged me down as I drove along in my little blue Subaru pickup (I'd traded in the Hilux – what was left of it – for this smaller, more economical truck). I thought it was something important he had to tell me, but all he said was, 'Watch thi speed, t'road's slape.'

Like I didn't know already. He was being nosy, he wanted a look at the mystery woman in the Subaru who was a regular visitor to Ravenseat. It wasn't just me that interested the locals. The farmers in this dale are very close, they've all been here a long time and they come from long-established families who have lived here for generations. Clive was a newcomer, even though he'd been here for several years when I came on the scene. So we were naturally a source of great interest and were maybe more scrutinized because of it. And it wasn't just our relationship that interested them. Folks here have always farmed traditionally, doing the same things, in the same way they've always done. To come to Swaledale with new ideas would have been frowned upon; it was a question of watching, listening and learning. Even though Clive had been there a few years, they were still watching to see he didn't stray from the old, traditional ways.

Folks saw me coming and going, but the only way to know what's really happening at Ravenseat is to come to Ravenseat, as we're at a dead end – the road goes nowhere else. So people had to find an excuse to drive up. And some of them were pretty transparent. Instead of ringing Clive up to tell him to collect a sheep that had strayed, it would be delivered back to him. People would come to talk to him about things they could easily discuss at the auction, friends would turn up with pots of jam. All just a ruse to see what was going on.

We were both very busy, Clive farming Ravenseat and me still contract shepherding and milking, but one evening we made a decided attempt to take some time off from farming and went out on a date for dinner. I made an effort, prised off the wellies and overalls and put on a dress, my one and only dress, and we went to the Red Lion pub at Arkengarthdale for a meal. I think it was the first time Clive had seen me scrubbed up and turned out, and he may have been impressed, but he's a true Yorkshireman – they hear all, see all and say nowt... On another occasion we went to Tan Hill, the highest pub in England. It's only three miles from Ravenseat as the crow flies but, as is often the case in the Dales and Lakes, it's a whole lot further by road. I even invited him for a meal at my place once. In hindsight this was a mistake ... I couldn't cook at all, but decided that a shepherd's pie would be appropriate. Now when I say I knew nothing about cooking, I really mean *nothing*. I had survived on a diet of pasta and CupaSoup and had never made any attempt to up my game. So when it came to concocting a shepherd's pie my lovely elderly neighbours were not only the suppliers of the shopping list but also the necessary pots and pans. It was only at the final assembly of my culinary masterpiece that I asked, 'How do you make mashed potato?'

I can't believe now that I genuinely didn't know.

'You've got a fork, haven't you? That's all you

need,' said Ruth.

Clive says it was the worst shepherd's pie he's ever eaten. If our life together had all rested on the shepherd's pie then it would have been over before it had even begun. Clive was a terrible cook too, living on his own, surviving on corn-flakes, shop-bought pies and Silk Cut Extra Mild. Thankfully, I've moved on from the shepherd's pie, learning how to cook by trial and error, and I'm now a dab hand at feeding the masses. Clive, on the other hand, has remained completely useless in the kitchen department and would revert back to pies and cornflakes in an instant. Even after all these years, he still cannot turn on the grill.

Clive, like me, started life as a townie. He was born in Doncaster, where his father, a joiner, built his own bungalow. His dad got a job over this way, working at a power station, and the family moved to Gaisgill, near Tebay in Cumbria, when Clive was seven or eight. His dad sold the bungalow for £3,000 in cash to a butcher who had won the money at Doncaster races. Gaisgill is a small farming community, and Clive's friends at school all came from farming families, and before long Clive was spending all his spare time with a farmer called Edward Metcalfe, known as Ebby, who was a renowned sheep breeder and sheepdog handler.

'I was the kind of kid who always wanted to know what was over the next hill, and the hill after that,' Clive says. 'I kind of had two homes: one where I slept and the other on the farm, where I spent all my time. I got the bug. He was a good farmer, a great stockman, and a grand fellow. He inspired me. There was never any doubt what I was going to do.'

Clive's parents' house had a field and a shed, and from the age of twelve Clive was buying and rearing calves. He'd do work for people and they'd pay him with a calf or a recklin pig that needed hand-rearing. (The recklin is the smallest in the litter, the one people call the 'runt', but I hate that word, it's an insult to the animal.) He worked one Christmas Day mucking out a loose box for a local farmer, on the promise of the next calf that came along. There used to be a baby milk factory in Kendal, and some of the women from the village worked there, so they'd bring back supplies of rejected powdered baby milk for Clive and his brother, Malcolm, who was in the little business with him.

Clive was much younger than me when he started farming. When he was fourteen he left school and home, and went to work on a farm in Arnside, on the Lancashire coast. The people were pleasant enough, but he was very young and homesick, and after a year he moved back and started working on a farm near his parents' home. But he didn't want to work for someone else: he dreamed of a farm of his own, and he knew he had to raise money, and to do that he had to work where there was money to be made. He worked at walling, fencing, road building and, during the summer months, sheep shearing, while all the time building up his own livestock. An old retired farmer in the village rented him more land and buildings.

Clive was desperate to be farming in his own right full time, and he applied for many tenancies, but it was difficult for a young fellow, as not only do you need a good reputation but also a substantial amount of money. A steadfast determination, saving every penny he could, eventually secured his first small hill farm, on Stainmore, which is in Cumbria but close to the borders with Yorkshire and County Durham.

There's something very special about hill farming: the sheep go with the farm. Centuries of breeding mean that the sheep have an inherent homing instinct, a knowledge that means they will stay on their patch of moorland even though there are no physical boundaries to retain them. It's a unique situation: the sheep belong to certain parcels of land. Even within one farm, certain sheep will go, every year, to the same patch of moorland. They know it, and they will travel miles to get back to it. They teach their lambs that this is *their* home. The word for this is 'heafing' and the sheep are 'heafed' or 'hefted' or 'hoofed' onto their part of the moors, for life. It's remarkable, because the moor is bare, without trees, just large expanses of heather and wiry, blow-away grass punctuated by peat bogs, nothing much to distinguish one area from another, and yet the sheep know their territories as well as any city dweller knows the suburb where they live.

Neighbouring farmers can turn their flocks out into thousands of acres of land with no boundaries between the flocks – and yet, remarkably, each group remains intact. There are occasional strays, of course, and a little bit of blurring at the edges. But for some deep, primeval reason, the sheep know their heaf, and they stick to it. When a tourist drives through the beautiful Swaledale countryside, they may wonder how the individual farmers sort out their sheep on these huge tracts of unfenced land, and the answer is that, by and large, the sheep do it for them. They stay on their own territory. When it's time to gather them, the farmers work together, each rounding up their own flock and passing over any that have strayed. The heafs all have their own names. We have four at Ravenseat: Black Howe, Side Edge, Robert's Seat and Midtown, three of them on Ravenseat land and one (Black Howe) on Birkdale Common, which we share with five or six other farmers. The sheep have different marks on them to show which heaf they are from.

The farm at Stainmore wasn't the farm of Clive's dreams, but it was a start, with a flock of 120 yows and forty gimmer hoggs, and twenty cows to milk. He married for the first time and had his older children, Robert and Rosie, while he was living there. Robert has caught the farming bug and works with us now.

Then, in 1989, the tenancy for Ravenseat came up. Ravenseat is on the 32,000-acre Gunnerside grouse-shooting estate: all the land for miles around is owned by Robert Miller, a multi-millionaire who made his fortune by co-founding Duty Free Shoppers, which pioneered duty free airport shopping. He is American by birth but an anglophile who has British citizenship. He comes in at number 91 in the *Sunday Times* Rich List, with an estimated £967 million. His passion is grouse shooting, and it's a hobby you have to be very wealthy to pursue because, unlike pheasants, grouse cannot be artificially reared as they feed on heather and the insects that flourish in the wild sort of terrain we have here.

Back when Clive applied for the tenancy the landowner was Lord Peel. This *was* the farm of Clive's dreams, a proper hill farm with a noted stock of sheep. Farms like this didn't come up to rent very often. He put his application in, but after three weeks or so he'd heard nothing. He rang up and was told that a shortlist had been drawn up, but that his name was not on it. He was very disappointed.

The very same day he heard he wasn't on the list he met up with Johnny Beckwith, another farmer, who said, 'Has ta gotten that farm tekken yet?'

Clive told him he wasn't in with a chance. Johnny said, 'I's gonna mek a phone call tonight.'

Later that night John Porter, another Swaledale farmer held in high regard, rang Clive.

'I'll have a word with Lord Peel. He doesn't always listen to me, mind.'

That's all that was said. A day or so later Lord Peel's agents rang and asked Clive to go for an interview. Before he saw them, Clive came to Ravenseat and he walked the entire perimeter of the farm. It took most of a day. He said he wanted to have a proper look, get the feel of the place. When he got to the interview, he was the only candidate who had done this and, what with the recommendations from other farmers who respected him, he got the farm. He brought his cows with him, walking them eight or nine miles across the moor to get here. In the old days people walked their stock everywhere. There is still a field at Kirkby Stephen owned by the church in Swaledale, bought centuries ago to give the Swaledale shepherds somewhere to turn out their flocks overnight when they'd walked them all day to the market.

Unfortunately, Clive's marriage started to go wrong, and by the time I met him his wife had been moved out for more than a year, and he was living at Ravenseat on his own. As he says, 'T'last thing I needed was another bloody woman.'

Then I turned up...

A few months after meeting Clive I was still living in my little cottage, working wherever I could, splitting my time between home, work and visiting Ravenseat. When I wasn't with Clive, we'd talk endlessly on the telephone. But typically for us, even a romantic chat on the phone could turn into something else. Once I was house-sitting at an old vicarage for an eccentric old lady who had gone into hospital for a hip replacement. She had a real menagerie: two dogs (a crazed ex-police dog German shepherd and an incontinent Boxer, both of whom wanted to tear me limb from limb), fifteen cats, all living in en-suite bathrooms (must leave a tap running as the cats don't like drinking from bowls), two donkeys and a flock of chickens. I didn't particularly relish spending my nights there. In its heyday the house was an imposing and splendidly grand Gothic edifice but it had fallen into disrepair, its past glories hinted at by the dusty leather books, heavy lacquered furniture and grand piano. Still-life paintings, intricate and beautifully realized depictions of dead birds, adorned the walls of the hall and staircase. Clocks in every room chimed constantly throughout the day and night, never quite in unison.

Having spent my second sleepless night in a four-poster bed, trapped under a cumbersome bedspread with the heavy tapestry curtain pulled tightly shut around to try and insulate me from the draughts and the sounds of the house, I persuaded Clive to join me for the evening. He was just as nervy as I was and the following morning was eager to leave, so much so that as he hastily pulled out of the driveway in his old Land Rover he hit one of the large stone gateposts with the pineapples on the top. The metal hanging gouged through the door panel and scraped down the entire side of the motor. This was especially annoying as he had earlier that week negotiated a deal to part exchange the Land Rover for a newer one. That was his first and last visit to the vicarage and I had the feeling I was being held partially responsible for this mishap. It wasn't long after this that I rang him.

'How's things? Sorted t'Landy?'

'Job done, took a lal' bit less for her on account o' t'damage but I've got a better, newer yan now.'

Then silence.

He's cut me off, he must be really pissed off with me.

It wasn't many minutes before the phone was

ringing. 'You'll nivver guess what I've done.'

As he'd been talking to me, gazing through the kitchen window, he had seen his pride and joy, the new Land Rover, not where he'd parked it, but perched on the edge of the stone bridge twenty yards away, its front end concertinaed into the wall.

'I munt 'ave put on't handbrake.'

I couldn't help laughing and soon we were both laughing together. There was no way he could blame me for that one...

It was the following spring, March or April 1996, when I actually moved in with Clive. I was lambing at Ash Fell for Martin and with lambing being an all-consuming job, there wasn't time to be going to see Clive at Ravenseat. One day he said to me, in his most romantic way, 'Don't yer think tha' it's time tha' you (and yer dogs and tha' bloody goat I suppose) gotten yerselves moved in here?'

So that's how I came to live at Ravenseat, and to live with Clive. I had loved and been intrigued by the place since my first sight of it, but I didn't come with ideas to change anything: Ravenseat moulds the people who live here. I didn't feel isolated or lonely, just deep contentment. As far as me and Clive went, it was all very understated. Clive says, 'I didn't exactly sweep you off yer feet, did I? It just kind o' happened. And I still marvel at how well suited we are.'

Moving here meant giving up my cottage, but the actual removal wasn't hard: whatever sticks of furniture I had were only fit for the tip. The main job was my animals. Through a friend of Clive's I'd bought another horse, Stanley, as a companion for Bruno. He was a Cleveland Bay crossed with an Irish Draught horse, a really big lad. Clive had to bring his trailer to take the sheep and, begrudgingly, Flymo the goat, and then returned for the horses. Deefa and Red came with me wherever I went, both riding in the back of the open-top pickup and never, ever jumping off unless given the command, even when we were stationary. Deefa barked every time we drove over a cattle grid – she knew that where there were cattle grids, there were sheep. Red would stand majestically with the wind blowing through his coat, surveying all around him.

Now, at this time Clive had a really good dog, Roy. He was far bigger than an average sheepdog, had a smooth tri-coloured coat and half-pricked ears, and was a wonder dog who knew everything about Ravenseat and could interpret all of Clive's moves, the sort of dog every shepherd needs. Roy was as loyal a dog as you could wish for. He was never tied up and never confined in a kennel; a short sharp whistle and he would be at Clive's side. He could fly-jump any fence, gate or wall with ease and when off duty would often swing by his teeth from a branch in the sycamore tree below the farmhouse. This was part of his daily routine; he spent many a happy hour swinging, accompanied by a deep growl of pleasure. Clive was genuinely concerned that Roy might not be willing to accept me or my dogs on his territory: he wasn't known for being overly friendly. As it was, he took it all in his long, lolloping stride and accepted both me and my two with a good grace.

Bruno and Stanley must have been the first two horses here since the demise of the working horses and the advent of the tractor. Dales ponies had been used to fodder the sheep until relatively recently in the high dales because the rugged terrain makes it impossible to get a tractor to many places. But the quad bike rang the death knell for the working ponies. In some ways it was a retrograde step, because shepherding on a horse gives you a terrific vantage point as you can see a lot further, and the sheep do not take fright as they can do when approached by a vehicle. Horses seem to have a sixth sense for boggy ground, and we don't bog the horses like we bog the quad bike. They pick their way, stopping every now and then, almost feeling whether the ground will take their weight. They hurry on through the wet ground and even take a leap, when necessary. Their instinct for self-preservation is something that no quad bike can ever match.

There was an occasion when breaking in Bruno that I turned this to my advantage. Bruno was a feisty and headstrong pony, full of youthful exuberance, and he could go like a rocket, not always in the right direction. I decided to ride him around the moor, the same route that Clive walked before he got the farm, to – in theory – wear him down a bit. Off we went, through the sheep pens, turned right and began the steep ascent up to Robert's Seat, Bruno showing his usual enthusiasm and me hanging on for dear life.

I was relieved to reach the old gamekeeper's

hut, Bruno out of breath but still going strong. Here the ground changes to typical moorland, tussocks of wind grass, knots of heather and then blacker peaty ground. We picked our way as best we could, Bruno now on a long rein, me whispering words of encouragement while his ears flickered with uncertainty. Suddenly, without warning, the ground fell away and began to swallow us up. Bruno floundered and panicked and although I was still in the saddle, I found my feet touching the churning, black ooze. Bruno was sinking, it was time to abandon ship. Keeping hold of the reins, I literally rolled sideways out of the saddle and onto all fours, levering myself out of the bog by grasping a clump of seeves (rushes).

Once Bruno had my weight off his back he was able to get a foothold (or rather a kneehold) and hauled himself clear. He stood, panting, then shook. We were both covered with the stinking black mud. I decided it was time to head for home and after a few minor alterations to the saddle, which had slipped because of his thrashings, we were homeward bound. I removed my mud-plastered clothes on the doorstep and then hosed down Bruno and his tack, and all was back in order. It certainly knocked the wind out of Bruno's sails: he was never any trouble after that and was always super cautious when crossing the moor.

A few weeks later, over a pint of beer at Tan Hill, one of our neighbours, Alan, asked how the horses were coming on (they were still seen as a bit of a novelty by the locals).

'Fine,' I said, 'comin' on just fine.'

'Really? Yer looked as if yer were 'avin' a bit o' bother wi't baldi [piebald] t'other day.'

I couldn't believe that right up on top of Raven-seat's open windswept moor, where you can feel so alone, I was being watched. But that's what it's like around here, the neighbours know more about each other than if we lived in a row of ter-raced houses.

Not everyone looked upon the horses as an indulgence, though. Sometime later I had acquired an old pony, Boxer. He was tied up in the yard when a neighbouring farmer, Jimmy Alderson, came to see us. Jimmy was in his eighties and not in the best of health: he'd had a heart by-pass and had been instructed that a little gentle exercise would be beneficial. This was a green light for Jimmy to carry on farming the same as usual. He was the epitome of a true Dalesman. He could have walked straight from the set of *All Creatures Great and Small* with his long, weather-beaten kytel (jacket) tied at the waist with a length of baler twine, an oversized ex-army sweater swamping his wiry frame and forming a spider's web over his checked shirt, coupled with heavyweight tweed trousers tucked into his rolled-over Argyll wellies. His gnarled, calloused hands told of a lifetime working the land and a flat cap worn at a jaunty angle partly concealed a shock of white hair. His face was furrowed and his skin nut brown from working outside in the elements for nearly eight decades. Even though I didn't meet him until the latter years of his life, he was still an incredibly tough, deeply religious man.

'I dun't nah how many years 'tis sen I was last on a Gallowa [pony],' he said.

'Now's thi chance, Jimmy,' I said, smiling.

I never really thought he would actually do it, but his eyes lit up at the offer. I gave him a leg up, and he rode Boxer round the yard. It was a very special moment: not a word was spoken but it was written across his face.

I've seen photos of him when he was young, shepherding the moors on horseback. He loved his ponies and could recall the names of all his horses from way back, and just for a few moments, he was able to enjoy that lovely feeling of being on horseback again.

I was twenty-one when I moved here and Clive was forty-two. He was divorced and had two children, so on paper we weren't a great match. But I never dwelt on the age gap between us, and I still don't. We both know we just fit together somehow.

At first I carried on with my contract farming, especially as I had things booked and I couldn't let people down. I continued to milk Martin's cows, until he, like many other small-scale farmers, did his sums and made the heartbreaking decision to quit with the dairy cows.

Anyway, it was soon clear that there was more than enough for me to do here, working full-time alongside Clive.

I don't know what the others hereabouts thought of my arrival but only a few weeks later I had the perfect opportunity to show them how well I fitted in. We were gathering the sheep for clipping up at Whitespots on Birkdale Common. There's lots of lovely mosscrop up there in the springtime, a cotton grassy sort of moss that is incredibly nutritious for the yows. Clive was helping Clifford Harker, another neighbour who also had sheep up there. Clifford and Jennie Harker lived at Pry House and farmed land adjacent to ours. Jennie's a great friend, and a great source of tales about the history of Ravenseat, as she was born and brought up in the farmhouse immediately behind ours, the one where the gamekeeper now lives.

For the gather I was standing down by the stone sheepfolds, ready to turn the sheep in. It was a very hot day, and the sheepdogs had been working hard and were now flagging. I saw the sheep coming in the distance, about a quarter of a mile away. Now, there were a few wily old darlings amongst the flock (probably Jimmy's), and they took full advantage of the situation and made a break for it. The air turned blue as they began streaming back up the moor and there was nothing anyone could do to stop them. The sheepdogs had no run left in them.

Clifford shouted at Tess, his dog.

'Git back, yer bogger, Tess.'

Tess slunk off out of sight, dog tired, so to speak.

'Send thi dog, lass,' he roared to me.

Deefa was with me, and because she had not been working all day like the others, she was fresh.

'Get back,' I yelled, my fingers crossed as I

100

offered up a silent prayer that she would come good.

She went off like lightning and made a wide-out run, everyone standing stock-still, their mouths gaping as she made away into the distance. She disappeared over the hill and within moments the sheep came back into sight with Deefa in full control of the whole flock. *Thank you, Deefa, you wonderful dog,* I whispered to myself.

Now, they don't say much, these tough old Yorkshiremen, it's not their way to praise people. But they gave me a nod when the sheep were all safely penned.

Yes, I was a woman, and an 'offcumden', a townie. But I'd shown them I could do it.

5

Hill Shepherdess

Coming to Ravenseat felt like coming home. I'd set off as a teenager reading the old veterinary books, then I'd worked at a succession of different farms, modern and traditional, some good, some bad. By the time I came here I knew what I liked, and this was it.

For me, it's the place I had dreamed about all those years ago when I watched *All Creatures Great and Small,* and when I pored over the book *Hill Shepherd.* The real-life James Herriot did not actually work at the top end of the Dales, his

101

practice was further south, some forty miles away near Thirsk. But when they made the television programme they came to Swaledale. It provided the perfect backdrop, as modern life had not really touched the highest outposts of the Dales; in fact, the money from the BBC for filming actually paid for the installation of mainline electricity to some of the outlying farms. So that's why I have a feeling of my life coming full circle, and I recognize the characters from the books: the details of their lives may be different, but the attitudes and lifestyles are exactly the same.

I am fascinated by Ravenseat and its past, and I'm always on the lookout for books relating to its history. I've got quite a collection now. Ravenseat captured me from the first time I saw it on that bleak night, and now it's part of me. And, for a time, I am part of it. We know, Clive and me, that we are temporary custodians, that the place went on for centuries before us and will go on for centuries after us. Looking down on the farmhouse from up on the hills gives me a feeling of timelessness, of the smallness of my part in the ongoing history of this amazing place. I feel connected with all the people who have farmed here in the past. We are doing the same things that they were, walking the same paths, repairing the same walls that they built and filling the same barns with sweet meadow hay (weather permitting). We face the same age-old problems: rain at hay time, deep snow in the winter, things that never change. Occasionally we get a more personal reminder of our predecessors in the shape of a clay pipe pushed into a wall, a clog sole behind a beam, a broken scythe blade and scratched initials in the ancient timberwork of the barns. Above all, there is a tremendous sense of continuity about the place.

The name Ravenseat comes from the old Norse word *hrafn*, which means a raven, and *saetr*, which means a place to summer animals. The Norsemen may not have stayed here in winter, but probably kept cows and sheep here in the summer. Ravenseat is the most wonderful place for summering animals, but wintertime is tough on both people and the livestock, so maybe those Norsemen were smarter than us. The 'raven' part was probably the name of an early settler who claimed Ravenseat as his own. We do occasionally see ravens soaring overhead and we hear their distant cries, but ravens are a mysterious bird, rarely glimpsed, as they inhabit only the highest and remotest areas, and we do not know if they actually nest here. We have an amazing variety of birds here, including one of the largest concentrations of lapwings in the British Isles. Although a lot of ground-nesting birds are in decline they appear to flourish at Ravenseat, with snipe, redshank, black grouse, golden plovers, sandpipers, oystercatchers, woodcock, curlew and skylarks in profusion.

I was out doing our regular evening walk with the children recently when we spotted a freshly hatched curlew, only hours old, hiding amongst the seeves. The light greeny-brown speckled eggshell from which it had hatched was lying, relatively intact, nearby. The children were puzzled as to how that chick's beak could ever have fitted inside the shell. I hope that Clive's knowledge and love of birds rubs off on the children as, quite frankly, I hardly know the difference between a seagull and an eagle (slight exaggeration).

Ravenseat is one of the highest, most exposed farms and is known as one of the toughest in the Dales, with our short summers and long winters, and it's a testing place to rear livestock. We were once at the auction mart and an old fellow who had spent a good while leaning against the pen looking at our sheep said, 'Thoo's got bestest stuff in t'auction, and thoo's come off worstest spot.'

That was a big compliment, as good as it gets.

Ravenseat sits at the head of its own little valley, two small rivers running within a hundred yards of the farmhouse. Whitsundale Beck, the larger of the two, flows from the west, and is spanned by the ancient packhorse bridge. Hoods Bottom Beck flows from the north, from the spectacular High Force waterfall away in the distance to Jenny Whaley Falls, a series of smaller tumbling and rushing cascades only a stone's throw from the farmhouse. It is a mystery as to who Jenny Whaley was and why the waterfall would be named after her. I like to imagine that she perhaps flung herself in after a doomed love affair, but my history books have given no clues about her. Another far smaller but equally timeworn bridge sits below the falls, a remnant from the days when coal from the Tan Hill pit was carried in panniers on the backs of ponies through Ravenseat and then along what is now part of the

Coast to Coast walk, and away into Cumbria.

The two rivers join to become one, which keeps the name Whitsundale Beck, meandering through the Close Hills valley, gradually gathering strength and speed, then culminating in another series of falls below Hoggarths Bridge. Here it meets another tributary, Birkdale Beck, to form the River Swale.

In days gone by, Ravenseat was a very busy place. In 1820 there were eighty-eight people here, according to the parish records. There were five farms on what is now Ravenseat land: the two farms in Ravenseat yard, ours and the gamekeeper's place, and Black Howe, Close Hills and Hill Top. The people who farmed here long ago farmed much smaller parcels of land, and farming was not their sole source of income. Coal and lead mining were big business in the upper Dales and many of the men relied on these for employment.

Tan Hill coal mine was about three miles from here. It was a small colliery which produced poor quality coal until early last century. Coal was expensive, and the farmers would have relied on peat as the fuel to keep the home fires burning. Turbary rights were important for the people in this area, entitling them to go to the moor and cut their own peat. They must have felt the cold, as I have yet to sit against a hot peat fire. We have tried them, but the fire just smoulders and glows without throwing out much heat at all.

Then there were the lead miners. Lead was mined all over the upper Dales from Roman times, when lead was important for making coffins. Mining was a grim job, and it's difficult to imagine that in the seventeenth and eighteenth centuries, when the industry boomed because new methods of roofing and building became popular, women and children worked down the mines. Our friend Jennie Harker is one of the Whitehead family, who used to live in the farm-house right behind ours, and she and her siblings remember talk of the days when the menfolk would leave home in darkness to walk to the mines and return in darkness during the winter months, never seeing daylight except on Sundays.

Below the road end that leads into Ravenseat there was a lead mine called Lonin End. Little remains of what once was, in its heyday, an innovative and substantial mining operation employing fifty people. I sometimes take the chil-dren down to Lonin End, and they are awed by the enormous, gaping open shaft. I have to be very attentive as, intriguing as it is to the children to drop pebbles and count while waiting for the splash, I don't want to hear a far bigger splash.

It is not a great place to take our metal detector, as it bleeps constantly. The children were determined to find a lump of galena (lead ore), but I broke it to them gently that this was very unlikely, as it was highly sought after by those early miners. Just to prove me wrong the children soon found a substantial lump and by the time we had taken turns to carry it home we were all thoroughly fed up.

Cheaper imported lead from Spain meant that the mines were abandoned from 1870, although one or two survived until the end of the nineteenth century. There was an exodus of people from the Dales to the woollen mills of West Yorkshire and the cotton mills of Lancashire and even further afield to the gold mines of the Americas. The few remaining in Swaledale now had to survive from farming alone.

Everyone made some extra money by knitting stockings, a trade which began in the early seventeenth century. Even the men knitted: as they walked to and from the mines the lead miners would make woollen stockings using a knitting sheath tucked into a belt. This held a needle so they could knit using one hand. Knitting sheaths varied in design from area to area and in Swaledale the goose-wing variety was most common. Some were ornately carved affairs with magnificent detailing, but the majority were crudely made and often carved only with the initials of their owner. They were sometimes given as a love token to a girl from her admirer. I'm still waiting for Clive to produce one for me but if he is after a pair of woollen stockings then he may be waiting a while: using these required an incredible amount of dexterity which sadly I lack.

The wives would knit as they walked from barn to barn to tend their cattle and sheep. From the earliest age, the children were taught to knit too, and the women would spin the raw wool given to them by the wool merchants into yarn for the whole family. The merchants would also visit the cottages and farms to collect and pay for the stockings. Payment was poor, but it helped towards the subsistence living the farmers made.

Back in the seventeenth century, there was a

stocking merchant known as Blue John, probably because of the wool dye on his hands, who visited the Swaledale farms to buy the knitted wares. When he left Ravenseat he still had a large sum of money, and he set out from here to walk the lonely route across Birkdale Common and into what is now Cumbria. He was never seen alive again, but a couple of years later his body was found among the peat haggs. A farmer was charged with the murder, but the evidence was very shaky, coming from a miner who contradicted himself and gave a description of events that nobody else supported. So, in the end, nobody was held to account. His name has been immortalized, as the place where his body was found is known to this day as Blue John Holes.

In addition to the farming and mining, there was a quarry at Hill Top supplying stone to build the houses and barns in the vicinity. The poorer stone was carted away to build and repair drystone walls. At the turn of the twentieth century, there was a family of thirteen brothers working there. People came from far and wide to buy the flagstones, which were of very high quality. The quarry was worked until relatively recently, supplying flagstones, quoins and lintels for the many barn conversions that need to use traditional, local materials to conform to the original builds.

Whenever I get a spare moment (not that often), I research Ravenseat, not only with my books, but by talking to anyone with memories of what it was once like.

Instead of it being a place in decline, a remnant

of busier times long ago, I love the fact that we are re-stocking Ravenseat with people. We have all the children, we have guests staying in our shepherd's hut, we have walkers stopping for a break and other visitors just driving up to sit in the sunshine, or the barn if it's raining, and eat my cream teas. During the shooting season we see the shooting parties come up through the farmyards and out onto the moor, a real cross-section of people from beaters through to the well-heeled set who have come to spend the day grouse shooting. There have been times when we have caught a glimpse of well-known faces, Elle McPherson looking splendid in tweed, or even Prince Charles.

Actually, it was Prince Charles who caught a glimpse of me, in a wetsuit and wellies, standing at the side of the road after taking a dip in Wainwath Falls. I like to imagine that I looked rather like Ursula Andress emerging from the sea in a Bond movie, but it's more likely that I just looked a twit...

There are farmers' days when we are invited to go and shoot, but it's not our thing. We are usually presented with a few brace of grouse but, despite it being a sought-after delicacy, we find the dark, strong, almost soily flavour quite unpalatable. Rather than waste them I take the breast meat off and wrap it in streaky bacon to disguise the taste.

Although neither Clive nor I were born into farming families, we both understand the feeling that farmers have of preserving the land and the way of life for future generations. Clive says, 'I am honoured and privileged to have Ravenseat for my time, and so I see it as my duty to keep it as good as I can for whoever comes after me.'

So we are connected forwards as well as backwards with the story of the place. Even when the weather is filthy and horrible, and I'm having one of those days when things are not going to plan, where else would I rather be? Nowhere.

Some of my favourite books about this area were part of a series written by two ladies who were travelling the Dales in the 1920s and 1930s. They were visiting the area at a crucial time, just as some of the old traditions and equipment were being abandoned and newer methods were being adopted. They collected much of the old farm memorabilia which is now in the countryside museum at Hawes. They wrote about visiting Ravenseat, where they were made welcome and ate trifle with the family. They described an old man, hunched over and crippled with arthritis, sitting by the range, and they talked of the feelings of sadness that permeated the house because of the recent death of a young child. She had fallen ill so the family had taken her by horse-drawn sledge to see a doctor at Kirkby Stephen. I imagine that if you weren't dying already, that journey would certainly finish you off. The little girl had peritonitis, and it proved fatal.

I asked the Whiteheads whether they had any recollection of the tragedy but they didn't remember anything being said. It was, after all, before their time, but I reasoned that it would have been spoken about. Jennie suggested it may have been a tale made up just for the readers of the book. But a few years ago we had a visit out of the blue from a man called Tom Cox. He came back to see his childhood home for the first time since leaving as an eight-year-old in the late 1930s. His family had come over from Orton in Cumbria with all their possessions on a horse-drawn cart when he was a babe-in-arms. He remembered life here: the long walk through Close Hills laden with eggs and cheese to meet up with the butcher's trap, the return journey carrying flour and sugar, and during a heavy snowstorm filling the boiler at the side of the range with armfuls of snow gathered through the living-room window.

It was his father who had plumbed in the first water supply to the farmhouse from a spring high up on the hillside; previously they had faced the constant, laborious task of drawing water from a well at the back door. It was only recently that the same spring moved to below the water tank, which was bad news as gravity dictates that the water source needs to be above the tank. A lot of digging was needed, with spades, sweat and curses, as the hillside is totally inaccessible by machine. A new tank was installed and, as long as the spring stays in situ, we will keep our running water.

Tom's memory was lucid and after talking to him at length about life back then I remembered the tale of the little girl. 'Do yer know owt about a lal' girl who died here?'

Silence...

'How's ta know about that?'

111

'I's read 'bout it in a book.'

He sighed, looked to the ground and chewed his lower lip. 'That were a varry lang time sen.'

He said that the story was true, that the old arthritic man was his uncle Willy and that the little girl was his younger sister, Hilda. He said that she was buried in an unmarked grave at the chapel at Keld, and even he did not know exactly where. The family had no money for a headstone to mark the spot. You could see the sadness in his face as he recounted those unhappy times. To romanticize about the old days is all well and good, but life was certainly hard back then.

It wasn't long after that the family left Ravenseat, never to return. I reasoned that this was due to the tragedy that had befallen them and that perhaps the memories were too painful. We kept in touch until he also passed away. A part of me feels good that a forgotten little girl now lives on, if only in my memories of Tom. She, too, is part of the history of Ravenseat.

Another visitor was a well-spoken, dignified, elderly gentleman who drove up our road one day with his wife. He introduced himself as Ingram Cleasby, and I knew from my research that Cleasby was one of the family names from Ravenseat's past. Our visitor had been brought up at Sedbergh, but he told me that his name, Ingram, is Anglo-Saxon for raven, or raven's nest, and that he was named this because his family had farmed here. It was a Cleasby who built the house behind ours, in 1820.

As he was leaving he took a photograph of a double rainbow over Ravenseat, and later sent it to me, with a letter. I didn't know until someone told me later that he was a very distinguished clergyman, who served as the Dean of Chester and the Archdeacon of Chesterfield.

There is a track that runs down through Swaledale called the Corpse Road, which dates back to the sixteenth century and was the route the locals had to take to give their relatives a proper burial at Grinton church. It is twenty miles long, and the journey took a day and a half from the upper dale with the dead body carried in a wicker coffin, and then the mourners had to make the return walk. We have a small field at Ravenseat that is known as the 'graveyard' and is rumoured to have been used to bury the bodies that didn't make the arduous journey to Grinton. After all, if you didn't like someone much in life, you might not want to walk for a day and a half there and then back again just to give him a Christian burial.

The illicit burials became such a problem that a church at Muker was built in 1580, during the reign of Elizabeth I. A special dispensation was given for it, because folk were becoming desperate about not being able to give their nearest and dearest a proper burial.

The 'barn' where I serve the cream teas when it is raining may at first glance look like a traditional stone barn, but if you look inside you can see that it has slit, arched windows. It was once a tiny chapel, used by a group of Inghamites, who were a nonconformist sect who followed the preachings of Benjamin Ingham and broke away from the Methodists and Moravians in the middle of the eighteenth century. After it stopped being a place of worship, a pair of large doors was added to the front and it was used as a cart house. Jennie's grandfather remembered a pulpit in the corner. I don't think it was ever ornate, but still, nobody knows what happened to it.

We know that the barn was originally thatched with ling (heather); you can see the line of the steep pitched roof at the back, and we know that the barn was once used as a house, before it was a chapel. We've had an architectural historian up here looking at the buildings, and he wrote in his report that the barn is the second oldest building in Swaledale, to his knowledge. I forgot to ask him which is the oldest.

It is only one of many barns on our land. A famous feature of the Swaledale landscape are the stone barns, seen in almost every field. The barns were used for the storage of hay and the over-wintering of cattle and sheep. Some of the barns are known as hog houses and these have two storeys, with flagstone floors to the upper level. They needed flagged floors because of the sheep peeing: wooden floors would have rotted away.

Most of the barns are between 200 and 300 years old, although they were still being built up to the late 1800s. When the farm-workers had cut the hay by hand with scythes, it was stored near to where it was needed later in the year to feed the animals. Most of the barns had stalls where cattle were tied up by the neck and fed on the hay until spring. We still sometimes over-winter stirks and tup hoggs in these barns if there is a spring or beck near enough to make it easy to water them.

Many of the barns had, over the years, fallen into disrepair, but nowadays there is a grant to restore and maintain them, which has enabled us to return all our barns to their former glory. Most of the barns and fields have lovely names, some referring perhaps to their original owners: Miles's cow'as, Peggy Breas, High Bobby Dale. Others relate to their topography or position: Round Hill, West End, Close Hills. Now, sadly, the maps show only the hectarage and field numbers, not their beautiful names. We prefer to use the original names and encourage the children to do so as well, aware that there is a real danger the names will be lost forever.

As for the farmhouse, I've traced it back to 1580 when there were two houses and six cottages at Ravenseat. The house is a typical Dales building, with thick outer walls, low ceilings and small windows. Not a grand affair, but warm and homely.

That's a small sample of the history of this place and I like the idea that we, too, are making a living in pretty much the same way as the people before us. Sometimes the walkers who pass through ask, 'What does a hill farm do? How does it work?'

I tell them, 'We're very good at rearing animals. There's not much point up here trying to fatten them up, we haven't got the crop for grazing and our seasons are too short. But what we are good at is rearing first-class animals.'

We sell them to lowland farmers to either fatten or to use as breeding stock.

We have about 900 breeding yows, and every year we keep 250 gimmer lambs (a gimmer is a young female sheep) to replace the older yows, which are sold, so the stock numbers and ages remain constant. In September and October there is the 'harvest of the hills' when all the hill farmers gather their sheep and sort them out, then take their surplus to auction. We sell gimmers, keeping only the best to replenish the flock, so the standard stays as high as possible. Other farmers buy them because hill sheep are hardy and healthy and thrive well in kinder climes.

Out of the tup (male) lambs born at Ravenseat, we keep about thirty as potential breeding stock. Then gradually they get whittled down to four or five of the best which go to the tup sales every autumn. Clive can often be found studying his tups, sometimes for hours. It beats television…

The tup lambs that aren't good enough to keep are fattened and sold during the winter. We lamb late up here so these lambs are nearly a year old when they go to the market, having spent the summer with their mothers high up on the moors amongst the heather. We believe this gives the meat a superior flavour to more intensively reared lambs.

We bring the yows down off the moor into the fields near the farm to lamb, then afterwards they go back to their heafs with their offspring, to teach the little ones their heaf. We only let those with a single lamb go back to the moor as the grazing is too sparse for a yow to be able to rear twins and there are many perils up there – gutters (water channels and small becks), rocks, grips (drainage ditches) and bogs. A sheep can only keep her eyes properly on one lamb. Hill sheep do not have as many multiple births as lowland sheep, but we do always have plenty of yows with twins, and we summer these up in the 'allotments', an area above the farm that was allocated to Ravenseat in 1828, when parcels of land were handed out to local people. It was at the time of the battles against enclosures, and it was done to give poor farmers a chance to work their own land.

Our allotments are kinder and sweeter grazing than the moor, and make it easier for us to keep an eye on the twin lambs. In September we gather in all the sheep and the lambs are 'spained' (weaned). At this stage the lambs will come into the meadows, the land close to the farm where the grass is growing again after haymaking, and the new grass, which we call 'fog', is particularly nutritious and good for fattening them and getting them ready for sales.

Our lambs are not reared intensively on feed and cake. They grow naturally, running around, doing what lambs are supposed to do and eating what they are supposed to eat. It's a longer process, our lambs take time. I truly believe that animals reared in a natural environment are happier, and this is reflected in the taste. We eat them ourselves, of course, and the meat is delicious, but how many I keep for our freezer depends on the price they are making at the market: if they're fetching good money I only get to keep a cronky one; otherwise, when prices are not so good, I fill the freezer.

There is far more to lambing than the arm-length rubber glove. As we are lambing a pedigree flock, a large amount of recording takes place. Each lamb is given an ear tag with an individual number, and its sex, sire and dam, and its heaf are all recorded. Before they go out to the moor we mark them on their shoulder, the middle of the back, the back of the head or the loin for our four different heafs. The yows are horn-burned, the initials AC or CA being burned into their horns when they return from wintering away as hoggs at about twelve months old. This tells everyone that they are our sheep. Even if the heaf mark is lost or the ear tag falls out, the horn burn will remain. We don't really know the origins of the initials, but we know that Ravenseat was occupied by farmers with the surnames Alderson, Cleasby, Campbell and Coates at different times in the past. It's probably their initials immortalized on our sheep, but, of course, being Clive and Amanda these initials relate to us too.

We have what is known as a closed flock, which means we don't buy in any breeding yows. We introduce new bloodlines through buying in tups from other pedigree flocks. To some extent we can use our own tups, the ones we breed, but this has to be done very carefully to avoid inbreeding.

Every autumn we sell draught yows, our older yows that have bred three crops of lambs for us. They are still good breeders, have still got their teeth and two working tits, but we like to keep our flock young as Ravenseat is a tough place to live (for sheep and people). Clive says, 'There's only yan thing better than a good old'un, and that's a good young'un.' I'm not entirely sure that it's just sheep he is referring to...

There are some yows we never sell, a small flock of sheep who live out all their days at Ravenseat. We call them the 'crusties', because they are old and decrepit and suffer from similar problems in old age as humans do. They are greying, have arthritis, no teeth, and they're skinny with saggy udders. Just looking at them, nobody would understand why we keep them, but in their time they were star breeders and show winners. They have earned the right to live out their days here.

We had a really old tup who lived to the ripe old age of thirteen. His pedigree name was Rasputin, but we called him Mossy because he came from a farm called Mossdale. He sired many show winners and was a real character. Mossy was troubled for most of his life with a problem foot that would regularly require a pedicure, which he disliked intensely. One day Clive was trimming his foot and somehow accidentally wounded him quite seriously with the foot shears, and Mossy never forgave him. He mortally hated Clive, and would head for the hills whenever he was near. I looked after him for many years and would hand feed him twice a day. Then one day he wasn't waiting at the gate for his usual morning feed and I found him dead in the snow. It was only when we looked up his date of birth that we realized what a great age he was.

We know our sheep, even though there are a lot of them. It's just like running a big school: a head teacher gets to know all the children, though some are more memorable than others, sometimes for a good reason and sometimes for a bad reason. Some sheep are escape artists, some are incredibly greedy, some are flying machines and can jump (ratchin), some are always straying, some are wild, some are friendly, some make good mothers, some not. We ken (know) our sheep. In these parts it's the most heinous of crimes to not ken yer sheep.

Sheep are just like people: you get nice ones and you get nasty ones. People use sheep as an analogy for placid creatures that always follow each other. It's not true, you just have to take the time to stand and watch them to learn their personalities. Clive once did an advert for Xerox photocopiers, supplying a line of sheep looking exactly the same. The tag line was 'It's not just nature that can make perfect copies.' But they don't look the same, not if you look properly.

Clipping is one of the annual jobs I love the most. The first to be clipped are the hoggs. They have eighteen months of wool on them, everywhere: woolly bellies, woolly legs, woolly bums. And they have never been clipped before. Clipping is not at all painful but still they struggle. They are the hardest to clip but they produce the best wool in terms of quality and quantity.

Over the years I've discovered that the noise of the clipping machine is a great soother for babies. You know you hear of babies that fall asleep to the sound of the Hoover? Well, ours have all fallen asleep to the sound of the clipping machine. It's the one job I can't do with a baby strapped to me, but they lie nearby amongst the wool and sleep as soon as I switch the clippers on.

We usually clip in July, but like everything else, it's weather dependent. Sheep are easier to get in dry than hay, so hay takes precedence. If hay gets soaked with rain it is probably ruined, so when the good weather comes that's what we concentrate on. The wool also has to be dry, because you can't sell wet fleeces: they rot, and the Wool Board won't pay for the extra weight of water. It is also miserable clipping wet sheep.

Clive used to be a contract clipper in his younger days and clipping can get rather competitive. I can't decide whether he is slowing down or I am speeding up because occasionally I can beat him. We wrap the fleeces and pack them into large wool sheets that hold about fifty fleeces. When full, the sheet is sewn shut, labelled up and sent on a lorry, usually to Bradford.

Swaledale wool is used for carpets as it's very hard wearing, not the soft lustre wool that's used for sweaters. Nowadays it's also used for insulation: if you look in any DIY store you'll find the most expensive insulation is wool. So it beats me how little we get for it: in our worst year, five or six years ago, I got a measly cheque for £65 for 2,000 kilos of wool. In a good year it's about £400, but you can see that hardly covers the cost of clipping. We don't farm sheep for their fleeces any more. Years ago the wool cheque used to pay

121

the rent on hill farms.

Our land and situation doesn't lend itself to big, modern machinery. We do occasionally put on farm tours, usually for *All Creatures Great and Small* fans, but Clive agreed to another type of tour recently – a farming discussion group tour! Forty arable farmers from East Yorkshire arrived on a super-luxury coach, the ex-Tottenham Hotspur tour bus. It was a challenge getting this impressive vehicle up the dale, over the narrow bridges and winding roads. The locals must have thought the Rolling Stones were passing through.

In his wisdom Clive decided that a sure way to impress was to line up his fleet of machinery. The overall effect was that our yard looked like the forecourt of an agricultural dealer in about 1972. There was a knackered haybob, a trailer, a very rusty digger, a tractor and a quad bike. That's it. Quite honestly, it looked as if a visit from the scrap man was imminent. We're a dog-and-stick kind of farm. The farmers were taken aback by how we do things and were intrigued by some of our age-old methods. We had a grand old after-noon, and they went away happily albeit with more passengers than they came with, as the children wanted a ride on the fancy bus.

Clive has a love/hate relationship with horses – he's accepted mine but I have a strict quota. I am allowed two, so I've got seven. Stanley, who came with me, didn't like it here and we had to sell him. He was a big amiable fellow: he used to lean over the sheep pens and pick a sheep up by its wool, just out of curiosity. But he found it very

122

cold up here and, even when rugged up, shivered and shook. Once he managed to squeeze himself into one of the barns through a doorway that was considerably lower than he was. He could not summon the courage to squeeze himself back out and remained in there for a couple of days looking forlornly out of the window. I wanted to go and feed him but Clive was having none of it.

'Thoos not tekkin 'im nowt, silly bugger will come out when he's hungry.'

And of course he did.

Otherwise, our only rule is that the horses have nice temperaments. We can't have any that aren't good around the children. Only the other day, the children were playing hide and seek and Miles won. No one could find him because he had found the perfect hiding place, underneath one of the horses in the stables.

In the throes of first love, Clive was happy to let me bring Flymo with me, but the reality is that he is a hardened goat hater, and his reservations about goats running amok were justified. The sheep followed Flymo everywhere, usually in the wrong direction; she didn't allow them to go through gates and charged them as they attempted to pass by. She also ate the washing off the washing line: I found a pair of pyjama trousers with one leg missing. And she stood on her back legs and ate two hanging baskets.

But her worst crime was when a friend of ours who lives nearby dropped in one afternoon for a cup of tea, arriving in his beautiful shiny black sports car. It was polished to perfection, so much so that you could see your face in it. And that was the problem. While we were in the farmhouse chatting, Flymo was getting indignant with another goat: her own reflection. When we came out there was not a straight panel on his car, she'd been venting her anger at the intruder by butting it. There was little point in protesting her innocence, as the dents in the car were all shaped like a goat's head. It didn't go down very well. Somehow, we managed to stay friends, but he drives an ordinary car now.

Flymo's attack is not the only problem we've had with cars parked on the farm. We had an official from the Ministry of Agriculture up here once and I did everything to impress her, down to getting out proper china cups and saucers instead of mugs. We were sitting in the kitchen going through the paperwork when suddenly a sheep shot in through the open door, going full pelt, and headed down the hallway. Seconds later a sheepdog came past like a torpedo, and almost immediately the sheep returned with the dog in hot pursuit. She never batted an eyelid, she never even mentioned it; we concluded our business, and we shook hands as she left. I was feeling quite confident I'd made a good impression.

But when she went outside to her car we found she had parked on a set of chain harrows, and not one, not two, not three but all four of her tyres were completely flat. The harrows had been left at the side of the road several months before and the grass and weeds had grown up through them making them almost invisible. She sat patiently waiting for a tow truck to come and haul her car away while I kept a low profile.

The summers are short here, and often wet, thus we spend a lot of time in waterproofs. A couple of years back I bought some bright yellow fisherman's bib and brace waterproofs off eBay.

When Clive saw me unwrapping the parcel he laughed.

'What the bloody hell has ta bowt them for? You'll look like Captain Birdseye.'

'I bet yer any money that you're wearin' 'em before t'year's out,' I said.

He's lived in them ever since. He looks like he works for the council, but they do the job. When you are being lashed by the rain on the top of the moor, it's as wet as being in a storm at sea. But there is a drawback: he mustn't drink too much tea.

There are some modern inventions that make our lives much more pleasant than those of our forebears. We have warm, efficient clothes and boots. Underneath our waterproofs we stay dry. The children all have waterproof overalls, and we must own one of the largest collections of wellies ever. The old farmers did the same jobs wearing hobnail boots and heavy woollen clothes which must have been permanently soggy, and with nothing more than smouldering peat fires to dry them out.

There's only one downside to the children's wonderful all-in-one weatherproof suits: they can hide a very smelly nappy until you have a poop that is hotter than the middle of the sun incubating in there. My emergency supplies, which I have with me at all times, include a nappy and baby wipes, which you would understand if you'd ever tried to craft a makeshift nappy from a dock leaf, and dragged a child's bum through some sphagnum moss to try to clean it.

My emergency kit also includes a dog whistle (for summoning dogs or children). I can whistle with my fingers, but not as well as I'd like. The sound of a whistle travels further than a yell, and quite often the sheep will respond to a whistle without a dog. Clive can whistle very loudly without fingers and I am most envious. I carry a penknife, and some baler twine to tie up a gate, a sheep or anything else that needs to be secured.

I also always have a balaclava with me in winter. I've been caught out too many times to mention, and it's no fun in a torrential rainstorm, crouching at the back of a wall with a wailing baby on my back, my hair dripping with rain. The old Girl Guide/Boy Scout motto 'Be prepared' definitely applies at Ravenseat.

6

Married in My Riding Boots

Clive's marriage proposal was as romantic as the way he asked me to move in. In fact, he didn't propose; I did.

'Does ta think we should get married?' I asked him.

Grunt.

'D'you think we should?'

'Mebbe.'

'Does that mean yes?'

'I suppose so...'

So you can see he was not madly enthusiastic. I believe a meeting with the accountant, who explained the advantages of us being a business partnership, swung it. I was twenty-five when we got married, we'd been together for more than four years, and as far as I was concerned it felt right to make it official. We decided there was only one place to celebrate this wedding. It had to be at Ravenseat.

We were married in St Mary's Church, Muker, followed by a big party here. My mother and sister came, and my grandfather (Mother's father), gave me away. Our neighbour and friend Jimmy Alderson was one of Clive's ushers. We looked into hiring a wedding marquee but balked when we saw the cost, and instead borrowed the local show's blue-and-white striped beer tent. I asked everyone down the dale to help decorate it, and they brought balloons, banners, garden furniture, hanging baskets and tubs of flowers. This was a cause for celebration in Flymo's eyes too: she spent happy hours eating the trailing lobelia and munching the marigolds, and it was embarrassing when our kind guests returned to retrieve their baskets and only chewed stalks remained.

Clive and his friends held an impromptu stag night in the beer tent the night before. I, of course, know nothing of what went on, but knowing the company that Clive keeps I suspect that most of the chat revolved around sheep...

We married on 29 July 2000. I wore a wedding dress in gold shot silk, in an Elizabethan style with a tapestry effect. I wanted something special, but a white meringue wasn't my style, and wouldn't have been very practical. As it was, I could take the hoop off the skirt and feed the calves in it, on the evening of the big day. Nothing stops, even for a wedding: animals need feeding and the routines of the farm are the same.

There was an open invitation to the wedding and the party, anyone could come. We both dislike formal events so everyone was welcome. They could come to the church and not the party, or to the party, missing out the church, or they could be at both – and most people were. The church was packed, with a crowd of people gathered in the village and outside the church gates to watch our arrival.

I didn't want to arrive in an ostentatious limousine, so my plan was to ride my horse Meg side saddle to the church. I practised with her around the farm and along the road, wearing a sheet draped round me so she'd get used to the feel of the dress. Meg was probably about seven or eight years old then, although I'll never really know as she was bought from the side of the road on her way to the Appleby horse fair. Clive had been away looking at some sheep at Meaburn and had seen gypsies camping at the roadside as they made their annual pilgrimage to Appleby. When he got home he told me of a wonder horse he'd spotted, tethered against a hedge. I had seen the same horse too, while on the way to the supermarket, and so we went back and, after a fair bit of haggling, a deal was struck. We had a horse, and one that we both liked. We don't know her breeding, but she is a typical gypsy cob type, a stocky tri-colour, black, brown and white with a profusion of smooth, silky feather on her legs and a heavy mane and tail. I suspect there's some Clydesdale in her as she has big clover-shaped hooves. She's a good egg, a kind creature who is never sick or sorry. She is the only horse that Clive has ever sat upon, the only horse that has gained a place in his affections.

The day of our wedding dawned bright and clear. Instead of the normal bridal preparations – nails, hair and make-up – I was grooming the horse. I had spent the night at Pry House with Clifford and Jennie, our neighbours. Meg was loaded into a trailer and taken to Usha Gap, a farm on the edge of the village. A hay trailer was parked in the field as an improvised mounting block. We unloaded Meg and I saddled her up, everything was perfect. It was a very hot, sultry day, and the sky had remained clear until that moment, when a dark storm cloud blacked out the sun, and just as I was about to mount there was a rumble of thunder and the heavens opened. A bright fork of lightning split the sky and the violent downpour forced everyone to run for cover. All plans to ride the horse were off, and I bolted for the church, while Meg was loaded back into the trailer.

Is this a sign from above? I thought as I headed for St Mary's.

But the storm cleared the air, and for the rest of the day the sun shone on us like never before, so if it was telling me something, it was all good. I was married in my riding boots, as I was unable to prise them off in time. I was sure no one would spot this, but when I was kneeling at the altar they were on show to the congregation behind me. It could have been a sad moment, not having my father there to give me away, but I was too flustered with the rain and the riding boots to think about it.

Clive gave me a beautiful gold wedding ring but, as he never stops reminding me, within a few months I'd lost it in a grain bin.

Muker is a pretty little village tucked between the moors and the River Swale; the church stands amid a cluster of stone houses nestling in the hillside. Traditionally, the church gates are tied with ribbon and twine by the village children to stop either of the couple changing their minds and running away. When you come out, married, you have to bribe the children with sweets and coins to untie the gates and let you through. Luckily, we remembered, and Clive had filled his pockets with goodies to hand out.

After the service everybody set off back up the dale to Ravenseat. We had organized a hog roast and Clive's friend Alec, a renowned sheepdog trainer, was at that time the landlord at Tan Hill. He and his wife Maggie set up and ran the bar. We had hired a dance floor and jukebox and one of our guests brought a mobile toilet trailer with him as a wedding present. We kept everything very informal: none of those official wedding pictures where the family all line up in order. We asked a photography student we knew to record our big day and she really captured the spirit of the event, including snapping some of our friends looking rather worse for wear. She photographed quite a few unfamiliar faces too. The day had been uncomfortably warm, and for those brave and hardy souls who were walking the Kirkby Stephen to Keld leg of the Coast to Coast, the unlikely sight of a striped blue-and-white beer tent sitting in a remote field must have been a very welcome sight. I've got people with backpacks and rucksacks on in my wedding photos, people I've never seen before or since.

'We thought it was a mirage, that the heat had got to us, when we saw a beer tent,' they said.

Their presence sowed a seed in my head for the future: perhaps one day I could earn a little bit of money by serving refreshments to the tired and hungry walkers who pass through Ravenseat.

The following morning, after the festivities, I had quite a few bacon sandwiches to make. Some of the revellers had brought their tents and caravans and decided to make a weekend of it, and by mid afternoon the party was in full swing again.

We told everyone that we didn't want wedding presents, just their company, but despite this, we were given some very special ones. Steve Akrigg had been helping Clive out at Ravenseat for many years and in the months running up to our wedding he became increasingly excited about some secret project, dropping veiled hints between fags about the marvellous wedding present that was coming our way. At the same time we realized that Nick, another man who occasionally helped us out during our busy times, was also planning a surprise.

On the morning of the wedding Steve turned up dressed to the nines and bursting with pride as he proudly presented us with our presents, a pair of beautiful shepherd's crooks with Swaledale sheep carved into the horn handles.

'Every time thoo goes to t'auction thoo must tek thi stick, it'll be lucky for you.'

It had clearly been a labour of love and he'd spent many hours whittling them.

Later the same day Nick appeared, brandishing what looked suspiciously like two stick-shaped parcels. Sure enough, another pair of amazingly detailed shepherd's crooks, Clive's fashioned into the shape of a Swaledale tup and his sheepdog Roy, mine with a Swaledale yow and my horse Meg. Nick had commissioned a well-known stick-maker to make these especially for us. Neither Steve nor Nick had a clue about the duplication, and still don't to this day. We don't want to show any preference, so we don't use any of the sticks in the ring, and they're far too good for working the sheep. But we really value them and have them on display on the beams in the living room, and we'll hand them down as heirlooms to our children.

We didn't go on honeymoon for a week. It was clipping time, and that took priority, so a couple of days after our wedding we were side by side in the clipping shed: business as usual. When the last sheep was clipped we set off to Ireland. Alec had lent us his new car because our beat-up Land Rover would never have made it. We drove around Ireland, stopping off at various bed and

132

breakfasts, but I think that subconsciously we were always looking for somewhere just like Ravenseat. There is no place like home.

It's just a fact of farming life that holidays are few and far between. You have to make such careful arrangements for the animals and with so many jobs being weather dependent, it's difficult to make any plans. We once went to France in late June and the weather was glorious, which would have been good news for most folks. But not for us: Clive spent all his time watching the French farmers making hay. He was starting to get twitchy and kept ringing Jennie at Pry House.

'They're all mowing 'ere, 'ave you started?'

'No, Clive. It's raining.'

'It's red hot here. Are yer sure 'bout the weather?'

'Honestly, Clive, I promise yer, it's peeing down. Relax and enjoy yer holiday.'

Anyway, although I didn't know it, by the time we went to Ireland on honeymoon I was already pregnant with Raven. I thought it was seasickness on the ferry going over, but it didn't get better on dry land, and then I discovered that there was something more going on.

Having a baby was a natural progression; it was something we both wanted but didn't give too much thought. We hadn't made any big plans, we just make it up as we go along.

Clive says, 'If you'd said to me we'll have seven children, I'd have run a mile. It's funny where life has taken us, but having the babies has always just seemed right.'

We were both happy that I was pregnant, and

things carried on much the same as usual. I had no intention of slowing down or putting my feet up and we were busy with the normal routines of the farm. Our hoggs went away for wintering as usual in November. We sent them in three groups, one to a farm at Longtown, near Carlisle, one to a farm in southern Scotland and some, along with some older, special yows, to Catterick, near Richmond. They went to good farms: over the years you get to know the best places, and you make sure you visit and keep an eye on them. We go to see them regularly when they're away, and drench them with a wormer and a multi-vitamin dose. That's what good shepherding is about.

It was February 2001, when I was seven months pregnant, that we first heard the news about an outbreak of foot and mouth disease. It was all rather low key at that point, so we didn't take too much notice. It was happening somewhere down in the south of England, it didn't affect us or our area. But it wasn't long before we had to take it all very seriously – and so did the whole country.

The disease spread quickly, with one of the worst outbreaks centred on Longtown auction mart, where some infected sheep were unknowingly put into the auction. Some of our hoggs were only a few miles away and were slaughtered straight away in an attempt to contain the disease. It failed, and we now heard the word 'epidemic' being used.

Our farm was on lock-down; nobody was allowed in unless absolutely essential and we stayed at home and only left the farm for vital supplies. The postman left our letters further down the dale and I didn't go to see the midwife any more. With every trip off the farm we risked bringing the highly infectious disease back to Ravenseat. Our only contact was with our friends on the phone: we were all watching television to see where the latest outbreaks were. Looking back, it's odd to remember that we didn't have a computer then to give us all the news updates. Everyone was in a terrible state, all the farmers around here, just waiting for news, phoning each other with rumours and stories. It was heart-breaking; it was all we talked about and all we thought about.

Yes, it was our livelihood. But it was also the animals we cared about, animals we nurtured and loved. We knew they were slaughtering sheep and cattle that weren't infected, because there was a policy that there should be a three-kilo-metre zone around any infection, and all animals within in it would be slaughtered as a buffer. It caused massive problems: in the end seven million animals were killed in Britain, and only one fifth of them had the disease – the other 80 per cent were healthy.

Our neighbour Clifford Harker could remember when the disease swept through the country before, in 1967, and he decided to take matters into his own hands. He barricaded the road just along from our farm, to stop any traffic coming over from Kirkby Stephen, where animals were being slaughtered. He put an old trailer and some enormous boulders across the road and a carpet soaked in disinfectant. You needed a damned good reason to come into Swaledale before he would let you through! At first, when he told us about it, we thought it was overkill, but he was a wise old boy and he knew what he was doing. There is no such thing as overkill with a disease like this, it's highly infectious and can be spread on the wheels of cars and tractors, on clothing and equipment. If it had got into Swaledale the whole dale would have been wiped out completely, and probably it would have marked the end of the Swaledale breed of sheep.

Clive and another farmer, Raymond Calvert, helped build Clifford's blockade, but in the end somebody complained and the council removed it with a JCB.

We were very concerned about what was happening to the animals that had been slaughtered. There were terrible tales of lorries laden with dead sheep going through the dales. There were phone calls: 'I've seed a lorry an' summat's drippin' from it...'

There were even rumours that it was being spread on purpose, lots of suspicion and speculation. Were the Ministry of Agriculture disinfectant teams carrying it? We all became paranoid. There was even a story that was reported in *The Times* about a cow's leg being found in a bag behind a chip shop in Kirkby Stephen.

Farmers committed suicide when their animals were taken, that's how bad it was, and we were all worried about each other, clubbing together to support each other over the phone. The calls were usually grim: 'D'you know whose sheep

136

have gone now?'

You knew this unseen thing was moving towards you, they showed its progress on maps on television, and it was absolutely bloody awful knowing that you were powerless to stop it. The disease moved ever closer to us, and the Cumbrian sheep that ran on the shared Birkdale Common were slaughtered to act as a buffer. From our bedroom window we could see men on quad bikes cutting a line across the moor and taking the sheep away to their deaths. An imaginary line, the supposed line where Cumbria meets North Yorkshire, was what determined whether something would live or die. It seemed so wrong to be killing so many healthy sheep and cows. We watched as the disease moved inexorably onwards and people's lives were destroyed along with their sheep.

When we were told that the ministry men would come to Ravenseat to blood test our sheep, Clive and other local farmers held a meeting with them. We didn't want them on our land, in case they had been to 'dirty' farms before ours. We heard they were using their own mobile sheep-handling pens: could these be carrying it? It was a hellish time. Nobody knew the truth and everyone you spoke to had different stories, none of them good. Eventually a mutual agreement was made that our local vets, who we knew and trusted, would carry out the blood tests.

I didn't worry about my pregnancy: human beings don't get foot and mouth. Frankly, I didn't have time to think about myself and the baby because all our waking moments were preoccupied by worries about this dreadful disease. We were devastated when our sheep at Gretna, in Scotland, were culled. All that we had left out of the three hundred that we sent away for the winter were our eighty sheep at Catterick. We thought they would be safe, there didn't seem to be any disease in that area.

Jennie and Clifford Harker had a terrible experience, because some of their sheep had to lamb without anyone attending them. The sheep were wintering in the grounds of Brampton Castle near Carlisle, and should have come home to lamb, but they were not allowed to move. The farmer friend who was looking after them was not allowed to go near, because he had his own sheep, and in the end the only person who could attend to them was a gamekeeper. Jennie cried and cried at the thought of them lambing on their own, and she spoke to the gamekeeper and begged, 'Just don't let any of 'em suffer.'

She got the word that there were some lovely healthy lambs born, but less than two weeks later the flock had to be culled, even though they did not have foot and mouth. Jenny cried every time she saw another lamb, for weeks afterwards.

In the meantime, my pregnancy was going well. I was blooming, getting bigger, but feeling fit and still working hard. I always intended having a home birth and, with all the issues regarding travelling off the farm due to foot and mouth, it made sense. The midwife wasn't entirely happy because it was my first baby and we are a long way from medical help, but I forced the issue. They could see where I was coming from, and agreed. You can call me pig-headed, but because I spend my time calving cows and lambing sheep, it seemed to me that having a baby was going to be the most natural thing in the world. I am no earth mother, hippy type, but I am a great believer in nature and was sure I could handle whatever came my way.

I wasn't prepared for what actually happened. I had a rough idea of what to expect: labour pains, cramps, waters breaking, a bit of pushing and then a baby. But, typically, I don't do things the normal way. I've had seven babies now and I just don't have contractions. The only way I know that I am in labour is because I start feeling a bit off, grotty, queasy, not quite right. I can't explain the feeling, but now I recognize it. (And so does Clive – he's straight on that phone to the labour ward!)

Back then, with my first baby, I didn't really know for sure that I was in labour, but after a night of persistent tummy ache and feeling quite grim I decided to ring the midwife. It was 8 a.m. when she arrived at Ravenseat after a twenty-five-mile journey from Horton-in-Ribblesdale and a brief stop at a disinfection station to make sure she wasn't bringing with her any of the deadly foot and mouth on her car wheels.

'You're only about an hour away from having this baby,' she said.

'Brilliant, I've only felt a lal' bit icky.'

I was still walking about and feeling relatively OK. I even went outside to watch Clive calve a cow, with slightly more interest than usual because I was about to go through it myself. I wasn't in any real pain, but the hour came and went, then another, and another. The midwife was a little perplexed but not unduly concerned as with first babies things can sometimes take longer than expected. Clive kept coming backwards and forwards to the house with thoughtful words of encouragement: 'Flipping heck, you're taking your time. My cow's calved, the calf's footed and up and sucking.'

Eventually by lunchtime I started to have contractions, real hard ones. I thought this was good, that the baby was soon going to arrive, but still nothing happened. The baby was stuck, jammed in my pelvis, and the midwife hadn't realized I was having what is technically called an 'occiput posterior' birth, commonly called 'face up' or 'sunny side up', which is when the back of the baby's skull is at the back of the mother's pelvis. About 5 per cent of babies arrive this way, and it can cause longer labours and babies, especially bigger ones, getting stuck.

Which is what had happened. By this time everyone was starting to panic. The midwife rang for an ambulance when she realized that the baby was presenting wrongly. I had to get to hospital and fast. I wasn't allowed any pain relief, because they could not monitor the baby. I was experiencing unbelievable pain; I have never, ever been in such excruciating agony. It was as if my body was in a permanent contraction. I was writhing, the ambulance crew were trying to get me to stay still, the midwife was being sick into a cardboard kidney bowl because the roads here are like roller coasters and the ambulance was rocking and rolling down the dale with the siren wailing. Clive was following in the Land Rover trying desperately to keep up. It was when the ambulance crew decided things were looking bad and that we needed to get onto a faster road that we lost him. At the Scotch Corner roundabout we took the exit for Northallerton, whereas he just went 'North', heading for Newcastle...

At the Friarage Hospital they took me up onto the labour ward, attached an ECG on the baby's head, told me that she was in distress and that I needed to have an epidural anaesthetic and then an emergency Caesarean. I was still writhing and the nurses had to beg me to stay still while they got the needle into my spine. Then, at last, the pain subsided and I was wheeled into theatre. Clive had arrived just in time to see her born, on 12 April 2001.

Raven weighed nine pounds two ounces, much the biggest of my babies, and that explains why she got stuck. Apparently if a baby is in the occiput posterior position the chances of needing a Caesarean are much higher anyway, and if the baby is large, higher still, more than three times the normal chance. I was amused to read later that the experts think two of the reasons that women have babies in this position are because of their sedentary lifestyles and because they are small. I don't think either of those really apply to me.

It was 5 p.m. when Raven was finally born, and I was relieved it was over, after such a long, terrible day, and that we were both well. You would think I'd never have wanted to do it again...

Clive couldn't stick around because we were lambing what remained of our sheep, the ones that hadn't gone away for the winter.

Raven and I spent a week on the special care baby unit (SCBU) which was funny because she was such a big, chunky baby and we were surrounded by such tiny little things. She was puffed up, because she had been so squashed, and her head was very bruised and misshapen, but to me she was the most lovely thing I had ever seen.

Clive was unable to come and see us much because of the foot and mouth, and lambing, so I got the hospital to take a Polaroid picture of Raven. I faxed it to Raymond and Alison Calvert at Hoggarths Farm, two farms down the dale from us, and they took it to him. It was only just possible to see it was a baby from the black and white fax smudge. Talking to Clive on the phone was difficult. I had to wait for a nurse to bring the phone to my bed, and then he wouldn't be in the house to answer it. He'd got a farm to run and it was our busiest time of the year. I'd leave a message on the answerphone and he'd ring back and get the nurses' desk. It was very frustrating. I'd had plans to build our sheep hospital for the poorly yows and lambs, and I'd just assumed I'd pop a baby out and carry on working, but instead I was fifty miles away recovering from a C-section with a baby in the SCBU.

Because I'd been expecting a home birth I didn't have a hospital bag packed, and had only the clothes that I arrived in. The hospital found me some knitted cardigans which the League of Friends made for patients on the geriatric ward, but they weren't exactly flattering. I gave Clive strict instructions on what to bring for me on one of his rare visits.

'I want the denim dress,' I said, meaning, obviously, the tent-like denim maternity dress that I had virtually lived in for the last couple of months.

He arrived at the hospital with a bag packed with baby suits, nappies and a denim dress. Unfortunately I had forgotten there were two denim dresses in the drawer. One I had last worn when I was about eighteen to go out clubbing. It was short and skintight. The other was the billowing mumsy number. He had, of course, brought the wrong one. I spent the rest of my hospital stay bursting out of a bodycon denim dress teamed with a knitted old-lady cardigan.

I got quite friendly with the nurses and one day I was chatting to one of the young auxiliary nurses who had come to do my temperature and pulse.

'You're a farmer, aren't you?' she said.

When I said yes she asked whether we were affected by the foot and mouth.

'My goodness,' I said, 'it's been terrible. We've already lost over two hundred of our sheep.'

She nodded in sympathy, still staring down at her fob watch as she checked my pulse.

'It's spread to where I live too,' she said. 'I've had to close the curtains in my living room as they've killed all the sheep in the field at the back of my house. The bodies are laid in a big pile. I think they are going to burn them.'

'Really, where do yer live?'

'Catterick.'

My heart sank. I asked her a few more questions, she described where her home was, and I knew that the sheep she was talking about were ours.

I rang Clive repeatedly until he finally answered and, yes, he knew. He had kept it from me, he didn't want to upset me while I was in hospital. My nurse had inadvertently let the cat out of the bag. I suppose it was just a matter of time before we lost that final packet of sheep and in my heart of hearts I was expecting it, but I'd secretly harboured a hope that this last lot would be saved, particularly because among them were a few very special sheep.

When I moved in with Clive my own little flock of sheep had come with me. These were some of the pet lambs that I had reared and kept, as they were good female breeding sheep. We called them the Princesses, because they were big, fat, spoilt sheep, mostly mules (Swaledale x Bluefaced Leicester) and Texel x yows. They were obviously not as hardy as the Swaledales and so had gone away for the winter with the hoggs. The Princesses were all in lamb when they went away to Catterick and were not allowed to come back to Ravenseat because of the movement restrictions. The farmer who was looking after them did his best: he cared for them and our other sheep and even recorded a video of the Princesses with their newborn lambs which he posted to us. It sat on the mantelpiece, but before we had watched it, while I was in hospital, Clive got the terrible news: the whole flock was being culled. During

144

my stay in hospital Clive had appealed to the Ministry of Agriculture and got a solicitor on to the case because we had heard of some farmers getting reprieves for their flocks. But not us: they were all slaughtered, with their newborn lambs. Not one of them had the disease, they were just in the killing zone. It was a week or so after I had come home with baby Raven that I got the phone call from the Ministry confirming that our dead sheep's blood tests had all come back negative for the disease.

We never watched the video of the Princesses with their lambs: it would have broken our hearts. One day Clive just picked it up and hurled it onto the fire.

I really grieved for the Princesses. On the one hand I had the joy and wonderment of a new baby, but the pain and stress caused by the culling of our animals was almost unbearable.

We came home from hospital a week after the birth. Clive had been busy lambing and had constructed only one pen out of old wooden pallets and hay bales for any sickly yows and lambs that needed a night indoors. Not only had he been busy making everything ready in the lambing shed, he'd also been getting everything ready for his wife and baby's homecoming. He had clearly not mastered the washing machine and had decided that rather than strip the bed and get everything washed he would just drag the mattress and bedding out of the house and onto the bottom field and burn it. I couldn't really complain as he was muddling on, getting by as best he could.

Every year we have pet lambs that need hand-rearing, due to their mothers not having enough milk. I was forbidden from returning to full-on shepherding activities, as I wasn't allowed to lift anything heavy for twelve weeks after the C-section, and a compromise was reached by Clive bringing the pet lambs to the back door in a wheelbarrow, so that I could feed them without ever leaving the farmhouse kitchen.

Nobody could come to visit us to coo over the new baby as we were still on lock-down. But after a few days, parcels started to arrive. Our mail was being left in Keld because the postman could still not come to the farm. We collected it whenever we went out for supplies, and now there was an avalanche of parcels to bring home. People who I didn't even know that well from down the dale sent presents for the new baby. There was a great outpouring of generosity and phone calls with messages like, 'I've gotten a pushchair and I'll bring it when all o' this is over.'

It was as if folks wanted something good to think about in the middle of the foot and mouth gloom. I received some wonderful letters from other people who were in similar situations, trapped on farms, terrified to leave for fear of spreading the disease. Raven's birth was a joyful event, she was a symbol of the future. She was a ray of hope in very bad times.

I do a baby box for all the children, a collection of mementoes of their birth. Raven's is labelled 'Raven/Foot and Mouth' because the two events are so entwined. I've included all of the newspaper stories of what we went through, so that she will know of the terrible experiences we were having at the time of her birth.

We knew we would call her Raven even before she was born: it would have been the same name if she'd been a boy. I've never known the sex of any of my babies, and with the others we haven't chosen a name until after the birth, but her name was right: she was a child of Ravenseat.

I was clueless about babies, but she was an easy, sleepy baby who didn't begrudge me my inadequacies, and I loved breast-feeding. There were so many things I didn't know. Until I'd had Raven I had never even held a baby before and I'd never considered reading baby books. I wasn't one of those little girls who grow up thinking about marriage and babies, and I certainly never thought I'd have a large family. It wasn't until I was with the right man and in the right place in life that it suddenly seemed the most natural and important thing to do.

Clive was very good: he has always helped out with the babies, and they slot easily into our lives. Baby yoga and postnatal gatherings with other mothers aren't for me, we just want to farm, and I didn't see any earthly reason why a baby could not fit in. How hard could it be? She slept between us in bed and the night feeds were just a matter of sleepily turning over and plugging her in.

I'm not a parenting guru and I don't hold myself up as any kind of example, but I think if you are relaxed and do what feels natural, you'll be OK. If you worry about everything that could possibly go wrong you'll become neurotic, and that will communicate itself to the baby. Babies love routine, just the same way that animals do. Not that I treat my children as animals. But you can learn from nature. My children grow up knowing they are part of something, that they are important to the whole running of the world.

I didn't take much notice of the rule about not lifting anything heavy. It was soon time for clipping and I had no intention of taking a back seat. Raven slept in her travel cot on top of the wool sheets, setting the precedent for all the others who came after her: sleeping while the clipping machine was on, waking when it was switched off.

One fine, bright day when Clive wasn't about I spotted some sheep out on the moor and decided to go with the dogs to investigate. It was as I was up there amongst the heather, looking out on to the vast wilderness of moorland stretching away to the horizon, Ravenseat sitting huddled below the hills away in the distance, that I thought: *Summat's not right. Ma baby's down there and I'm up 'ere. I'm probably not supposed to do that.*

It sounds terrible when I think about it, as though Social Services should have been involved. It was complete naivety on my part; stupidly, I hadn't thought about it but I now had a tiny baby who was entirely dependent upon me, and much as I loved running about shepherding sheep and tramping the moors, I could not do this without putting her first. I wasn't going to stop doing what I did, but in future I needed to take her with me. So I got a papoose, a little soft blue one that I wear on my front for the first few months of the babies' lives, then when they are able to support their heads they go into a more solid, robust front carrier until they are about six months old, when they can go on to my back, and that's where they stay until they are old enough to climb the moors under their own steam. It works very well, and means that I can traverse the hills knowing the baby is safe and sound. It also helps to keep me fit: I think I have carried a baby either on my front or on my back continuously for about the last twelve years.

Foot and mouth ended in September 2001, but it was months before things got anywhere near back to normal. It was only the following January, nearly a year after the initial outbreak, that movements of sheep across the county boundaries were permitted. The few lucky people who did get their sheep back, some after as much as eighteen months away, found that their sheep still recognized their heafs on the moor. But our moors, usually speckled with white dots of sheep, looked sadly depleted.

People said to us afterwards, 'Just buy more sheep.'

We got compensation, but the problem is you can't 'just buy' sheep like ours. They are hefted sheep, reared on land they know. If we'd put new sheep up on the boundary-less moor they'd have wandered away for miles. The only way we could recover was to breed up from our remaining flock. We reckon it took us five years to get back up to where we were before foot and mouth.

In a normal year we keep 250 of the young sheep and sell on everything that doesn't make the grade for us. But now we had to keep every damn last thing, so the quality and purity of breeding took a nosedive. We were no longer keeping the cream of the crop, we were keeping everything. If you factored in that we were not making any money from selling our surplus sheep, then you can see how our income suffered a major blow. It was the same for everyone around here, we were all in the same boat and we've had to work very hard to get the quality of the breed back to where it was. We were lucky. We have, eventually, recovered. Not every farm did. 2001 was an eventful year, a year of euphoric highs and hopeless desperation, but we, and Ravenseat, survived, and with the birth of Raven, me and Clive launched our own private little flock. She really was a beacon on a very stormy night.

7

Reuben Ready or Not!

If Raven's birth wasn't dramatic enough, then Reuben's birth certainly was. I fell pregnant two and a half years after Raven. I'd adjusted to life with a baby on the farm, and hadn't found having Raven stopped me from doing anything I needed to do, so I wasn't overly concerned about the prospect of another little one. I can't say, though, that I didn't feel some pangs of nervousness as to what lay in store for me with the birth. But this time it was entirely the opposite problem: a tiny baby who took us all by surprise, born one stormy night at Ravenseat ten weeks too early.

It was a good pregnancy. I always feel bloody awful for the first three months, the 'morning' sickness that lasts from dawn till dusk. There's one smell that makes me nauseous every time: chicken. Not cooked chicken, I mean the walking, clucking variety. Every day I go to the henhouse to feed them, I throw up all the way there, then all the way back. Sometimes the first clue I have that I'm pregnant is when the merest whiff of a chicken makes me quite green. On a farm, life goes on, and pregnancy is part of it. After those first grotty weeks, I feel fine and life carries on the same as usual. I haven't got time to spend nine months worrying and fussing, there's always so much to do.

The night of Reuben's birth, 2 November 2003, there was a terrible storm raging. It had poured down all day, rain was lashing the front of the house and the river was in full spate. Raven was tucked up in bed and we had planned a cosy evening in front of the fire, watching the *Antiques Roadshow*. Clive had volunteered to go pick up a Chinese takeaway, which might sound very normal to most people, but for us involves a twenty-five-mile round trip, including edging the Land Rover over the packhorse bridge because the river was too high to cross the ford. You can drive across the bridge if you've got nerves of steel and a car you don't care about too much.

We enjoyed the takeaway. I had duck in plum sauce. It wasn't long after eating it that I started feeling unwell, then came the stomach cramps: stabbing, agonizing pain. I was bent double, sure that it was a bad case of food poisoning. But when I went up to the bathroom there was suddenly blood everywhere. This was bad: my baby wasn't due for ten weeks. I didn't know what to think. I yelled for Clive and he took one look. 'Oh my God,' he said.

He rang 999, but we knew it would take an hour, maybe more, for an ambulance to get to us. So he rang our friends Raymond and Alison who live two farms away, because Alison is a nurse. A respiratory nurse actually, but, hey, she had a lot more medical training than we did. She and Raymond were here within minutes, leaving their Land Rover the other side of the bridge and running up to the farmhouse. They dashed upstairs, where I was sitting on the edge of the bath. There was blood everywhere. I'll never forget the grim look on Clive's and Raymond's faces. At that moment, I was sure I'd lost the baby. Alison, thank God, took charge, but she, too, looked worried.

'Get t'phone,' she told Clive.

She rang the doctor, who said he couldn't get here and couldn't do anything over the phone, but told her to ring the hospital and talk to a midwife. The midwife, Anne, realizing the situation, told us to try to stay calm and that under no circumstances should I push.

'We'll talk you through it,' she said. 'But get her

out of that bathroom!'

They were worried I'd have the baby sitting there, but at the time I didn't understand and just refused to move because the pain was so bad, and because there was so much blood: it sounds ridiculous but I was worrying about the mess. I remember Raymond, a big tough farmer, putting his head round the door and, with a face as white as a sheet, commanding me, 'You've gotta come outta there.'

Now, as well as everything else, I felt utter humiliation that everyone was seeing me like this, but it worked. I let them get me out of the bathroom and onto the bed and only just in time because, with no effort whatsoever, something popped out. Clive was shouting, 'It's here, the baby's here!'

Then time seemed to stand still, a completely quiet moment. I was absolutely sure that the baby was dead. Alison handed the phone to Clive. The voice on the other end of the phone told him to pick the baby up, and as he did so there was a faint cry, the first sign I had that the baby was alive. I was laid out on my side with the baby still attached, not daring to look. I just didn't want to see. I was sure this tiny slip of a thing wasn't going to make it. Later I remembered someone saying, 'It's a boy,' but I've no idea who actually said it.

Alison wrapped him in a towel. Anne, speaking from the hospital, gave clear and concise instructions. Clive was told to find a hot-water bottle. Easier said than done – Clive's terrible at finding things, and he was shouting to me, 'Where's the hot-water bottles kept?'

'In the bloody drawer, where they always are.'

'Which drawer? I cannae find 'em...'

Eventually, the towel-swaddled baby was laid on a hot-water bottle and wrapped in tinfoil. He was placed on the bed in front of me, still attached by the cord. I still didn't look at him. I'd seen the expressions on everyone's faces; I can't put into words how shocked and devastated they seemed. I didn't want to see for myself how pathetic he looked. I felt as if I wasn't there, as if all the panic around me was nothing to do with me. Instead of feeling part of it, I felt distant. I can't explain it; it was as if I was frightened to get involved with a baby who might not survive.

Raymond was manning the door, watching for the ambulance lights, and eventually it came down the road, stopping at the other side of the bridge. The ambulance men ran up to the house, their heads bowed as the rain beat against their faces, clutching a holdall full of equipment. They came up to the bedroom.

'Right, first things first, I'm going to cut the cord. Dad, do you want to do it?'

'No, I bloody well don't. I'm going to get a cup of tea.'

The next challenge was to get me and the baby to the ambulance. Although I felt remarkably well I suddenly had a bad attack of the shakes, and it was decided that it would be best if we were loaded into the Land Rover and driven over the bridge to where the ambulance was waiting. Sterile it wasn't: I sat in the back amongst the sheep droppings and general farming detritus

154

while Alison in the passenger seat cradled the baby. Clive drove with his face pressed to the windscreen, squinting into the darkness, the wipers on full tilt as the rain fell in bucket loads and the wind whipped down from the moor. It was a fierce, bleak night for a tiny baby to come into the world.

I can't remember much of the two-hour journey to the hospital. I still felt very detached. I couldn't believe that within a couple of hours I had gone from relative normality to this. Only the day before I had been talking to a lady in Kirkby Stephen who had asked whether I was pregnant because there was hardly a bump to be seen: a multitude of sins can be hidden beneath waterproofs. I finally looked across to the baby when Steve, the ambulance man, was struggling to put an oxygen mask on him. He was so small that even the tiniest mask covered his whole head, so Steve had to scrunch one up and hold it over his face to get as much oxygen as possible into him.

After what seemed like an age we pulled into the ambulance bay at the Friarage Hospital. Anne, who had talked us through everything, was waiting at the entrance. She ran out, took the baby in her arms and took him up to SCBU. The next time I saw him he was in an incubator, covered with tubes and on a CPAP machine, which stands for Continuous Positive Airway Pressure. This pumped oxygen into his lungs at constant pressure, to keep the lungs inflated between his breaths.

His tiny head was about the size of a tennis ball and bandaged to hold the tubes in place. He lay

155

there, his matchstick legs splayed, an oversized nappy rolled down, his skin waxy and transparent, and his body covered with a fine dark downy hair. He sported a monobrow complete with mutton chops that gave him the look of a tiny wizened old man. He weighed just under four pounds, which was a decent weight for a baby born so early.

When she got a moment, Anne congratulated me. She was full of praise for how calm we had all been and how well we had done to get him to the hospital in such good condition. I rang Clive and gave him an update on what was happening and told him that we needed to think of a name quite quickly, and that we'd talk again in the morning when I knew more. I was physically fine, but still in shock. I was given a room next to the unit and spent the night wide awake trying to come to terms with the evening's events.

The next morning I rang Clive to see if he had come up with any baby names. The staff kept asking me for his name, which, reading between the lines, made me think that they thought he wasn't going to survive, although they never said it. We decided that we needed a lucky name, and because the previous day Ruby Walsh had been riding the winners at Chepstow, I said, 'How about Reuben?'

We agreed it was an excellent name as we wanted our little boy to be a runner. I felt cautiously optimistic as they seemed to have everything under control. This was the second time that I'd had a baby on the unit, so I was familiar with the layout, which was small, with maybe half a dozen babies in separate rooms. Two nurses were assigned to each baby. Everything seemed so orderly, safe and controlled, and I had every faith in those specialist nurses. It almost felt as if I wasn't needed, and in a way I wasn't, as there was nothing I could do except let them get on with their job.

I went home from hospital the next day, without my baby. I know some people think this is odd: I have read stories in newspapers about people who keep long vigils by the side of incubators. But what can you do, sitting there? I didn't know how I should be behaving or what I should be doing. I am such a tall, strong person and this helpless, tiny, jaundiced baby was so different from me. Some people believe that their presence helps, but I wasn't convinced, and I felt I should stand back and let the experts do their job. Sometimes on the farm we have to temporarily take sickly lambs and calves away from their mothers and give them a helping hand, and this was just the same.

Clive brought Raven with him when he came to pick me up and they both came to have a quick look at Reuben. Clive seemed shocked at his frailty; while Raven seemed intrigued. A plan was hatched with the nurses: I would try to express some breast milk at home and come back to the hospital every other day. This would mean a four-hour round trip, but there was no other way of doing it.

It felt strange returning home; it felt like a part of me was missing. I set about busying myself on the farm and convincing myself that everything was going to be fine – all Reuben needed was time to grow. On my first night back, when we were in bed asleep, the telephone rang. Bleary-eyed, I reached for it. Dr Damann, a soft-spoken South African paediatrician, told me Reuben had suffered a pneumothorax.

'What's one o' them?' I asked, suddenly completely awake.

A collapsed lung apparently. They had put a line into the lung, reinflated it, and that was the panic over. There was nothing we could do, he had rung just to tell us what was going on.

'He's OK, we've scanned him. He has had a bit of a brain bleed, but don't worry.'

Clive and I sat up in bed for a while, trying to absorb what we'd been told. Should we get dressed and head off to the hospital? Should I go on my own? What would it achieve? We didn't talk about the big issue, whether or not our little scrap of a son would make it.

I went the next day and there he was, now with yet another tube, this time into his chest, but he was still clinging to life. Once again, that night at home, we had another phone call: Dr Damann again. Reuben had suffered another setback, his other lung had collapsed, and again they had reinflated it.

'A double pneumothorax is unusual but it's OK, we're handling it. We'll ring you if we feel you need to come to the hospital. But if anything else happens we'll have to transfer him to James Cooke Hospital at Middlesbrough where they have more specialized equipment.'

I didn't like the sound of this, and Clive and I

had the same conversation as the night before. Should we set off for the hospital regardless?

But again, we didn't rush to his side because we didn't see what good we could do. Fortunately, he then started moving in the right direction: he came off the CPAP and the head bandages came off to be replaced with sticky tape. His ears had no cartilage due to his prematurity and could be moulded into any shape so they needed to be held in a normal position. If I'd been mean, I could have rolled them up and made them into Shrek ears. As it was we just stuck them down to the side of his head with nothing more complicated than a roll of sticky tape.

It was a momentous day when he moved from the fully enclosed, all-singing, all-dancing, high-dependency incubator into a normal fish tank-type one. He lay on a heat pad to keep him warm, under a blue light to deal with the jaundice which made him so yellow. It was at this point, when he was a week old, that I held him for the first time, sitting beside the incubator while a nurse deftly handed him to me. I expressed my milk into little pots and then he was fed via a stomach tube, only one millilitre at each feed. I tried to put him on my breast, but his mouth was so tiny that he could not latch on. It was another couple of weeks before the feeding tube came out and I was able to get him feeding as nature intended.

I was told that he would not be allowed to come home until his due date, which was well into January. But the weather was drawing in, with the temperature below freezing many mornings, and there had already been the first flurries of snow. We knew it wouldn't be long before I wouldn't be able to get out of Ravenseat to make the trip to hospital. I was facing not being able to see him for weeks on end if the snow came down. He needed to come home, and they knew it as well as I did. They could see our predicament, and they adapted the rules for us.

It was agreed that he could come home when he was four weeks old, six weeks before his due date. He weighed four pounds. We had to agree to create the right conditions for him and I went to Middlesbrough where there was a shop that sold specialist premature baby equipment: a Moses basket, minute little vests, extra-small nappies. With Raven I'd completely relied on people giving me things, but none of her old baby clothes would fit, everything swamped him: she had been literally more than twice his size. The hospital League of Friends who provided the cardigans I wore after Raven was born also knitted and crocheted clothes in miniature sizes for premature babies. Everyone who has a very premature baby is caught out, nobody expects it to happen, so nobody is prepared. Bless those women: I was taken into a stockroom to choose mini matinee jackets, hats, etc. I still have them, as a reminder of how tiny Reuben was.

To take him home I had the babyseat on the absolute bottom setting, and then I had to pad it with a rolled-up fleecy blanket in order to make it small enough to strap him in. It was snowing as we left the hospital, and I knew this was a bad sign, that the snow would get thicker and heavier as I drove towards home. I turned the heater on to its highest setting and we were soon on the A1 northbound heading for Ravenseat. We hadn't gone far when I noticed the engine temperature gauge going up and up and up. I'm no mechanic but I had a nasty feeling that the radiator had cracked and was spilling water behind us. I didn't know whether to stop and ring for help, or to try to get home with my tiny passenger. The A1 is a busy road, and there aren't many exits, but eventually I came to a turning with a sign for a B & B. I pulled off and drove down a single-track road and into a red-brick farmyard. I left the engine running while I went and knocked on the door. I figured that if the radiator was leaking slowly enough I could fill it with water and get home.

'I think that t'radiator's knackered, I could do wi' some water,' I told the man who answered the door.

He begrudgingly nodded and, putting on his wellies, ushered me round the corner to an outside tap. He became a whole lot friendlier when he saw the Land Rover, realizing that we too were farming folk. I explained my predicament and he quickly had the radiator replenished, and filled bottles for me in case I had to stop again.

I wound my way home, the roads becoming ever whiter with snow. I stopped a couple of times to top up, and it was such a relief to reach Ravenseat. Under instruction from the hospital we had a room that was constantly warm for the baby. The farmhouse relies upon the most basic of heating systems and an open fire. So we had bought an oil-fired radiator with a thermostat, and put it in the least draughty room, the shower room. We put the Moses basket on top of a large chest of drawers in there, raised the heat to tropical levels, plugged in the monitor that set off an alarm if he stopped breathing, and that was it: Ravenseat's very own SCBU with its very own small patient.

When Raven came home after her birth nobody could visit us because of foot and mouth, but this time people came from far and wide to marvel at this tiny chap. He pretty much lived in the shower room for the first few months of his life. Unlike my others, who have been out and about in the papoose within a matter of days, Reuben was not strong enough or big enough: his legs would not stretch wide enough and his head was just too wobbly. In the end I had to buy an inflatable neck brace to prevent his head falling forward and him suffocating in my bosom. He was the most difficult of all my babies: from not being able to feed at all he progressed to being a glutton and was sick constantly, to the extent that we were sent back to hospital to test for cystic fibrosis, which can cause sickness. The test was negative, thank goodness.

There was always one worry at the back of my mind all the time I was coping with this sickly little chap. What about the brain bleed? At a doctor's appointment I finally plucked up the courage to ask: 'I was told tha' he had a Category 2 brain bleed. What does tha' mean, 'ow will it affect him?'

'Well, there are four levels of brain bleed, and

we will just have to wait and see. We won't know until he is older if there is any residual damage.'

That was as clear as mud to me, so I never asked again.

Reuben is now a big, healthy lad with a brain that is fascinated by anything mechanical, which he will fiddle with and fix. I think he has inherited this streak from my father. It certainly doesn't come from Clive, whose idea of fixing things is copious spraying with WD40, and if that doesn't work, hit it with a hammer.

Of course, it had been a very worrying time, but I think that, being farmers and particularly dealing with animals, we tackle things methodically. We see the job we have to do and we do it – we don't sit around crying and worrying. It doesn't mean that we don't care, but we could see that the baby needed to grow and we needed to do certain things to allow that to happen, so we just got on with it. Clive still blames that Chinese takeaway and I have been forbidden from ever having duck in plum sauce again. They never did find out what had caused Reuben to have been born prematurely but I am sure the duck had nothing to do with it – however, it's off the menu at Ravenseat now.

It was in the months after his birth that we lost two of our dear friends. Clifford Harker died on Christmas Day 2003, and sadly Jimmy Alderson passed away the following spring. Jennie no longer lives at Pry House but is still close by, in the village of Muker, where I see her often and still ply her with questions about Ravenseat in the old days.

Reuben stayed a floppy baby for what felt like ages: the other babies have all grown out of the soft papoose after three or four months but Reuben was in it for a very long time, because he just didn't have the strength to support himself. I have never been a competitive mother, mostly because I have never been in the right places to be one. You don't meet many new parents at the auction mart or on the moor. But on one rare occasion I was in the playground at Hawes with Raven and Reuben.

'How old is yours?' asked another mother.

'Eleven months.'

'Oh ... mine is, too.'

You can imagine the look on her face: hers was walking, bouncing around, picking things up, just about bloody well juggling. Reuben couldn't even lift his head. When I finally did get him into the backpack he literally disappeared, his head didn't peek out over the top.

So I don't take them to the swings, ball parks or to the swimming baths, but I feel that my children have a great, busy outdoor life and, I hope, an idyllic upbringing in a million ways. They eat properly, rarely watch television and have lots of freedom. I'm proud of the way they are all turning out. But I am ashamed to say that I committed a terrible mother crime with little Reuben...

I'm not an expert at this business of being a mother. Who is? I believe that everyone has a scare story in their past, when it comes to bringing up children. I have a couple, and this is one of them. I still go cold when I think about it.

It was late afternoon and we'd been outside marking lambs all day. It had been a tiring day and we were filthy from working in the sheep pens. Raven had been sitting on the wall watching us work and Reuben had been on my back in the baby carrier. One of the last jobs of the day is always to get a bucket of coal and an armful of logs for the fire. Clive had gone to feed the dogs and I had fetched the coal and logs and put them in the porch. The front door was in a sorry state and in order to shut it you had to give it a bloody good slam. I leaned forwards to pull it towards me, slammed it really hard, and then, at the same moment, looked sideways. Just as I was pulling the door closed, little Reuben, who was about eighteen months old at the time, had extended his arm towards the door and his fingers were in the hinge. There was a frozen moment but it was too late.

'Oh my Gawdddd!' I shrieked.

Then silence, a momentary pause, before he let out a piercing scream.

I pushed the door open to see blood smeared onto the paint-work. Reuben's finger end was hanging off, held only by a stringy piece of flesh. The wailing started – mine. Reuben was strangely muted now, and gazed at the bloody injury with interest. Clive came running, bound it up in a clean tea towel and, scooping Raven up, we all set off for the hospital. Reubs slept, while I cried for the whole two-hour journey. I was mortified by what I had done. The journey seemed to take forever, but finally we reached the Friarage. I rushed in while Clive parked the Land Rover. I was a jibbering mess: I couldn't remember his name, my name, how old he was.

All I could get out was, 'I've ... chopped his ... finger off.'

The doctor looked at him, the finger, then me. Looking me in the eye he said, matter-of-factly, 'Mrs Owen, I think it would be best to amputate the finger off to the nearest joint.'

He explained how Reuben would be fine, and would adapt, especially as he was so young.

'You cannae do that, I'd feel guilty forever every time I looked at his hand AND he won't be able to be a concert pianist AND he won't be able to give two fingers to anyone...'

'I tell you what. I will take a photograph of his injury on my mobile phone and send it to a friend of mine. He is a specialist hand surgeon, I'd like his opinion.'

Who knew there were surgeons who specialized in hands?

We had the most tremendous luck. It appeared that his doctor friend had dashed up to Middlesbrough that day to operate on the hand of someone who had been involved in a car crash.

'Send them over to Middlesbrough and when I get this guy done I'll operate on him,' he said.

So we loaded ourselves back into the Land Rover and set off again. It was late in the evening when we arrived in Middlesbrough, another half-hour's drive away. We were taken up to the children's ward, where they were expecting us. What they weren't expecting was a family of scruffbags covered in sheep muck with wellies caked in mud. There were one or two disapproving looks.

166

I was given a fold-down bed next to Reuben, while Clive and Raven were put in a small room with no window and no light, basically a cupboard. We had no spare clothes, no toothbrush and we couldn't get any food because the only facilities left open were vending machines, and all we had was a £20 note which Clive found in his pocket, and which was no use in a machine. In the end a nurse took pity on them and gave them some sandwiches which were left over from dinner time. I was so stressed with guilt I couldn't eat.

The next morning the surgeon operated and saved Reuben's finger. What a brilliant, wonderful man! He repaired it so well you can't see where the injury was. He told us after the op that Reuben could still one day become a concert pianist. (Not that any of my children show any interest in the piano we have. Clive saw it advertised as free to anyone who could pick it up, and he got it for me because I can play a bit, but only very badly.)

We drove back into our yard almost exactly twenty-four hours after we left in such a hurry, and Reuben still had his finger. Calm was restored.

As well as adding to our brood, we increased our responsibilities in a different way: we took on the tenancy of another farm. Sandwath is a much smaller farm than Ravenseat, 120 acres compared to the 2,000 up here. It's on the other side of Kirkby Stephen, twelve miles away. We wanted somewhere to over-winter some of our sheep. It is in the Eden Valley, which is synonymous with fertile, good-growing land, with lots of quality grass for rearing animals. It can be farmed more intensively than up here, and much as Clive and I prefer the Ravenseat way of doing things, it helps us a lot to have this other land available to us, and the two farms work together well.

Clive's son Robert runs Sandwath day-to-day. Every morning we speak on the phone to compare problems and decide which are the most pressing. Clive or I will go down to Sandwath when we are needed, or Robert comes up to Ravenseat.

We keep the majority of our cattle there in the winter as Sandwath has modern buildings which are ideal for cattle, easier to muck out than our traditional buildings at Ravenseat. We bring them up here for the summer months. We have about a hundred beef cattle which we rear up until they are nearly two years old, and then sell them on to other farmers who either fatten them or breed from them. We have in the past bred fancy continental-style cattle and on a few occasions won prizes with them, but we're moving back towards traditional cattle for much the same reasons that we love Swaledale sheep: it's more natural and we encounter fewer problems. We had some difficult calvings with the continental cattle, which occasionally necessitated Caesarians, and there were a few fatalities along the way. So now we are establishing a herd of Beef Shorthorns, a traditional, hardy breed.

Sandwath gives us another, unexpected, small income. Every September, Kirkby Stephen hosts its annual Cowper Day Fair, which is a big horse sale. For one day every year, Kirkby Stephen becomes cowboy country and all hell breaks loose. The fair originated with hill farmers selling their young Dales and Fell ponies but now a whole range of horses turn up, from heavy Clydesdales through to donkeys, but the majority are gypsy horses with more than 500 changing hands on the day.

One of Sandwath's fields is close to the auction mart, and we open up the field and charge people to park their cars in it. When we first came up with the idea a few years ago friends warned us that everyone would refuse to pay and we'd get beaten up for even asking. Clive had a cunning plan: he put me on the gate taking the money, because he believed (correctly) that they wouldn't beat up a girl. The only problem we have ever encountered on Cowper Day has been entrusting our car park money with the children. On one occasion they snuck off and bought a pony...

We once acquired twelve Galloway cattle, not by choice but in settlement of a bad debt. Galloways are those dark brown shaggy cows without horns, rather cute looking, like little teddies, which come originally from Scotland, hence the name. They are often a bit wild, so we decided that instead of trying to tame them we would run them into the Close Hills allotment at Ravenseat, where no walkers go, and we would be able to watch them from a safe distance.

We would go up the road, into the Black Howe pastures, and look across into the Close Hills, count them, and say, 'Yep, there's twelve, that's fine.'

Then one day, we counted and got to eleven. Counted them again, still only eleven. We set off to search for the missing bullock. We looked everywhere. There is a lot of ground to cover, but there was not a sign of it. It was only as we came back down towards the gate that we looked inside the hog house, one of the barns. A quick glance in the downstairs barn bottom revealed nothing, but when we looked on the upstairs floor we found him. The door had been left open, probably by a lost rambler who had perhaps gone in for a wee. The nosy bullock had gone inside and was trapped when the door closed behind him. It's the last place we thought to look.

We opened the door, and it took a moment for our eyes to adjust and see into the darkness. He was standing in the middle of the loft, wild-eyed, looking towards us. He backed up towards the wall, considering a charge, snorting all the while. Just as we were thinking that we needed to dive for cover he disappeared as the stone-flagged floor suddenly collapsed. He crashed down onto the ground floor of the barn and, shocked, stood stock-still for a few moments, surrounded by debris. Remarkably, he was fine, just a few scrapes here and there, and as soon as he gathered his senses he set off at a rate of knots out of the lower door and up into the allotment.

We thought that would put an end to his inquisitiveness, but only two or three days later we looked across to the Close Hills, and there were only eleven again. Clive counted them, then said, 'You count, I can only get eleven.'

He was right, one was missing.

'Flippin' 'eck, we'd best go and see what's going on.'

Away we went again, checking the hog house en route, just in case. It wasn't long before we spotted him: he was stuck in a bog. When he'd fallen through the loft floor he had grazed his legs and although they were only minor wounds he had clearly been bothered by flies. The first thing an animal does when it's got fly problems is head for water. It's what nature tells them to do, to go in the water to get rid of the flies. But in this case it was a stagnant, reeking bog, and he was up to his belly in it, and he couldn't move in any direction.

'He's not 'avin a good week, is he? Go back down to't farm and get a halter an't Crovect.'

Crovect is a special fly repellent that we use on the sheep and lambs; one stripe down the back and no fly will come near. As well as a line of Crovect, we gave him an injection of penicillin to ward off any infection. We knew he wouldn't stand for any of this treatment once we got him out so it was a question of treating him while he was unable to put up a fight. We got the halter on him, tied it to the back of the quad bike, drove slowly and pulled him free from the mire. There was a great squelching noise as his chunky body freed itself from the swamp. For a moment he was prostrate on the ground, still attached to the quad bike, and all that was needed was for someone (Clive) to remove the halter and release him. I suggested that a penknife might be the answer, just cut through the halter and let him go. Clive was having none of it.

'Nivver, I's not cutting it unless I 'ave to, we's short o' halters.'

The bullock clearly blamed us for everything. To say he was angry would have been an understatement; he was livid. Once Clive had taken the halter off and the pressure on his head was released he was on his feet and heading in Clive's direction. I've never seen Clive run so fast. In fact, I've never seen a bullock run so fast. It was like watching a cartoon, Clive running with a furious bullock literally inches behind his backside. Luckily, Galloways don't have horns, or it might have had him. Clive legged it, then jumped over a wall, leaving the bullock bellowing on the other side.

It was a lucky escape. Speaking from bitter experience, having a cow on top of you, trying to grind you into the ground, is not good and best avoided at all costs. Clive recovered from this near-miss and, physically, the bullock did. But from then on he was a complete head case, a real psycho cow. He was totally unhandleable. He was OK out in the wilds of the allotment, but with winter approaching there was no way he could remain out there. The only problem was: what to do with him? He wasn't going to adapt to being housed in the barn, and taking him to sell at the auction was a no-no. There was only one place he was going, and that was into my freezer. We have never had any problem eating our own animals – you can eat meat with confidence if you know that the animal has lived a happy life and been well cared for.

He's not the only animal we've had in bogs. We've had to winch the occasional cow out, but more often it's bogged sheep. The sheep are usually very good at avoiding the bogs as the hefted sheep know their own land and follow the trods (sheep paths) that have been used by their mothers and grandmothers before them. Sometimes in very hot weather you get one who will go looking for water to cool down, and if they are ill they might wander off the trod. But normally you see them 'bog sniffing', with their noses to the ground to be sure where they are walking.

The main reason we find them in a bog is if they've been panicked, for instance if a military helicopter has flown over very low. We once had to pull twelve sheep out of a bog on Ravenseat moor. It was sheer luck that a walker had come across them, as they were in up to their chests. They were so heavy and claggy with the weed and the mud that they could not stand. We brought them down into the farmyard in the bike trailer and put the pressure hose on to wash them, then left them in the garth, the little field opposite the house, in the sunshine to dry.

When you have animals you have to be ready to deal with any emergency; day or night. We had a terrible incident with a cow one night. Clive's got a gay good eye for when a cow's going to give birth: he can spot the signs. He usually tells me that I'm about to go into a labour before I know myself. The cow starts 'panching', trotting up and down, restless, can't bide herself. He says I do that: when I start getting ratty, impatient and

173

busying myself with all manner of household chores, he knows I'm near.

Anyway, we had put three or four cows in the barn ready to calve, as the last thing we wanted was for any of them to calve away in the pastures in case anything went wrong. The cow in question was very unsettled and clearly unhappy about being in an enclosed space, so we decided that she would be better off in the garth, which we can see from our bedroom window. We put her out and she headed for the corner, the stone wall giving her some privacy and shelter. We went to bed and awoke in the early hours to hear the most terrible bellowing. I have never, ever, before or since, heard a cow make such a harrowing, heart-rending noise.

'What the bloody hell was that?' Clive said. 'I think we'd better ga an' 'ave a look-see.'

I could hear from the rattling sash windows that it had come on a bad night, with furious rain and clashing winds.

The custom here is to leave everything we need in the kitchen in case we have to go out in the night: wellies with leggings still attached, coats, hats and gloves. We pulled everything on over our pyjamas, but as usual we couldn't find a torch, so we nipped into the building, brought the quad bike round and aimed the headlights into the garth. As Clive said, 'You wouldn't have walked into that noise without knowing what it was.'

I've been around a lot of cows, enough to know that something was badly wrong. We managed to pick out her eyes reflected by the headlights, and we went cautiously towards her, Clive carrying a

174

stick. It soon became clear that the blummin' cow had calved, she still hadn't cleansed after the birth, but there was no sign of her calf – and she couldn't find it, neither. She was beyond distressed. There was only one little hollow in the whole of the field and that's where we found it, lying in about six inches of water: I peered into the mossy green pool and it was clearly dead.

The cow was going mad and was inconsolable. The best we could do for her was to drag the calf out of the puddle and put it where she could see it. We now had a cow with a bag full of milk, and no calf to suckle. As soon as it was a civilized time, Clive rang a farmer down at Kirkby Stephen who sold calves, and off we went to get one. Our cow had produced a beautiful big beef calf, but what we needed was an altogether smaller calf to wear the skin of the dead one. The changeover was not going to be easy.

Clive drove into the field on the quad bike and grabbed the dead calf from under the nose of the cow. She was not keen to part with him, and this was in our favour for persuading her to adopt the foster calf. Clive skinned the calf – much more difficult than skinning a lamb – to the unnerving accompaniment of the cow flinging herself at the metal gate to the field. She knew that we had her calf and she wanted him back. All we had to do was give her a replacement calf that smelt like her own, so we put the skin on the new calf. Usually we would have liked the introduction to have taken place in a confined space, but she was so upset we decided it was better to put the new calf in the field with her and then watch from a safe distance.

Then it was a question of whether she would take to the new one. You never know if it will work. She didn't realize it, but she had a line of spectators watching her: Clive, Robert, me and the kids. She acted quite confused for a bit and we didn't know which way it would go. There is one thing worse than total rejection, and that's utter indifference. If you get a cow or a sheep you've mothered a baby on to and it just ignores it, that's a nightmare. Rejection gives you something to work on and quite often you can eventually get them to accept it. Total indifference means it will probably end in failure, and you'll have to hand-rear the calf or lamb.

She hovered about a bit looking perplexed. The calf looked pretty pathetic, a skinny little thing with an oversized jacket dangling from its meagre frame. She'd go to it, have a look, a sniff, then look around as if she was still trying to find the other one. Fortunately, the calf was very sensible and was not trying to force itself on her. Eventually she must have decided it was better than nothing and allowed it to suckle. There were sighs of relief all round.

We hand-rear a few calves every year. We're very successful with hand-rearing, but we only do it when necessary. Nothing beats being reared by a mother, whether it's lambs, calves, foals or babies.

Robert rang up from Sandwath one day to tell us a cow had calved before her time, and she'd managed to drop the calf in a load of muck. I don't know what she was thinking: this sickly

176

little calf was covered in cow muck, and the mother had no milk. The calf had the dome-shaped head, velvety coat and odd eyes that premature animals have.

Robert put her in the footwell of the van and brought her up to Ravenseat. Clive was convinced that she would not survive – premature calves have a tendency to develop breathing problems or to be troubled with scour (diarrhoea). But I always feel that where there's life there's hope, and give any animal my best shot. I put her in the porch with a fan heater and defrosted some colostrum (I keep a supply in the freezer for moments such as these). I then reared her on ordinary milk from the Co-op supermarket. We called her Ginger George, and she did so very well that we kept her into old age.

When Raven was three we acquired another dog: Clive bought her a puppy for her birthday. A friend of his had a litter of Jack Russell cross Lakeland terriers and Clive chose one of these for her. We called her Pippen, and she's a great little dog. We've been very lucky in having some wonderful dogs over the years, and the terriers especially live what can only be described as a perfect dog's life.

Roger Red, who came with me, was already elderly, but he remained active until his last breath, dropping down dead doing what he loved, working in the pens chasing sheep through the race. Deefa died in 2007. I went across the yard one autumn morning and up the stairs to the upper part of the barn where she slept, cosy in the hay with the warmth from the cows, horses and sheep below. She followed me down the stairs, not bounding as usual, but with a slow, unsteady gait. She followed me into the farmhouse and straight away curled up next to the range, on a bed of blankets and cushions where Pippen slept during the day. I went round my sheep that morning without her by my side, the first time she hadn't shadowed me on my chores.

When I returned to the farmhouse, I could hear that her breathing was laboured, but she wasn't in distress. She was old, and I knew she was near the end. I hunkered down next to her, stroking her head, tears streaming silently down my face. It was over soon: she died peacefully and naturally, with me holding her. She'd been mine from a few weeks old, and we had never been separated, a faithful and dear friend. There is a deep understanding between a shepherd and a working dog, a bond forged from constant companionship and mutual reliance, and I felt her absence from my side for a long time. I couldn't face moving her body immediately, so she stayed there all day, until Clive had dug a grave in the garden.

Clive's dog Roy never wanted to retire. Working dogs don't live as long as pampered pets, but they live an action-packed life. As Roy got older, we acquired two new sheepdogs, Sky for me and Jess for Clive. But Roy was a worker, and nothing would persuade him to take life easy. He would trail behind, occasionally showing his displeasure at the young dogs' exuberance. He had never been kennelled or tied up in his life, and he valued his freedom. Sadly, he had a stroke, and one side of his body became weaker. It was heart-breaking watching him struggling to stand, and we were beginning to consider the idea that this loyal, clever sheepdog perhaps deserved a more dignified end.

Early one morning I looked out across the garth from the bedroom window and something caught my eye, a dark shape floundering in a wet spot among the rushes. It was Roy. For reasons known only to himself he had decided to take a walk across the field and had keeled over in the mud. I went out, in my dressing gown and wellies, and picked him up. It was the only time that I had ever done that: he would never normally have tolerated it. He had lost a lot of weight, but he was still heavy. He put up no fight as I carried him back to the barn. He lay quietly in the straw, gazing at me with misted eyes.

I went back to the farmhouse to clean up and get dressed, and talk to Clive. We knew his end had come. Roy had never travelled well, not even on the quad bike (he always preferred to run alongside), so to take him in the Land Rover to the vets' would have caused him unnecessary stress. We went out to him, taking him some left-over sausages. Clive agreed with me that the time was right. I went back to the farmhouse to call the vet, but Clive stayed with him, never leaving him until the vet had been. I didn't go back out to the barn until it was over. He was Clive's dog and they had a very special relationship, right to the last minute.

We have had other sheepdogs, and we love

them all, but with some it goes very deep: any shepherd will tell you the same. Deefa and Roy were two who will always, always stand out in our memories.

Chalky, another terrier, this time a pure Jack Russell, came into our lives as a companion for Pippen. We bought her from our local builder. She's pure white, but there's usually a grubby grey look to her, unless the children have decided to bathe her. She has a longer coat than most Jack Russells, which we reckon is a natural adaptation to the arctic conditions at Ravenseat. She and Pippen live perfect terrier lives, coming into the house for the occasional doze and to hoover up any food the children have dropped. They are outside the rest of the time, never on a lead unless the children are attempting to civilize them. The last job we do at night is to let the terriers out. They sleep in the straw or on the hay, and patrol the farmyard, keeping their beady eyes out for unwanted visitors, like rats.

When I was first with Clive, he always had a packet of fags with him, and his way of coping with stressful times was to light up. I asked him about giving up, and he did try: he had a go with nicotine patches, but that meant he was wearing numerous patches and smoking at the same time. He tried cutting back. He has friends who can make ten cigarettes last a few days, but not Clive; it was all or nothing, and I soon learned that nagging made no difference. It wasn't a deal breaker for me, because he smoked when I met him, and I accepted it as part of him.

Every winter I lay in supplies in our dairy to see us through if the snow cuts us off, but no matter where I hid the stash of cigarettes, he always found them and smoked them. One winter, during a particularly bad snowstorm, he became so desperate for a cigarette that we had to dig our way out of Ravenseat. We battled through the ice and snow to get to Muker, only to find that the shop had run out of cigarettes, then on to Reeth where the shop was shut, and finally to Richmond, in thick snow, a round trip of fifty-four miles for his fags.

Finally he gave up the smoking of his own accord. It was the day of the Tan Hill Show, and he started the day by getting a pack of twenty from the vending machine in the pub. Now, on show days you get some old chaps who spend the entire time in the pub, talking tups. One old boy, sitting next to the machine, spoke to Clive when he returned for another packet.

'Yer back again?'

'Aye, I'm having a couple o' packets today, it's bin a stressful sort o' day.'

'Two? Yer've bin back here for three.'

That was when the reality of just how many cigarettes he was smoking became clear to him and he stopped. That was it, no nagging from me, no patches. He just quit. He's never had a fag since.

8

Miles To Go

The most magical time of year for me is lambing time, but it is also the toughest month of the year. We lamb our sheep late – spring is slow to reach Upper Swaledale – and many times our first lamb will arrive when there is still snow on the ground. It really begins in February when the yows are scanned after tupping to see if they are pregnant, and to see how many lambs they are carrying. Although we farm in a traditional way, we're not against some modern technology. The yows are brought down into the pens and then run through a race where they are temporarily held while the scanning man uses an ultrasound scanner to determine if they are in lamb, and how many lambs each one is carrying. Each yow is marked according to whether she is carrying a single lamb, twins, triplets or no lamb at all (geld). This allows us to manage them accordingly: lots of grub for twins and triplets, meagre portions for geld yows.

The aim is to have not too many geld yows and not too many multiples, with ideally each yow having one big strong single lamb which she can take away to the moor. The geld yows go away to the moor too and we hope they make up for their non-productive year with twins the next. Old

Jimmy always said, 'Geld yows would nivver break a fella,' meaning that a year off would give you a bigger stronger yow for next year.

We shepherd the sheep very carefully all year round, but especially when there's deep snow, when they are heavy in lamb. The stress can make them sick. There are two ailments they can get when they are in lamb. One of them is staggers, which is when their calcium levels drop. It's an old name, and it's a perfect description. The lamb is taking all the calcium. The yow goes off her food, then she gets a glazed look and wobbly legs, and eventually she keels over and will die. But it's easily remedied. You warm a bottle of calcium solution to body heat and then with a syringe inject it under her skin, usually on her ribs, in a couple of places. Lo and behold, she's up and running very quickly. We put a marker on her, because once she's had it she's susceptible again, and we know to keep an eye on her.

The other ailment is twin lamb disease, and it looks similar to staggers but is caused by a drop in sugar levels, like diabetes. It occurs mostly in the yows that are having twins, so you keep a lookout. They will become blind and if you sniff their breath it smells of pear drops. We inject them with calcium and mixed minerals and feed them with treacle, my favourite stand-by. There's no miracle cure, the prognosis is not good, but the nearer she is to lambing the better her chances.

One year Clive brought a yow into the yard on the back of the bike. She'd gone down with twin lamb disease.

'She's knackered, she won't survive.' Clive is a

glass half-empty kind of a guy. 'Sham, she'll 'ave a good lamb inside 'er, she's scanned for two.'

I said, 'Let's give 'er a go. I'll give 'er some treacle and mess on with 'er.'

'If thoo can mak 'er live you can 'ave t'lambs.' He never learns, does our Clive.

I did make her live. I went out to her in the barn so many times during the snow, giving her treacle, tempting her to eat. Eventually she lambed twins, one (the best) stillborn, and the other an incredibly weak tup lamb.

Usually when a sheep has been sickening and has been nursed it cooperates, but not this old bitch. There wasn't the slightest hint of appreciation. She steadfastly refused to let me milk her, put her foot in the milk jug every time, and would stomp all over me and her sickly lamb. She was horrible. Like I say, sheep have different temperaments, like humans. They're certainly not all nice. But she survived, and so did her lamb.

We always gather the yows down from the moor a few days before their due date. We know which are going to lamb in the first week as we rely on the age-old method of rudding our tups. This involves mixing powdered colour with oil to make a very thick paste (rud) that we smear on the tup's brisket. Every day during tupping time (November to December) we reapply more colour and give our lothario a small bite of feed to keep his spirits high and lead in his pencil. The rud is transferred onto the yows' rumps when mating and we change the rud colour about every eight days to help us predict when the lambs will appear, five months, minus four days,

184

after tupping.

The yows carrying multiples, twins and triplets, come into the barns to lamb. The majority of yows carrying singles will stay outside but come down into the pastures where there should, we hope, be some spring grass and a bit more shelter from the elements.

I oversee the yows lambing inside and Clive oversees the lambing outside. The barns are bedded up with straw and the racks filled with hay, and the yows soon settle down to the routine of life inside. Nature dictates that an animal will distance itself from its companions and find somewhere private and hidden to give birth, and obviously this is not possible when lambing inside a barn. So it's very important to keep a close eye on which ones are lambing to avoid mismothering or abandonment. If two yows lamb in close proximity the lambs can get muddled up and perhaps be rejected. The yows are watched very, very closely by everyone, even the children who all know the telltale signs: panching, restlessness, an inability to settle, building a nest in the straw and, eventually, lying down and straining.

The first visible sign that lambing is imminent is the protruding water bag, usually closely followed by a pair of front feet. After a few minutes a nose will appear, then in a short space of time the head, followed by the body. The yow will quickly spin round to begin licking and nuzzling her newborn. It's a critical time, as the lamb may still be inside the membrane, and it's vital that the combination of the yow licking and the lamb shaking breaks the sac so it can take its first breath. There is nothing worse than looking into the barn and seeing a big healthy lamb lying dead with the sac over its head. It could easily have been saved if someone had been there at the crucial moment.

The majority of our sheep lamb without assistance, a watchful eye being all that is needed. A newborn lamb is soon on his feet (footed) and taking his first wobbly steps: his aim is to suckle and he must find the tit as soon as possible. A lamb that fails to suckle quickly loses strength as the first milk, colostrum, contains vital antibodies and energy. The dangers of lambing outside are that sometimes the weather and terrain can mean that a lamb is lost, either through being dropped down a bank or into a beck while taking those first faltering steps. A yow can be so intent on hiding away that she will lamb in the most unsuitable places, on the edge of a stream or amongst rocks and screes. A lamb will soon succumb to the elements if he doesn't get that vital first feed and it's these situations that Clive is watching for.

'A shepherd spends all his time looking for things that he doesn't want to find,' he says.

We have our own version of a hospital, an ovine hospital, in a small building with a row of a dozen individual pens, a warming box, medicine chest and all the paraphernalia that goes with lambing time. This is where yows and lambs that require more attention are nursed and it's the hub of the whole operation. It's in here that decisions are made. We prefer our shearlings, the first-time mothers, to go back to the moor with just one lamb – rearing two lambs is a big ask for a young sheep.

If an older yow is struggling to feed twins, we may have to take one off her. This is where our pet lambs come from ('pet' lambs is what we call the hand-reared ones). People assume that a pet lamb is an orphaned lamb, but in reality it's more likely that its mother just didn't have enough milk. This happens more if the weather is bad, as less grass means less milky yows. We hand-rear about forty pet lambs every year, although in 2013, when the weather was so bad, we had seventy. I used to use a device known as a 'shepherdess', which is basically a bain-marie. The milk powder is mixed with water and then it sits in a bucket of warm water, kept at blood heat by an electric thermostat. The lambs actually feed themselves from the rubber teats after the first two or three days, so the milk is available to them all the time in the same way that it would be if they were reared by their mothers. But I was flat out trying to keep up with them as they got bigger, and was mixing, filling and scrubbing the feeders several times a day. Then Clive bought me a present, an expensive one at that, a wonderful machine that only has to be filled once a day with the dry milk powder, is plumbed into the water supply and has an automatic cleaning programme. It took us a while to get it calibrated, but it's a godsend, and proved a good investment.

Clive will sometimes come roaring up the yard on the bike with a yow in the trailer, sometimes a yow in denial with a lamb she refuses to acknowledge as her own. She needs a few days in a pen to get her head around motherhood. Sometimes he will return with a small woolly corpse. Providing that the dead lamb's mother has plenty of milk, this is a good opportunity to mother on a pet lamb. The dead lamb is carefully skinned, its jacket fitted onto the pet lamb, and if all goes to plan the yow, after a bit of sniffing, will accept it as her own. We remove the skin after a day, and then the yow with her 'new' lamb can return to the flock.

Occasionally we may need to assist with the birth of a lamb. Sometimes the lamb will not be presented correctly, perhaps in a breech position, or perhaps twins coming together at the same time. You only realize that something is not right when too much time elapses with no result. There is one sure-fire way to find out what's going on, and that is to put on the shoulder-length orange plastic glove and investigate. In most instances the problem is easily solved, perhaps by the straightening of a leg or a gentle pull, but in very difficult cases where the lambs are tangled together a great deal of patience and dexterity are needed to get them into a position in which the yow can lamb them.

On one occasion during lambing time we had some overseas visitors who were doing the Herriot tour, a Japanese couple who were intent on seeing a yow giving birth.

'Not a problem,' I said. 'Follow me an' we'll go an' 'ave a look at what's going on in t'barn.'

We stood quietly in the middle feed passage. It

was a scene of contentment, the yows all quietly eating their hay. I explained that we needed patience, so we sat down on a bale of straw and watched intently. It wasn't too long before an old grey yow started to show all the signs that a lamb was imminent. She headed off to a corner and began pawing at the straw with her front foot. She sat, then stood, then lay down. It was looking promising, and I explained to our visitors that it wouldn't be long. The video cameras came out, focusing on the yow. Then the noises started, terrible, agonizing groans coupled with an eye-popping strained expression. I was beginning to feel a bit uncomfortable – though perhaps not as much as the yow. My visitors thought this was entirely normal and the cameras kept rolling. I reassured them that there was nothing to worry about, trying to keep up the pretence of nor-mality, while hoping that Clive would put in an appearance. Lo and behold, he did, alerted by the dreadful noises coming from the barn.

I looked at Clive, he looked at me; the Japanese couple happily chatted to each other. Whatever was said was unintelligible to me but the smiles told me they had no idea things were going a bit wrong. I explained to them that we were going to go to the labouring yow to make sure she was all right, muttering to Clive under my breath, 'Just keep smilin'. I 'aven't a clue what the problem is. She's scanned for two.'

We knelt down next to the yow, and quickly realized that both lambs were coming at the same time, jammed like a cork in a bottle. Clive whisp-ered, 'Turn t'owd bugger around, away from t'camera. We're not guaranteed to 'ave a happy ending here.'

In a case like this, both lambs need to be pushed back, making for one incredibly unhappy yow. She was already being pretty vocal, and this procedure did nothing to quieten her. Clive lifted the rear end of the yow up into the air and off the ground and I did the shoving, all the time smiling for the camera. Eventually the lambs moved back far enough to be able to be realigned and I was able to grab two front legs, luckily both belonging to the same lamb. In an instant we had a lamb, with a round of applause from our visitors, the second lamb following immediately. Both lambs were none the worse for their ordeal. We left the now-quiet yow happily licking her offspring.

The Japanese people said it was one of the most amazing things they had ever seen. We thought we were amazingly lucky to have got away with it – it could so easily have ended in disaster.

We always give an injection of penicillin to yows we have physically helped giving birth, to ward off any infection, and the following day this old girl went out into the fields with her two lambs, all fit and healthy.

For a whole month we lamb day and night. We take turns sleeping, one of us working late into the night, the other starting very early. It is exceptionally tiring, but it was even more so for me in 2006, when I was heavily pregnant for the third time, with Raven just started at school and Reuben a very active two-and-a-half-year-old. The government advice is that pregnant women should avoid all contact with sheep, especially at lambing time, because there is a risk of picking up infections that can occur in sheep. I was faced with a real dilemma: no one wants to be accused of being selfish or reckless with the life of a baby, but there was a job to do. Whether I was out in the lambing shed or inside the farmhouse, I was always going to be in contact with sheep, directly or indirectly from dirty wellies and clothes. The only way to avoid contact would be to leave Ravenseat for the duration of lambing, and I wasn't going to do that. I was careful: I took extra precautions, scrubbed up, wore surgical gloves and slathered disinfectant everywhere. I avoided physically lambing any yows unless it was necessary, but sometimes a yow in difficulties just needs a smaller hand.

By this time I knew I didn't go into labour the normal way, with contractions and waters breaking, the textbook signs. I knew that when I started feeling just a bit out of sorts then I ought to set off to the hospital. There was no way the medical profession would let me have a home birth after my two previous experiences. And I was very organized this time: I even laid out the clothes for the other two children, so they would look splendid when they came with us to the hospital.

It started at 5 a.m., just a couple of weeks before my due date, when I began to feel sickly. There was no pain, but I recognized the feeling and woke Clive.

'Come on, it's time we were going.'

It was a beautiful May morning, clear and bright, with a hazy mist just lifting over the moor. Clive nipped out into the yard to do a few jobs, and I got Raven and Reuben dressed in their best clothes and put them into the back of the Land Rover, and off we set. Clive was driving sedately down Swaledale towards Richmond, a lovely route that winds its way through Muker and all the other pretty villages down the dale. Even when you know this area like the back of your hand, you can still marvel at how beautiful it is, and Clive loves to drive slowly, doing his 'visual farming', keeping up a running commentary about so-and-so having his cows out, should ours be out, who's feeding their tup hoggs and so on. There was no sense of urgency.

I was feeling a bit uneasy, shuffling around in my seat, but I suffered in silence.

'Get a move on, will ta?' I said to Clive eventually. I really didn't want to stress either him or the children.

He looked slightly concerned and went a bit faster, but there's a limit in a Land Rover.

'Do you want me to stop and get a feed bag for you to sit on?' he said.

'No, I don't want a bloody feed bag!'

Was he worried I'd mess up the Land Rover? It wasn't exactly pristine.

'Just drive a bit faster, yer dozy bugger, ne'er mind who's cleared 'is meadows,' I yelled at him.

He put his foot down, but I realized it was getting urgent.

'Clive, we 'ave to stop.'

I knew there was a military hospital at Catterick

A beautiful summer evening at Ravenseat. I have no idea why some of the children are in pyjamas. Their childhood is so very different to mine.

Aged six and living in Huddersfield.

Holding my baby sister Katie, with Dad, Grandma and Granddad.

Dad would take me with him when he went motorcycle trialling and sometimes let me ride pillion on his bike.

Sitting in the back of my old
pick-up with Red and one of my
pet lambs.

My first sheepdog, Deefa.

Clive with Deefa at Ravenseat.

I wanted something special for my wedding dress but white wouldn't have been practical — I fed the calves in it later that evening!

Below Clive, me and Meg on our wedding day.

I'm fascinated by the history of Ravenseat. This photo was taken in the 1950s, before the road went in. Aside from that, it looks much the same today.

The old barn (the second oldest building in Swaledale) was once used as a chapel — you can see the tiny arched window.

Our friend Jimmy Alderson, the epitome of a true Dalesman.

Baby Raven was born in 2001 , during the foot and mouth crisis.
Here she is with a very old Roy, as loyal a dog as you could wish for.

Miles trying to stowaway on the mobile clothes van that calls at Ravenseat.

With Reuben in the baby backpack. This is how I carry all the children from about six months until they are old enough to climb the moors under their own steam.

As Raven knows, when you live in the middle of nowhere you can wear what you like to feed the cows.

Edith and Chalky.

Violet with our Tamworth pigs,
Dandelion and Burdock.

At Hawes auction mart selling our lambs, with Edith and Annas in the papoose.

A proud moment for Clive with his champion tup Glory.

OPPOSITE PAGE Raven amongst the globeflowers at Ravenseat. Swaledale is famous for its traditional wildflower meadows.

Giving a lamb a top-up of milk
using a stomach tube on a
bitterly cold April evening.

Violet feeding one of the pet lambs.

Violet helping with a pedicure on
a tup lamb.

Raven tonsing (tweezing out stray
white hairs) so the gimmer lamb
looks its best for Muker Show.
Reuben, Edith and Violet cast
a critical eye over proceedings.

Above It takes about a fortnight to clip all our sheep and it's one of my favourite times of year.

Below The children enjoy helping out by wrapping the fleeces and squashing them down into the wool sheets.

I don't mind being snowed in, but when the pipes freeze, watering the animals as well as the humans can seem like an unending task.

The green waterproofs. Not very flattering but my everyday wear for about six months of the year. Bill and Fan (who is on the wall) don't mind the weather.

A roaring flood at Ravenseat. If you have nerves of steel, you can drive across the packhorse bridge on the right when the river is too high to ford.

The children love haytime. Raven is standing, then from left to right: Edith, Reuben, Sidney, Miles, Violet and Pippen.

We serve cream teas to walkers on the Coast to Coast route —
I've perfected the art of making scones.

Baby Annas was born in 2013, making seven children in all.

OPPOSITE PAGE *Top* We often have unexpected visitors. I came in one
day to find Little Joe in the living room. Luckily I'm not house-proud.
Bottom Out for a ride. I'm on Josie, Raven is on Meg and Reuben is
on Little Joe. Edith is without a pony and looks distinctly unhappy
about it. Very Thelwell I think.

From a town girl engrossed by James Herriot books to becoming a shepherdess, my dream was realized the day fate brought me to Ravenseat.

Garrison, the army's infantry training camp, but also that the out-of-hours GP service was run from there, so there had to be a doctor and some help at hand. We were only halfway to the Friarage Hospital, and there was no way I was going to make it through another hour of driving. This baby was imminent.

Clive pulled up to the sentry box at the gate and got out. Two soldiers emerged, carrying rifles.

'I need to see t'doctor, wife's 'avin' a baby right now,' Clive said, hopping from leg to leg. He was getting seriously twitchy now.

We didn't, of course, have the right slip of paper for admission to the military hospital: they send you one if you go there for a routine appointment. But this was not routine. The two young soldiers didn't know what to do. Maybe they thought we were terrorists, in a battered old Land Rover, with two little kids and a heavily pregnant woman... But they had a job to do, and they were doing it.

'Sorry, we can't let you in without a pass,' one of them said.

Clive said, 'Come on, lads, this's a proper emergency. She'll 'ave t'baby in yer sentry box if yer don't ler us in.'

They kept looking at me, and I suppose, like everyone else, they expected me to be writhing with labour pains, which I wasn't. Eventually they capitulated and waved us through.

We screeched to a halt outside the doors of the hospital. Clive rushed in and appeared moments later with a doctor who said that an ambulance was on its way, and that she would give me a quick examination. Clive began to unload the children from the back of the Land Rover but the doctor said, 'There's no need to get the children out of the car, you'll not be stopping.'

I followed the doctor into a treatment room, while Clive played his deaf card and manhandled the children into the waiting room. The doctor was probably praying for the ambulance to arrive, and it did, very promptly. But as soon as the ambulance men took one look at me they said, 'We can't move her. She's too near.'

So then there was no choice. I had the baby there, on that narrow examination bed, with my foot resting on a wall socket. The look of relief at the safe delivery on the doctor's face was a picture: it had certainly livened up her night shift. I had a healthy seven-pound baby boy who cried immediately.

Outside Raven said, 'Babby's 'ere, I can 'ear it crying.'

They popped their heads round the door to have a quick look at the new arrival, and then Clive took them off to the garrison McDonald's for a celebratory breakfast while I was loaded into the ambulance with the baby and taken to the Friarage. It was good that this birth had been witnessed by a doctor as she told me that he was born in the occiput posterior position, the same way that Raven had presented, but, thankfully, as the baby weighed less than she did, I had been able to deliver him.

Clive and I had both decided that he would be called Miles. We have a field called Miles's field complete with a barn called Miles's cow'as (cow house) so it figures that there had been a Miles at

Ravenseat long ago. We also like names that are short or can be shortened, so they can be easily yelled at high volume from the farmhouse door when the children are just specks in the distance.

Miles was a very sleepy, contented baby and fitted in well to life at Ravenseat. I carried him with me everywhere as I went about my work on the farm. My babies have always been good at sleeping through the night from very early on. I always think it must be because they are in the fresh air all day long.

I try to keep the children safe, of course, but I also like them to be busy outside. I'm always keen to introduce them to country pursuits, but on one occasion it ended in tears: Miles's and mine. We had a burgeoning population of rabbits at Ravenseat, and I decided it was time to make a rabbit pie. I had been rabbiting before but I have always been hopeless at killing them. On the one occasion I reckoned I had caught enough to make a family-sized pie, I got home and realized that my rabbits had clearly not been dead, merely concussed. They had woken up and escaped out of my bag.

Clive was equally unsuccessful at controlling them. He got so annoyed at the number of rabbits sitting in his newly mown hayfield that he decided he was going to shoot a few. He sat on the tractor and fired at them with his air rifle. His target would jump, look a little startled, peer quizzically at its rump, scratch, and then carry on grazing.

We had a ferret called Brian, Brian Ferret, and

the children were excited when I announced we would take Brian rabbiting. Many of our steep banks are a maze of warrens which are perfect for rabbiting, the idea being that you put nets over all the holes then send Brian down to scare them. The rabbits take fright and run out into the nets. That's the theory, anyway... Brian was a lazy so-and-so and never took his job very seriously: we were sure he went down the hole, found a cosy corner and had a doze.

We set off on a lovely autumn afternoon: me, Raven, Reuben and Miles, just a toddler in the backpack. We had Brian and all the time in the world. There was great excitement among the children, they could hardly bide themselves. It didn't matter how long Brian spent down the hole, as I'd brought along some Milky Bars as a treat and to keep their spirits up while we waited. And waited. And waited. The children nibbled away on the chocolate, willing a rabbit to appear.

Ferrets don't have very good eyesight, but they must have a damned good sense of smell, be-cause unbeknown to me Brian had come out of the hole, rabbitless, walked across to Miles, sniffed the air, smelt chocolate and then sunk his teeth into Miles's cheek. There was a piercing scream. I ran over and tried to prise Brian off, but his jaw was locked on to Miles, and the more I pulled the more I was pulling Miles's face. I remembered being told that the way to get a ferret to release his jaw was to stub a cigarette on him, but I don't smoke, so that was no good.

It's all a blur how I managed to get the ferret off, but I did. I shoved him back in his box and ran back to the farmhouse, me in floods of tears carrying an inconsolable Miles. There were fang marks on his face, he looked like he'd been savaged – which he had – and I was beside myself. I was convinced that if I took him to the doctor I'd be reported to Social Services.

'Clive, they're gonna take t'kids off us,' I wailed.

Clive was calm, as usual. Miles was up to date with his tetanus jab, so that was all right, and we squirted some penicillin into the wounds and dressed it ourselves. He stayed in hiding on the farm for a while, until it was all nicely recovered. Because the wounds were only puncture marks they healed beautifully, and left only the tiniest of scars.

A few superficial injuries are bound to be picked up along the way if you let the children run free.

BEWARE: FREE-RANGE CHILDREN.

That's what my sign says on the road down to the farm and that's exactly what they are: free range. They play in the fields, ride horses, dig, build things from the rocks they find in the river and generally make their own amusement. They also have a freedom that is probably rarely found in this day and age.

We live so far from anywhere that they don't have 'play dates' and friends round for tea – not very often, anyway. We did have one little boy who came round to play with Reuben, dropped off for the afternoon by his mother who arranged to pick him up a couple of hours later. The responsibility of someone else's child weighed heavily on my shoulders, and I forbade the children from straying any further than the farmyard. A little while later I went to check on them and found them in the corner of a barn very much engrossed in something. We'd had an invasion of rats and had put down some traps for them. A rat had been caught in one of the traps, and Reuben had decided it would be interesting to see who would win in a fight between a rat and a ferret. So he got Brian and put him in the trap with the rat.

Although it wasn't really my idea of a cracking way to while away your afternoon, I didn't mind too much. Brian could see off a rat with no problem and I despise rats. But I don't think the other boy's mother thought much of it, when her son excitedly told her all the gory details after she came to pick him up. Needless to say, he never came back to play.

It was after Miles was born that I started up my cream teas enterprise. As I've mentioned, we're slap bang in the middle of the Coast to Coast walk, and there's a constant stream of walkers, in good and bad weather, throughout the summer months. In fact, we get them most of the year: the only time they don't come is in the worst of the winter weather. They often pause here to rest their weary limbs after crossing miles of bleak, boggy moorland. Ravenseat is a welcome sight, the first habitation they will have seen in nearly ten miles.

Although the idea of serving refreshments to the tired, weather-beaten walkers had first crossed my mind when we had the invasion of them in our wedding tent, it took a while for my idea to come into fruition, what with foot and mouth, babies and other things putting it on the back burner. What I needed was a nudge to get me started. It came when we found that the old chapel, which was used as a barn, needed repairing. It's an ancient building, so it had to be done sympathetically. The beams needed repairing and the roof had to come off and be reinstated as it was. This meant we had to clear out the rubbish that had accumulated over the years, everything from clogs, milk churns and rakes to a catering-size tin of ravioli that expired some twenty years ago – it all had to go. We were left with space for people to sit inside with their cream teas and shelter from the weather. A couple of toilets were installed and a couple of picnic benches provided, and I was in business. I have built up gradually since then, and although I haven't exactly gone global I do now have six benches, with customers sitting on the wall or in the grass when we are really busy. The majority of people who visit are outdoorsy people anyway, thankfully, and all they want is a hot drink and somewhere to sit to enjoy it. I sometimes think that I influence the weather at Ravenseat: if I have all the benches outside it will rain and when they are dragged into the barn the sun will come out.

The barn has a loft accessed by stairs on the outside and you have to duck to get through the door. Inside there are a couple of pews. Scrawled on to one of the ground-floor beams are the words: 'If you are lish, there's more room upstairs.' 'Lish' means fit ('crammly' means that you're not) and of course the walkers on the Coast to Coast are definitely lish.

It used to be just walkers and ramblers who stopped at Ravenseat for a brew, but now I also get people calling in cars who have been for a drive out in the Dales. The first thing that happens when someone in a car turns up is that I get a telling-off for being 'difficult to find'. There used to be a sign at the end of our road advertising that afternoon teas were available, but I couldn't cope with the number of people who would turn up. Then a camper did me a huge favour by using the sign as fuel on their barbecue. I never replaced it.

I had a visit from a woman from a business enterprise organization, with all sorts of ideas for promoting the business: flyers, adverts, etc. She said I could get a grant for a proper sign at the road end and suggested I get some tablecloths. I politely declined: people who call at Ravenseat don't want to take their muddy boots off or to sit down in palatial surroundings, and as for advertising for more customers, I am working to capacity as it is. Cheap and cheerful, that's my motto. As far as we are concerned, it started out as a minor thing, a sideline to the farming, which is, and always will be, our main job.

I serve the teas in the afternoons; the last walkers usually come through at about teatime. I've spent years trying to work out if there's a pattern as to what times I will be busy, but there really isn't one. I can have a beautiful day when the sun shines and see hardly anyone, and then a terrible wet grim day and be madly busy. Sometimes I will look out of the window and there will be nobody and the next time I look I will have a coachload of Czech tourists. We get a fair few foreigners walking the Coast to Coast, especially Americans and Australians. I recently had an email from an American who had been on a tour of Britain and had stopped off here for a cream tea. He said he thought Ravenseat Only (which is what it says on the sign at the end of our road) was one of the most beautiful places he had ever seen.

Of course, making teas and coffees wasn't a problem at the outset but making any sort of cakes was. I was a seriously bad cook and although I had improved in many areas, baking just wasn't my forte. I had to devise some kind of fail-safe recipe, something I could make quickly and easily, and that we liked too so if it wasn't sold the family could eat it. I tried making all kinds of things but the one thing that consistently came out of the oven looking OK and was reasonably edible was my scones. I make them fresh every day. My baking has improved considerably since and I bake other things as well, like Chelsea buns, Devonshire splits and tarts. I never advertise these because I would need a more extensive menu, and would have to make everything on it. But if someone says, 'I don't like currants,' then I can usually find them something else, although I may be muttering under my breath, 'Yer keisty bugger.'

I originally put a note at the bottom of my basic menu saying: 'If it's not on the menu, then please ask.'

I soon scribbled it out after requests for anything from massages through to cash machines and taxis, not to mention macchiatos with a double shot.

'It's not bloody Starbucks tha'knows,' I say.

'Well, what sort of coffee is it?' they ask.

'The variety tha' costs yer a quid,' I retort.

As I said, I couldn't cook at all when I first came to Ravenseat, but I had to learn pretty quickly. Clive would announce, 'I've got thi a bullock for t'freezer.'

Nothing like half a ton of beef to expand your repertoire. I knew I couldn't mince it all and turn it into cottage pie, or even a lot of cottage pies.

I've had plenty of opportunity over the years to hone my cooking skills. What with all the children and occasional workers, it isn't unusual to have a dozen people sitting down for supper.

I'm now an accomplished cook and, surprisingly, I really enjoy it.

When we are clipping or working together in the sheep pens Clive is quite likely to say, 'You ga an git dinner sorted, Mand.'

Sometimes a small argument ensues about who is clipping the fastest, sometimes resulting in Clive disappearing to the kitchen to make a plateful of sandwiches and a pot of tea.

Equal opportunities, I say.

Clipping can be punctuated by visitors wanting refreshments. I have a variety of signs that I put up on the farmhouse door – 'I'm in the clipping shed/sheep pens/barn/wherever' – and then an arrow to show them where to find me. The only official time of year that I am closed is during lambing time when I feel that a visitor requesting a cream tea may be put off by the shoulder-length rubber glove.

The children are very helpful with the teas. A basic cream tea is £3, so the children are good at their three times tables. Raven can now bake and take control of the whole thing; Reuben will help to serve the teas and has perfected the art of charming the ladies. Miles, on the other hand, from time to time rings the bell to alert me that a cream tea is needed, and then eats it himself. When he was smaller he used to wait until the customers had gone and then round up their leftovers and disappear behind the chapel to eat them.

We believe it's important that the children realize money has to be earned and I'm sure that learning to deal with people and being polite and helpful will stand them in good stead in the future.

Occasionally – very occasionally – we get someone who is difficult, stroppy even. I can remember one dismal day when it was chucking it down with rain and a group of walkers came in. It's about a hundred yards from the kitchen to the picnic barn, and I was walking up and down, sheltering the food and drink from the elements. They were tricky customers: they had a mix of teas, coffees and hot chocolates, with crisps and scones – some buttered; some no jam – then they asked for more coffee, then for more scones, then hot water and then another teabag. Each time I did the walk through the pouring rain, trying my best to keep everything dry and the drinks hot. I gave them the bill and one of them examined it forensically and said, 'I think you've overcharged us by fifty p.'

I was at the end of my tether. I'm cheap enough. I threw the money pot at them and said, 'Just put in whatever thi think fit,' and I stomped back up to the farmhouse. I sat down with tears streaming down my face. They'd pushed me to breaking point.

It was all quiet for a while and then there was a timid knock on the door. One of the group was standing there with the money pot.

'We're really sorry. We miscalculated.'

They were the exception: most people are really appreciative.

I'll take a day off for maternity leave, but the day after I've had the baby I'm usually back serving teas. Occasionally I put the CLOSED sign up, when I just have to. Recently I was away, seeing the midwife, and a chap came through doing the Coast to Coast and, despite the sign, he asked Clive for a cream tea. Clive told him we were closed and he said, 'I've been coming through here for years. I've been having a cream tea ever since you started serving them, and I enjoy a break and a chat. It's very disappointing.'

'Well, thoo can use t'loo and get some water from t'tap, but you're going to be even more disappointed, cos I'm off now, an' all,' Clive said, climbing on to the quad and driving off. I guess Clive maybe needs more training on the customer relations front.

We occasionally get passers-by who want to camp, and we have some lovely places on the river edge for them to pitch their tents. We get quite a few groups of teenagers doing their Duke of Edinburgh Gold award. Our biggest camping group was a motorcycle club from Hull, thirty of them. They were mainly middle-aged men on super bikes with the missus on the back. I said I'd do a barbecue for them, as well as breakfast. They took their leathers off and to my surprise they all had onesies on, mostly animal ones. We had tigers, penguins, cows, Santa, all sorts. The children insisted on digging out their onesies, and the party went on until the small hours, only ending when a person dressed as a penguin fell out of a tree.

We did once have a walker who sadly collapsed and died in Close Hills. The first we knew about it was when a woman came into the farmyard, clearly upset, and stuttered that there was a body on the footpath. Clive's hearing is not so good and there was a mammoth misunderstanding, him assuming that one of his cows had expired. He was not very happy about this and set off to investigate, muttering under his breath about how annoying it was that things always chose to expire on the footpath. It was only as he neared the body that he realized it was not a cow after all: it was a rambler. (So it wasn't as bad as he thought. JOKING!!) He came back to the farmyard, rang for an ambulance, picked up a horse blanket and returned, covering the poor man, as by now he had a group of curious cows surrounding him. When the ambulance arrived Clive took the crew on foot to the scene, and as they drew near one of the ambulance men said, 'What's that?' pointing towards the striped hump in the field.

'That's thi' man,' said Clive. 'I's covered 'im up.'

'Yer shouldn't have done that,' said the ambulance man, 'we've got to try an' revive him.'

Clive said, 'Yer a pair o' marvellous fellas if yer can bring 'im back...'

On seeing the body they had to agree there was nothing they could do except carry him back to the ambulance.

It was all very sad but I reckoned that he can't have been feeling at all unwell to have set out walking in such a remote place, so it must have happened very suddenly, without suffering, and I like to think he was doing something he enjoyed. Not a bad way to go at all.

9

Edith on the Way

Edith was born on a lovely hot day in August 2008. I was very busy serving cream teas, and the customers were all lapping up the sunshine and the scenery. It was a perfect summer's afternoon.

I told Clive at lunchtime that I was feeling a bit rough, but I was so busy with the teas that I pushed the thought aside. Clive will tell you that he has to nag me to take the feeling seriously. As soon as he hears I'm feeling a bit off, he's on full alert.

I'd been given a whole set of instructions by the

midwife: 'Do not under any circumstances set off for the hospital in the Land Rover. Call for an ambulance the minute you think the baby is coming.'

They were getting to know me: very rapid births, no contractions. I hate ringing for an ambulance, I feel I'm a drain on the system when there are people in more need than me. But Clive was very much in favour. As he says, 'If she's gonna have t'babby in a lay-by, I don't wanna be t'one delivering it.'

The midwife primed the ambulance service control centre by letter explaining that they should expect this woman to ring up feeling only slightly ill, but they were to take her seriously and send an ambulance. That's the theory: but every time we ring up ambulance control the person at the other end has no idea what we are talking about. When we tell them the baby is coming they imagine me lying on the floor counting the gap between contractions.

Instead, I was busy sorting out whether Clive had enough scones to carry on with the cream teas, whether he should put the CLOSED sign up, wondering whether the older two, Rav and Reuben, would be home from school in Gunnerside before I went, deciding what they would all be having for their tea.

Our local ambulance depot is a forty-minute drive away, over in Wensleydale, and if there's an ambulance on standby it can be with us in that time, which may sound a long wait if you live in a town, but up here it's pretty good. By the time they arrived I'd decided to turn the sign round to say we were closed, but it makes no difference, the customers still come. As it was such a lovely summer day some of them were still sitting there, drinking tea in the sunshine, so new arrivals couldn't understand why they couldn't have a cream tea too. It's no good telling them I'm in labour, because I'm busying around clearing tables, not looking like I'm going to give birth in the next hour or so.

I began to feel a bit more tetchy, so sat quietly on the garden wall in the sunshine. We can see every car that turns into our road a good five minutes before it gets to us, so I watched the ambulance approach.

'Oh, it's you again,' the ambulance man Steve said, as I leapt healthily up into the back of the ambulance. I had previous form: Steve was with me after Reuben was born so unexpectedly. I didn't feel the need to lie down so I perched on a seat feeling a little embarrassed about the whole drama. Clive waved and gave me a thumbs-up, glad to see the back of me. He's very happy not to be the driver on these adventures any more. He stood in the farmyard and watched us go along the Ravenseat road, but we'd only got as far as Black Howe barn when I said to Steve, 'Yer know what, I think I do need to lie down.'

They pulled off the road to let me get onto the stretcher. Clive, who was watching from the farmyard, thought, *Uh-oh, babby's here before she even gets off our road.*

But in fact I wasn't quite ready to have the baby, and we set off again. They turned up and onto the Buttertubs Pass, the road climbing steeply as it leaves Swaledale, twisting round tight bends and rapidly descending into Wensleydale.

The ambulance crew were unconcerned about me because, as usual, I showed no signs. We were chatting away, discussing the weather, hay time, the sheep trade and catching up on all the local gossip. As we went past their depot they decided to pull in and collect some supplies, bits and pieces they were running out of on the ambulance. By this time I had a really heavy feeling in the pit of my belly, not in waves like contractions, but as if something was weighing me down. It wasn't long after we set off again that I felt the heaviness increase and I knew the baby was coming.

'Would yer tek a look, I think it's happening down there,' I said to Steve, gesturing downwards.

He was very reluctant.

'No, yer fine,' he said.

'Please, 'ave a look. Quick.'

He was in denial, holding the blanket down as I tried to lift it up and make him look. He wasn't at all convinced.

'Please, please...'

I'm surprised I was still being so polite. Very gingerly, he lifted the blanket and glanced under, and then suddenly he was hammering on the glass window partition that separated us from the driver, yelling, 'We've got to stop. Pull over as soon as you can. She's having the baby.'

We ducked into a wooded lay-by and the driver rushed round the side of the ambulance and slid the side door open. I turned to see a group of middle-aged people in striped deckchairs having a picnic, a bloke with a Scotch egg in one hand and a mug of tea in the other.

Just as I'm looking at them and they're looking at me in amazement, the ambulance men lift up the blanket and with one easy push the baby slides out.

The ambulance men popped the baby, a little girl, onto my front, wrapping her in a towel, and then off we went to the hospital, leaving one little picnic party totally traumatized. They'd probably driven out into the countryside to see a bit of nature, and ended up seeing rather more of it than they wanted. I bet they still talk about it.

Edith was a lovely six-and-a-half pounder, feeding well straight away. We were both declared fit, and a few hours later Clive arrived to collect us from the hospital with the other three kids in tow. Clive is good with the children, he's happy to take charge of them. He always tells me he'd have no trouble getting another woman if I died, because when he's out on his own with the children, women flock to help him.

'The more they squawk, the better it is,' he says.

I once left him looking after the children at the visitor centre at Rheged, while I did a mole-catching course. I returned, feeling bored with my day, to listen to Clive telling me how much he had enjoyed his afternoon.

'There was a varry friendly lady helped out wit' lal'uns,' he said.

That very same friendly lady turned up at Ravenseat the following weekend. I don't think Clive had mentioned the small matter of a wife to her. I still tease him about it.

It was about a month after Edith was born that Clive had a close encounter with Julia Bradbury, the television presenter most famous for fronting *Countryfile*. She was filming a series called *Wainwright's Walks*, in which she retraced the walks popularized by the famous fell walker and author Alfred Wainwright. We were told that she and the film crew would be walking down Whitsundale and passing through Ravenseat on the Coast to Coast route, and that they might want to film Julia walking over the packhorse bridge. We were busy getting our mule gimmers ready for sale the next day and were not unduly worried when nobody showed up. It was a horrible day, the day from hell, with rain and thick mist up on the moors. We just assumed the filming had been postponed due to the bad weather conditions.

Our sheep were finished, the light had gone as the nights were already drawing in, and I was in the farmyard putting the dogs to bed when I saw a car approaching. A young man got out and jogged up the yard, introducing himself as a runner for the BBC. He asked if we had seen Julia and the crew. I looked at him blankly and said that I had seen and heard nothing, not a sign. He was almost having a panic attack: as far as he was concerned, they were lost, in awful conditions. There is no mobile coverage in our area so there was no way of knowing where they were; all he knew was that they had left Kirkby Stephen that morning and no one had seen them since.

'Calm down, I'll fetch Clive,' I said. That's my

answer to emergencies: get Clive, he'll do summat.

'I'll ga an' see if I can spot 'em,' Clive said.

He jumped on the quad bike and set off in the direction of Whitsundale, following the Coast to Coast route. It's a real wilderness up there: remote, boggy and heathery, hard-going for walkers at the best of times. Clive had to skirt Fawcetts intake (one of our fields) on the bike because it's full of grips and tussocks, and took a detour round the wire corner (it's a route we use when gathering sheep). At the stile at the far side he found them. One of the crew had twisted her ankle badly, and they were sitting there in the rain, with no mobile signal, unable to contact anyone, at the mercy of the elements.

What people don't realize when they watch programmes like the TV series *The Dales*, in which we have featured, or *Wainwright's Walks*, is that filming takes a long time. On the walks programmes you see Julia striding out with a small backpack, and you get the impression that the whole thing is filmed as she goes along. But in fact it's: 'Do it again, Julia... Just go back up there again... Let's try that again.'

And while Julia isn't carrying much, the crew are lugging all the gear. It's not as easy as they make it look.

Anyway, they were very relieved to see Clive. The hero of the hour got his priorities right and put Julia, the glamorous star of the show, on the back of the bike and brought her back down to Ravenseat before going up with the bike trailer to bring the others down. Julia jumped on the bike, sitting astride behind Clive and holding on for dear life. This impressed Clive.

'Look wha' I've found at t'moor. Can I keep it?' he said when he brought her back, clinging to him and soaking wet.

'Nooooo, Clive, you can't...'

We sat by the fire, warming up and drinking tea, while he rescued the others. After arranging the next day's filming at Ravenseat, they headed off to their hotel for the night.

Fortunately the next day dawned bright and clear and we filmed a small piece down at the picnic benches with baby Edith in the papoose.

Our bit is only a short segment of the film, but it has made our picnic benches a must-visit part of the Coast to Coast for those who have watched it. Julia's series of *Wainwright's Walks* have sold very well on DVD; they are classics for walkers because they tell it like it is, a true reflection of what it's like doing the walk in foul or fair weather. We get a lot of Julia fans – we have learned that Clive is one of a not-very-exclusive club. They want to know where she sat and what she said. The most popular question is: 'Did she actually walk it?

The answer is yes, but filming takes bloody ages so it's not, for her, like doing it as a normal walker.

Anyway, I never heard the last of it from Clive. It was Julia this, Julia that, for the next few days. Then a few weeks later I got an email from her: she wanted to know if we would mind her writing about Clive rescuing her for an article in the *Countryfile* magazine. She has to write a piece every month, and she wanted to feature her knight in shining armour, the man with the quad.

Clive said, 'Yeah, yeah, not a problem.' Obviously.

A couple of weeks later he was at a cattle sale at Kirkby Stephen auction, and he came home puzzled.

'They call't mi Colin, all day lang.'

'What do you mean, they called you Colin?'

'They aren't calling mi Clive, they're calling mi Colin, they seem to think it's funny.' He was perplexed.

We soon discovered that Julia had written a lovely, glowing article about him for the magazine, but all the way through she called him Colin. There was a picture of him with the caption: 'My knight in shining armour, Colin.'

He was devastated. Clearly, he wasn't as memorable to her as she was to him... But I have to admit that I had to turn my back to enjoy a secret smile.

Every day at Ravenseat starts at 6 a.m., for everyone. There are jobs that have to be done every day, jobs that have to be done every week, and jobs that change with the seasons. In the winter there's a lot of feeding to do. 'Bullocking up' is what we call the everyday feeding of every animal that is incarcerated in the barns around the farmyard: the horses, cattle, calves, sheep, lambs and pigs. The majority of the sheep are outside but are still fed once or twice a day on hay and cake. We work it between us, I have my sheep and Clive has his. We only have one quad bike, so he'll go out first thing while I'm seeing to the kids, and then when he's back for his breakfast, I'll go out. Plus, of course, I have to feed the humans, including anyone who's working or visiting, which takes a bit of forward planning.

The rest of the year there's lambing, clipping, dipping, trips to the auction, not to mention household chores. I do loads of washing. It's a filthy job, farming, and I like everyone to at least start off spick and span in the morning, but I never iron anything: I try to hang things straight on the line or flake (that's an old local name for a clothes rack, and like other bits of Yorkshire dialect, it's originally a Norse word). Then I fold it, and it's the job of one of the children (Miles at the moment) to put it away. Miles is a good choice, as he's a very tidy, organized child.

For me and Clive the day usually ends about 9 p.m., when we try to have an hour on the sofa together, catching up about the kids and the farm. We're never off duty. Occasionally we socialize with our neighbours and other farmers over a meal, but it's rare. We have a chance to catch up with everyone at the auctions, and when we're gathering sheep and taking strays back. There are also big events like weddings and funerals. I'm not great at funerals, so Clive always goes as our representative. He loves singing hymns.

It's very unusual that we do days out but sometimes we have to, like a trip to Darlington to buy some school shoes. But our trips usually seem to tie in with looking at sheep. Once, when Clive knew I had a scan appointment at the hospital, he said, 'You wouldn't tek some sheep to Arthur's field, would yer?'

We have a friend who has some land bordering Teeside Airport and every winter we take him a trailerload of sheep to look after.

Being an idiot, I said yes, of course I would take the sheep. So there I was, trying to park a long-wheelbase Land Rover with a triple-axle trailer on the back and forty-five sheep in it, in a hospital car park. I did three circuits, couldn't find anywhere to put it, so in the end pulled into an ambulance bay. I was sure when I came out that I would have been clamped, but clearly everybody who saw it thought there must have been a terrible agricultural emergency. Why else would anyone park a trailer-load of forty-five bleating sheep in a hospital car park?

I took Edith and Raven to the county hall at Northallerton a couple of years ago when I was asked to speak at a rally opposing the down-grading of the maternity and children's services at the Friarage Hospital. William Hague, our local MP and the Foreign Secretary, was talking immediately after me. He had security men with him, and there was someone between him and the window at all times. It was very much frowned upon when I made a joke about there being a grassy knoll directly opposite the balcony from which we were making our speeches.

Afterwards I took Raven and Edith to the shops, but they're no more interested in shopping than I am. They're not used to shops and don't really know how to behave in them. I remember one incident outside WH Smith. I was looking through the window when one of the children,

216

who shall remain nameless, squatted down to have a wee on the pavement, because that is what you do when nature calls at Ravenseat. Carrying a baby on your back makes getting round the shops far easier than using a cumbersome pushchair but also means that you can be entirely oblivious to the baby's shoplifting activities. After leaving a shop on the High Street I realized with horror that one of my little ones had swiped a very cheap-looking, badly made thong from a discount store, and was waving it aloft for all he was worth. It had obviously caught his eye.

I do want to give the children a normal childhood. We've always had it in our minds that we should try to give them a proper beach holiday, take them to the seaside and watch them dig in the sand. And we've tried, we really have. Before Edith was born we actually booked a weekend in a hotel in Blackpool for us all. Clive had spoken very highly of Blackpool, he had many happy memories of times spent there as a youngster. Later I discovered that Clive's recollections were based on boozy trips with a bunch of mates when he was eighteen or nineteen to watch the Miss Blackpool beauty pageant, his memories distorted by the copious quantities of beer taken on board. Not quite the same as going with the missus and three kids in tow.

The place just didn't do it for us. We don't really like the manufactured fun, but we thought the children might like it, just because it's the complete opposite of what they are used to. In the event, they didn't like it any more than we did. Staying in the hotel was a nightmare, with other people complaining about the noise of the kids, banging on the ceiling. It wasn't a child-friendly hotel, which is odd in a town supposed to be designed for family fun. We walked miles up and down the seafront in the rain, looking out onto the muddy shoreline and counting the worm casts. They weren't even impressed with the donkeys – and why would they be, when we have our own ponies at home that they can ride whenever they want and as fast as they want. As Clive says, 'Blackpool's just not us. It's fine for them that likes it, there's nothing wrong wi' it. It just isn't us.'

So we came home. Early.

It's not always a total fiasco. We decided to take the kids to Edinburgh once. I looked through a brochure and found a flat that looked spacious, in a good central location, opposite a park and with a lovely view across Princes Street to the castle. It was cheap, too, and I thought, *That'll do nicely*.

We went on the train and at Waverley station all piled into a taxi. I told the driver the address and he looked puzzled.

'I knaw Edinburgh like back'o my hand but I dinnae knaw what holiday flat ye're goin' to.'

'Honestly, it's the right address.' I was starting to get worried now.

Then the mist lifted.

'I've got it now, I knaw where you're stopping, wee hen'.'

We found out why he was confused when he dropped us off: the holiday flat was above a sex shop, and there was a nightclub next door. This wasn't mentioned in the brochure and, admittedly, when I rang up to make the booking, I didn't specify that I *didn't* want to be next to a nightclub and above a sex shop. But the apartment was brilliant, once we were inside. Every time we went in or out we had to shield Reuben's eyes: he wanted to peer through the door at the display of nipple tassels, and the grubby-looking men in raincoats who were thumbing through magazines in there.

But we liked Edinburgh, and once we crossed the main road the children had space to run around in the park. Late at night Clive and I amused ourselves watching from our window the drunks coming out of the club trying to climb over the roadwork barricades, round the area where the new tramlines were going. Edinburgh was a success.

Then there was the day out to Whitby, when Edith was a toddler. This was Clive's great idea. He saw an advert in the local newspaper for a day trip by rail to Whitby. *Great,* he thought. *Let the train take the strain, and all that.* Well, it was the day out from hell.

First of all, we had to get to Bishop Auckland by 8 a.m. to catch the train. That's an hour's drive for a start and what with getting everything packed up for the day, and doing all the usual farm jobs, it meant an early start even by our standards.

Then we discovered that what the glowing advert failed to mention was that the train stopped at every station along the way. It even went back down a branch line at one stage to pick up more passengers, making it a three-hour journey. The train got more and more crowded, the kids got more and more bored. Our kids are used to being able to wander outside, doing their own thing. They don't know about being confined like that, and there's only so long a colouring book will keep them amused. I lost count of the number of times we heard 'Are we nearly there yet?' as I slowly lost the will to live. All I could think about was how we were going to have to repeat the same journey later in the day.

At last, at noon, we arrived in Whitby. It was cold, and it was raining, and we only had a few hours there because we had to be back on the train at 3 p.m. for the nightmarish journey home. What a disaster. We couldn't see the place through the rain, we were all miserable. All in all we spent two hours in the car, six hours on the train, and three hours there, eating fish and chips behind a windbreak. It was a memorable day at the seaside for all the wrong reasons.

I have come to the conclusion that holidays just aren't for us. Our hearts are never very far from Ravenseat, even if we do fancy a change of scenery. It's not only that we feel this place calling us back, but we also have a niggling feeling that while we are away something could be going wrong. As I've said before, you are never off duty when you live on a farm. Even when we decide on a lovely day to sit outside to eat our tea, one of us will look up the moor and say, 'That gate's down up there.'

'No, it's not.'

'I's sure it is...'

Next thing, the field is full of sheep and you're up there chasing them back out and fixing the gate. There's always something going on and we like it that way.

Even though the farmhouse was not looking at its best the first time I saw it, I could see it was a warm and homely place, a place that had a history and held echoes of the people who had lived here through the centuries. It needed renovation, but not modernizing: in fact, what it needed was to be restored to how it originally was. We need modern amenities like flush toilets, washing machines, fridges and freezers, but we also want the look and the feel of the place to be traditional.

The first job was to make the place watertight. Until then, I shut the door and ignored the damp carpet in the living room. When we were able to lift the carpet we found underneath there were layers of felt stuck with bitumen tar to the original flagstones. It was hard work scraping it off, but worth it to uncover the perfect floor for a farmhouse. Now I just have two rag rugs down, very practical, and I don't have to yell at the children when they come in with their muddy wellies on. The flagstones between the living room and the dairy have been worn away by the iron soles of clogs over many years. We thought that if we turned them over we could start afresh on the unworn side, but when we did it became apparent that one of our predecessors had had the same idea, and they'd been worn down on that side too!

The children and I wear clogs during the summer months to give our feet a rest from wellies and they love making sparks with the iron corkers on the stone flags. In years gone by, particularly fine sand from around the edge of Birkdale Tarn, at a place called Lops Wath, was scattered onto the stone flags in the house and walked over by clog wearers, to clean the stone. I'm tempted to try this (anything to avoid scrubbing with caustic soda) but I suspect it would just be used to build sandcastles.

The other living room was even more wrecked. It had been used as a proven (feed) store and had scribblings on the plaster-work detailing how many pounds of feed was to be given to the animals. It took a lot of digging around the exterior walls to prevent water seeping in, then a good deal of replastering before a habitable room emerged.

There were originally four bedrooms but the bathroom was through a bedroom: it didn't make sense so we've changed it round to get a good bathroom with a shower. Now we have two big bedrooms and one really substantial one. When I came there was no shower, just a bath. It wasn't practical after a hard day's work on the farm to come in and have a bath, especially when the water was heated by a back boiler on the open fire, which limited the amount available. The spring water was very, very brown, full of peat. It looked like we were being very generous with the whisky when someone asked for a Scotch and water. We were used to drinking it, but any newcomers would usually succumb to a bad attack of the heebie-jeebies for a few days until they got used to it. Now, although the water comes from the same spring, we have a filtration and cleaning system making it safe for anyone to drink. It still has a slightly brown tinge, but it's 100 per cent pure: we just don't want to pump in loads of chlorine to get rid of the discolouration.

There was a double earth closet outside, and another single one across at the pig hulls. The double one amused me: who do you like well enough to sit next to them on the loo? I suppose I could have put a couple of the children on it, side by side. The earth closets are still there. The children went through a phase of using them, just to hear the long plop, but when I made them empty the bucket the novelty quickly wore off.

A big thick wall runs through the middle of the house, which was the original outer wall. The farmhouse doubled in size when the newer bit was built at the back. But even this 'new' bit predates 1820, as I've found a reference in an old book to a Mr Cleasby, the farmer who decided he'd had enough of the cold and damp in Ravenseat farmhouse and built the other house where the gamekeeper now lives. He wrote that he hated the leaking valley gutter that ran between the roofs of the older part and the newer part. Even now it still leaks.

The big stone dairy is wonderful: I now use it as a pantry and a storeroom for all the supplies I have to keep in for the winter. It has stone shelves, which would have been used to keep the milk cool before the days of fridges, cheese shelves, and hooks for hanging meat and game.

In the kitchen there used to be a white Rayburn – well, it had been white once upon a time. There had been so many spillages baked on to the enamel it was impossible to get them off. It ran off bottled gas, which scared me, and it had a very nasty habit. Every so often the pilot light would blow out, everything would go deathly quiet, and a few minutes later the bottom door would blow off with a huge bang, travelling at high speed right across the kitchen. It was a momentous day when that contraption was removed, and replaced with a new one that runs off kerosene.

It has taken a good while to get the house the way we want it. Things happen slowly here, because there's so much work to do on a day-to-day basis and time is at a premium. It's also true that, given a choice between being outside shepherding or being inside painting a room, then there is no contest. Outside every time.

The most ambitious work on the house took place during the summer of 2009 when I was pregnant with my fifth child. We had to move out and live in a caravan while the whole of the front of the house was taken down and rebuilt. Over the centuries, the relentless, driving rain from the west had penetrated the exterior wall, causing the whole front wall to belly outwards, and rotting the upstairs floor beams. In fact, the porch was all that was preventing the entire collapse of the front wall. If you looked at the house square on from the front then it seemed fine, but from the side it too looked pregnant, bowing outwards in a frightening way.

The weather up here is so fierce that the life-span of the wooden sash windows is only a few years: no matter how much you paint them, they rot. The wind whistles through them, and in an attempt to stop the draughts I roll up towels and place them between the upper and lower panes, only for them to blow off. You can see where the house used to have mullions, and it still has its small 'fire window' that lets light into what was the inglenook fireplace.

An architectural historian showed me the original wattle and daub foundations, and all these factors, on top of the fact that it's a listed building, meant that the job of repairing it had to be done meticulously, with every stone carefully numbered and replaced in its original position.

I knew that we would have to move out of the house while the work was being done, so when I saw a beautiful big blue and chrome caravan advertised in the paper I decided to buy it. It was flashy, and I realized it must be a gypsy caravan because there was no toilet inside: gypsies con-sider it unsanitary to have a toilet in a caravan. It didn't matter to us because we had a toilet in the yard. The caravan was at a scrap-dealer's yard at Morecambe and I arranged to pick it up, as I was planning on parking it out of the weather at the back of the building at Ravenseat until it was needed. I am used to towing trailers, but this cara-van was exceptionally wide as well as long so Clive was specific in his instructions as to how I should tow it home: do not go on the motorway, do not exceed 40 mph and give yourself plenty of room past parked cars. I told him in no uncertain terms to shove off and returned home later in the day with one large caravan in one piece, after driving down the motorway at more than 40 mph. I pulled up into the farmyard and Clive came to admire our new acquisition.

'Great, tha's done well to get tha' back in ya piece. Now you ga an' get tea gaan, and I'll put it in t'building.'

Off I went, but before I had reached the kitchen door there was a nasty crunching sound. Clive had backed the caravan right into his sheepdog Bill's kennel, and the back fascia and light were cracked and hanging off. Needless to say a heated exchange, with a wealth of adjectives, followed.

The work on the house took ages. It was supposed to be six weeks, but it was nearly ten before it was finished. By this time the fun of living cramped up together in a caravan had worn distinctly thin. Special experts in ancient and listed buildings had to advise on the whole renovation process.

'Have you thought of planting a forest to the west side of the farmhouse to act as a windbreak and stop the weather hitting the house?' one of them asked.

Clive was indignant. 'You cannae grow trees up 'ere: just tek a look round an' count the number of trees thoo can see. Besides, 'ow can we plant a forest of fully grown, mature trees to stop t'house collapsing when it's already falling down?'

Luckily, the work, including these consultants, didn't cost us anything: the estate footed the bill.

While the builders were in we decided we wanted a traditional range in the living room, in place of the tiled monstrosity that was there. So when the work was underway I set about looking for one. There is an antique shop that I drive past every time I visit Hawes, and I knew the owner, Ian, had a big working black range in the cellar of his shop. I decided that he would be a good person to ask.

'Aye, I've just gotten one, it's in pieces in t'out-building. I'll get it all fished out an' yet can come back an' 'ave a look-see,' he said.

Clive came with me and we were confronted with an array of pieces of cast iron, propped up against a wall. It was difficult to imagine what it would look like when put back together. It had belonged to a drover at Hawes auction known as Lal' Ed (Little Ed), because he was small with a hunched back. He used to drive the animals into the pens on auction days, a local character, everyone knew him. He'd recently died, his house had been sold and the new owners did not want the old range.

Clive took a bit of persuading. He wasn't convinced that the pile of rusty-looking iron could ever look the part, but I liked the fact that it had a stone sooker (that's a local word for the bit at the top that sits over the open fire, forming the flue and sucking the smoke up the chimney). By Victorian times the sooker was made from metal, so I knew this was a really old example. The stone had been daubed with thick chocolate-brown paint over more layers of green paint. It was a lengthy job removing it, two whole days with a

227

steam cleaner and a scraper, but eventually the flakes of paint came away to reveal the beautiful, intricately shaped stone.

We bought the range knowing that we needed two things: a bloody big hole to put it in, and somebody who understood it, who could get all the flues working for us. I didn't want it to be just decorative: I wanted it to work.

The first problem was easily solved. When the builders took the plasterboard off in the living room, they found a huge inglenook behind, just the right size for the range. Ian, the antique shop owner, gave us the number of a retired chap who in his youth had worked with open fire ranges, and taken many out as people replaced them with newer electric and gas fires. He came up to Ravenseat and worked with our builders in an advisory capacity, keeping a beady eye on proceedings as it was slowly reassembled. Garbed in his bib and brace overalls, he would park himself up on a stool with a mug of tea doling out instructions. Every so often he would get on his hands and knees, look up the chimney, move some stones a fraction of an inch and then sit down again, pondering and sizing up where everything should go. It was a precision job and needed someone who knew exactly what he was doing. He frequently became exasperated with the young builders who weren't happy with the fine tuning needed to make this contraption fully functional.

The range has an oven and a boiler, and an open fire which I have burning every day of the year, even in summer. Reckan hooks are suspended from the bar above and can be used to hang a cooking pot or girdle over the fire and there's a sliding rack on the grate for a kettle. If we look after the fire properly it never goes out. It's a bit like the Olympic torch: an eternal flame. It heats all the hot water for the house and dries all the washing on the flake. Whenever there's a storm I tour round in the Land Rover, loading up branches that have blown down. My quest for firewood knows no limits, there is no branch too big for me to pick up. The children keep an eye out for wood while on the move and any shout of, 'Muuuuuuuuum, I can see some wooooooood,' signals an emergency stop.

I like to remind the children that the wood will warm them up twice, once when chopping it into manageable logs for the fire, and again when they're lying in front of the hearth. It is Reuben's job every morning to stoke the fire, rekindling the glowing embers, while Miles fills up the coal bucket and log box. They know, from past experience, that no fire equals no hot water, equals cold shower. Now they never forget: that's how they learn.

Once the work was done on the house it was lovely to settle back in, and I've been collecting antiques and bits and pieces that fit the age of the place ever since. I've got my goose pot, and a girdle for making oat cakes and drop scones, and of course the range is great for making bread. These jobs are more suited to the winter months when I have a little more time, and it makes more sense to be self-sufficient when getting to the shops is sometimes impossible.

I want Ravenseat to be homely, a warm, comfortable place where the children can be happy and relaxed, a place where it isn't the end of the earth if muddy terriers stretch out in front of the fire, or pet lambs are allowed to curl up by the hearth. There is nothing fancy about the place, though I do like to cover the walls with paintings and prints that relate to us and resonate with the place's history. Recently, when looking through the window of a gift shop in Reeth, I saw a print that I knew needed to be on the wall at Ravenseat.

We had an old neighbour, Tot (short for Christopher), who farmed at Smithy Holme, two farms away from us. The farmhouse had been abandoned after his mother died, and Totty, who had just a small flock of sheep, had farmed the land and lived in a caravan. I loved talking to him: he remembered life in the Dales so far back. He was very fond of his mother, and he never married.

Eventually he went to live in sheltered housing at Gunnerside further down the dale, but still kept his handful of sheep. I'd see him almost every day across in his fields pulling thistles or repairing the walls. I would sometimes visit him in his little bungalow next to the school. We and other neighbours would lend a hand at certain times of the year when his sheep needed clipping or if he needed a pet lamb to mother on to a yow.

When he became ill he was taken into the Friarage Hospital, and I went to visit him. All he wanted was to go back to Smithy Holme. We knew, and I'm sure he knew, too, that he'd never get there again, so me, Clive and the kids went there, gathered up his sheep and made a film on the iPad. I saw him in hospital a few days before he died, and showed him the video. He was quite lucid and he loved seeing his old home. He was naming all the sheep and telling me stories from way back.

Clive was a pallbearer at his funeral, and that morning the children and I picked flowers from the meadows – lady's mantle, marsh marigolds and wood cranesbill – and tied them together into a small bouquet. At the funeral people commented, 'Them's some o t'bonniest flowers 'ere.'

A few months after his death I was in Reeth waiting for the garage to repair the Land Rover and had a bit of time to kill. I walked onto the village green and, glancing through the window of the gift shop, saw a picture I recognized. It's of Tot's mother, sitting by a black range, with a sheepdog pup at her feet. I'd seen the picture hanging on the wall at Totty's house. I bought it straight away. In years to come the memory of who the lady in the picture is, or even where she is sitting, will have faded, but we know. It may not be at Smithy Holme, but it's at Ravenseat, the next best place for it.

10

Our Little Flower

I am, as you've gathered by now, a regular at the Friarage Hospital, and not just because all my babies have been taken there, wherever I've given birth. We've had a few other medical problems that have required trips there. One that puzzled the doctors (but not me) was when Edith caught orf when she was a baby, still in nappies.

Orf is a skin disease that sheep can catch, sometimes called scabby mouth because that's what they get. It's a virus, and you can vaccinate against it, but even after vaccination it still happens occasionally and there's not much you can do but let it run its course. You treat the lambs and their mothers (who sometimes get the scabs on their teats from the lambs' mouths) to stop the scabs becoming infected. The pet lambs, the ones we hand-rear, are more susceptible because they share the feeding teats and pass it on to each other and they don't have the same immunity a mother's milk passes on.

It looks terrible, but it's not really harmful. There are various remedies that people suggest – spraying it with vinegar, giving the lambs zinc supplements – but nothing I've tried works. I hate it, it stinks.

It's what's known as a zoonotic virus, because it

can be passed to humans, and when you are dealing with pet lambs you have to keep your hands very clean. I wear surgical gloves. I've had orf and Raven has had it: just the odd pustule on our hands. They hurt a bit and look pretty unpleasant but eventually they disappear.

I was bathing Edith one night when I noticed a little warty thing on her bottom. I ignored it but the next day it was bigger, and alarm bells started ringing. I said to Clive, 'There's summat on Edith's bum.'

It looked suspiciously like orf, but I was trying to play it down. Unfortunately, he agreed.

'Looks like poor lal' bugger's got orf.'

I must have given it to her off my hand when I changed her nappy. I was hoping it would shrink away of its own accord, but when it didn't I took her to the doctor.

'She's getten orf,' I said.

'Yes, it's orf,' said the doctor. 'But I've never seen a case of it there.'

Our GP practice is a rural one, used to the problems of farmers. I told her my theory, that I had likely passed it on to her when I changed her nappy. She gave me some cream, told me to keep it clean, and said it would run its course, which was what I already suspected.

Keeping it clean inside a nappy wasn't easy and no matter how much cream I slathered on it kept on growing, getting bigger and bigger. I remember having her in the backpack on a warm day in June when I'd been selling bullocks at Penrith auction. All the while I could smell the awful orf smell that I was so familiar with from

233

the pet lambs.

Back we went to the doctor, who said the orf was infected and Edith had a temperature, so we were sent straight to the hospital.

'Right, well, we'll run some tests to see what exactly this is,' the paediatrician said.

'It's orf,' I said flatly.

Edith was put on an antibiotic drip, and we were put into an isolation unit, Edith in a medical cot bed and me on a fold-down bed. Nobody was allowed in or out without good reason, and the staff who came in wore plastic suits.

'We'll have a result soon, we'll soon know what it is,' one of the nurses told me.

'It's orf,' I said.

We had an endless stream of medical professionals and even a medical photographer.

'My God, what is that?' they all said when they saw it.

I gave the same answer: 'Honestly, it's orf. Sheep ger'it.'

I told everyone who would listen that it was orf and that it was a common sheep ailment. Nobody actually contradicted me, but clearly they weren't about to accept my diagnosis. In the meantime, the thing on her bottom grew ever bigger and the doctors began treatment with antiviral drugs. We were in isolation for about a week until eventually we were given the diagnosis 'ecthyma contagiosum'. Which is the medical term for orf in human beings...

It didn't make any difference that we had the official name, there was no new treatment. Like I said, orf just has to run its course. I was a bit

234

relieved to know this: it means that when I leave my sheep to get on with it I'm not depriving them of a cure, because there isn't one.

Eventually, the big growth began to shrink, probably of its own accord, and we were allowed to go home. I had to take Edith back for check-ups, and weeks later the medical photographer came back to take a picture of her perfect, blemish-free little bum. I expect she's in some obscure medical book somewhere.

The upside for Edith is that she can be around the pet lambs as much as she likes: she'll never get orf again.

It was while I was taking her backwards and forwards for check-ups at the hospital that I had two customers for cream teas who looked a little bit out of the ordinary. It was late afternoon, and a big, executive-type car came up the road, and two men in immaculate suits got out.

Uh-oh, these guys is lookin' official, I hope I'm not in some sort of trouble, I thought. We have farm inspections, hygiene inspections, animal assurance inspections ... you name it, someone inspects us for it.

The men ordered cream teas, and I got chatting with them. It turned out that the one with the *really* expensive suit had flown in to Manchester Airport from Chicago, and the other one, who met him at the airport, had promised him a trip to the Yorkshire Dales and a traditional cream tea. They were brokering a deal to supply cutting-edge technology to hospitals to combat hospital infections: it was at the time when there was a lot in the news about MRSA and other hospital bugs.

I told him of my limited experience with viruses and bugs, and all about our recent orf incident. He wrote down my address and a couple of weeks later I received a large parcel full of special dressings, antibacterial wipes, hand sanitizers and disinfectant sprays. I've still got some of it.

It was so kind and such a coincidence that I met them at that time.

Just a few months later, I was back at the Friarage. Violet was born twenty-one months after Edith, and she is the holder of a record in this family that still stands to this day: she's the only natural birth I've had in hospital (Raven was in hospital, but she was a C-section). She was born in May 2010, and it was half-term so Raven and Reuben were home from school. We'd had a busy day: we'd decided to take the quad bike and trailer and go stick-picking. This means we pick up all the sticks and move anything else that will stop the grass growing in the fields where we make hay, and move anything that will knacker our hay baler. Or, I should say, knacker it any more than it already is.

We filled the trailer as we went along with bits of sticks, broken fence posts and rails, and we were putting fallen topstones back onto the wall tops. Then we pulled up outside the barn at Hill Top. Builders had been working there, doing repairs, and they'd thrown down a lot of old beams and laths, and we decided to saw them into lengths and load them onto the trailer too, which was quite strenuous.

I was feeling very pleased with our efforts. I knew Clive would be delighted to have his fields cleared, and there was the bonus of wood for the fire. It was a beautiful evening as we wandered our way back home. The fields were teeming with birds: curlews, redshank and lapwings plunged and dived around us. The children half ran, half rode, stopping every now and again to investigate some previously undiscovered place. They were tired and after a bite of tea were soon in their beds. Then that familiar feeling of being slightly unwell started. The baby wasn't ready to hatch for another couple of weeks but as soon as I told Clive he said, 'I's ringing for t'ambulance reet now.' Which he did. Then we had the usual interrogation:

'How fast are the contractions coming? How long is the gap between them?'

'She's no 'avin' contractions, she just feels sick.'

'She's not in labour until she has contractions.'

'Yes, she is, thoo should 'ave a letter from t'midwife there explaining it.'

An ambulance was eventually dispatched, but this time it was coming from Skipton, which is a good hour and a half away – if the roads are clear. Before it got to us a paramedic turned up, a first responder. He came from Richmond, which is nearer, but still an hour away. He shot up the yard at full speed and ran into the house carrying a heart monitor and blood-pressure gauge. He seemed pretty disappointed not to find me prostrate on the floor in the throes of labour. Feeling a bit of a fake, I allowed him to check my blood pressure which, of course, was fine. By the time the ambulance arrived, more than two hours after we called, I felt awful, but was still thinking that I could be mistaken.

Off we went, slowly.

'Could yer turn off t'blue flashing light, please?'

I didn't want the horrible embarrassment of everyone down the dale finding out that I had been shipped off to hospital with nothing more than a bad case of indigestion.

This was new territory for the Skipton ambulance crew. The sat nav was out of action and I sat up, peering out from the back through the windscreen and giving directions, as they were not so sure where they were going.

'We usually go to Bradford and Airedale Hospital, we've never been to Northallerton,' they said.

A few wrong turns were taken and there was a narrow miss with a deer, but eventually we reached the hospital.

'We'll have to put you on a stretcher.'

'Is ta kiddin? I can walk.'

I picked up my hastily packed bag and took the familiar route to the labour ward. I still wasn't feeling in great fettle, but wasn't wholly convinced that I should be on the labour ward at all. The midwife, Jan, looked at me a bit sceptically because, as usual, outwardly there was no sign of labour.

'I'll put you in one of the labour rooms and check you over,' she said.

I followed Jan into the room, popped my bag on the chair and climbed onto the bed. I lifted up my tunic and she carefully felt my distended tummy. She checked my pulse, blood pressure, the usual. She looked up and smiled.

'You're not in labour,' she said.

I felt so embarrassed. I had got it wrong this time, phoning for an ambulance so soon. I was going to look a right idiot calling Clive to pick me up and take me home, still with the baby on board. The humiliation didn't bear thinking about.

'I'll just leave you quiet in here for a little while,' the midwife said. 'I'm not hooking you up to anything because there's nothing doing.'

As soon as she left I started pacing up and down. The supposedly soundproof room couldn't muffle the screams from a neighbouring room where someone else had clearly got their timing right. I stood at the window, looking out across the rooftops of the hospital, trying to breathe in some fresh air from the small opening in the window. I thought, *People are going to think I'm proper stupid. How can you not know when you are in labour, especially when it's your fifth?*

I went into the bathroom and while I was sitting there I had that feeling, the one I get when the baby is ready to come. I scarpered out of there and rang the alarm button, the only time I've ever rung an alarm button in my whole life.

Jan popped her head round the corner of the door. 'What's up?'

'I think–' I started to say, and then had an urge to push.

She took one look and pressed the emergency button. The room filled with people, and within a matter of seconds Violet had been born. I'd gone from first to third stage of labour in eight minutes. I was delighted to see Violet – and relieved I wasn't going to face the embarrassment of going back home without a baby. At least Clive and I were vindicated: we had recognized the signs.

Once again, like all the others, she came out face up, occiput posterior. Midwives are trained not to show any signs of panic or surprise, so it was only after the birth that one of the student midwives commented, 'I've never seen one born like that before.'

I was also quite pleased that the professionals had witnessed and could corroborate my story of there being no signs of labour, as they had checked me over and declared that there was nothing happening only minutes before I had given birth to a healthy six-and-a-half-pound baby.

Whenever I'm expecting, people say, 'Shouldn't you be having a rest? Shouldn't you sit down for a bit?'

But I'm convinced that keeping busy means I don't have big babies. I say, 'I don't want any twelve pounders when I'm giving birth in a lay-by without any pain relief, no thank you.'

Sometimes the walkers who pass through Ravenseat ask whether I have walked the Coast to Coast and I tell them that I reckon I cover the same distance, all 182 miles, every week. I go up and down the moor and between fields, backwards and forwards between the kitchen and the picnic benches balancing a tray in one hand and with a baby under my arm or on my front or back.

Multitasking is what I do, on a whole new level. Clip a sheep, make a cream tea, drive a tractor, breastfeed a baby: there is no combination of activities that hasn't been tried and tested. Folk sometimes assume I have these babies so fast and easily because I'm some sort of super tough woman: not the case. I can't wax my legs without wincing. It's not a plan, it's just what happens. I have no problem with taking painkillers, I just don't get the chance.

In some ways I know I'm very lucky, but I also know it's a bit risky having them the way I do, so fast. I've never so far made a 'birth plan'. My plan is that there is no plan, take it as it comes. What's the point? You can't predict what's going to happen. All you need to know is where you are going and what to put in your hospital bag. And I've never felt the need to have anyone there holding my hand, I couldn't think of anything worse. I'm much happier knowing that Clive is at home looking after the children and the farm.

It was Clive who came up with the name for Violet. It was time he had a turn at choosing a name, and that's one he's always liked. It suits her – she seemed so delicate, like the flower.

I had to stay in hospital that night, of course: it was too late for Clive to come and pick me up and officially you are supposed to stay for six hours after the birth. So that's when I started my battle against the heat. I am acclimatized to Ravenseat and to me the room was much too warm. But every time I opened the window – and it would only open a crack – the nurse would slam it shut

241

when she came in, telling me the baby would get cold. Maybe she thought I was trying to have a sneaky fag or was thinking of jumping. When she went out I'd open it again and put my head down to the crack to breathe in some cool air.

The next morning I decided to go outside, to cool off and fill my lungs with some normal, fresh air. I went through the foyer into the covered area at the front of the hospital, where there were all sorts of people chuffing away on their cigarettes or chattering on their phones. There was an old dear sitting on a bench on her own, so I sat next to her and said hello. I thought she might be glad of a chat but I didn't ask her why she was at the hospital in case she had something terribly wrong with her. As it happened she *did* have something wrong: her attitude.

'Grand morning,' I said. 'My husband will be comin' to tek me an' t'new baby home soon.'

'Oh aye,' she said.

'Yep, it'll get a bit o' sortin' out gettin' t'other four ready to come wiv 'im, this is mi fifth.'

She turned towards me with a look of sheer disgust on her face.

'And I expect the taxpayers are paying for that,' she said. With that, before I had time to reply, she got up and walked away.

I thought, *No wonder yer on yer own, yer miserable owd bat.*

I would never, ever say anything so rude or be so presumptious. I thought, *I work very hard and enjoy doing so, but it's tough work. Don't ever suggest I am lazy and don't ever suggest we don't pay our own way.*

People jump to conclusions far too quickly, and sometimes their reactions are just downright unpleasant. For example, plenty of people don't like it when the Appleby Horse Fair is on in June, the big get-together when the gypsies invade the area and ride bareback through the streets on their piebald horses or race pacers in their sulkies. They believe there is more crime when the travellers are about, and there are certainly examples of quad bikes and even Land Rovers being stolen. But thefts from farms happen all year round, and I'm not going to say it's not the gypsies, but there are plenty of other rogues about.

One of the cheekiest thefts was from our neighbour Raymond. He'd been on the moor gathering his sheep with his dogs and he was in his Land Rover going along a beautiful, quiet little road with the flock in front of him, driving them back towards his fields. It was a hot day, and as always happens there was one yow who was slower than the rest and making heavy weather of the journey. She was obviously struggling, so he stopped the Land Rover, left the engine running and ran twenty or so yards after her. He intended to pick her up and put her in the back. As he was grabbing her a car came along the road, a man jumped out of the passenger side, leapt into the Land Rover and drove off at speed.

I've heard stories of thieves waiting outside the vets', and when someone jumps out of their car with a sick animal, too worried to lock the car and take the keys, they jump in and away with it.

So we all know there are people who come out into the countryside not just to enjoy the scenery, but with different intentions. They didn't plan to steal a Land Rover, but when they saw one, with the keys in and the engine running, they took the chance. Another neighbour had his Land Rover stolen from his yard, and the next day they came back for his quad bike.

But nobody knows whether these were gypsies or travellers or someone else entirely, and I'm never going to judge. They have a tough enough time. We get on well with the gypsies and travellers on the whole. When they turn up here, as they do sometimes, we make them tea and talk horses with them. We've traded horses with them, and I enjoy the Appleby Fair. It's not everyone's cup of tea, but it's very colourful. There are stalls selling videos of bare-knuckle fighting; they call them the tarmac warriors. Lasses as well, fighting each other. Raven loves coming with me – she'll wangle a day off school to come if she can, to see the horses, enjoy the colour and high spirits of the day. The only stipulation I have with regards to taking the children to the horse fair is that nobody drinks too much beforehand because the blue portable loos are to be avoided at all cost.

A couple of years ago, just after Appleby, I was coming back from the other farm, Sandwath, with three of the children in our battered old white pickup. On our way there we'd seen all the vardos, the traditional barrel-shaped gipsy caravans, and other horse-drawn vehicles heading home after the fair. Now, as we headed back towards Ravenseat, we saw a vardo at the side of the road, a coloured horse cropping the verge, and a woman bawling her eyes out. The vardo was cockled over at one side, something had happened to the wheel. There was a clutch of children sitting by the road. I pulled over and the woman told me that her husband had gone on ahead in the transit and trailer, and she'd been slowly making her way after him when her wheel had punctured.

I offered to take her to a phone box but there was nobody she could ring, so instead I decided to load her and the younger children up and drive to a garage where she could get help. Just as we were getting into the pickup, a car came up the road quite fast, then suddenly braked alongside us. The window came down and we were treated to a torrent of abuse, calling us all the names under the sun. He clearly thought we were all gypsies. He ended with, 'Why don't yer just f*** off back where yer come fra'?'

I opened my mouth to retaliate but couldn't get a word in edgeways, then his window went up and off he went. I was rigid with shock: I'm not used to being called names like those, and certainly not within earshot of the children. I looked at the gypsy girl and she shrugged and said, 'Tha' allus 'appens. I's used to it.'

It was a weird moment. I'm not a campaigner for human rights, or anything like that, but it was such a flagrant show of aggression when there was nothing to be aggressive about. When I got home, after dropping them at the garage, I told Clive and he said, 'Didn't yer get 'is number down?'

I hadn't, of course, but even if I had, and told the police, I don't think it would have gone to the top of their workload. So, what with the woman at the hospital who judged me for having a big family, and the man in the car who thought it was necessary to pour violent verbal abuse on two women and their children, I do sometimes wonder about the sheer hatred that festers in some folk. They should get out into the fresh air more, I reckon.

We had a gypsy friend, a traveller who no longer travelled, who used to turn up here every so often. We'd see a battered old flatbed truck making its way down our road, and we'd know it was Bomber. He was a big fat chap, and always wore a straw hat, a string vest and carpet slippers. In his youth he'd been a bare-knuckle fighter of some repute and even in old age commanded great respect from the younger generation. His arms were covered with tattoos of what were once shapely women, but as his arms had acquired more flesh the women had become heftier too. He also had the names of the women/conquests in his life tattooed up his other arm, which is never a good idea. He hadn't gone in for laser removal, he'd just had each name blacked out as his love life moved on. So there was a whole ladder of blotted-out blueish rectangles down his arm. The bottom and most recent name was that of Gloria, his wife.

He always had something in the back of his old truck to sell, maybe some logs, wire or a gate. But he never did any of the physical work, he just had all the patter, and regardless of whether you actually needed whatever was on the back of his truck you always ended up with it. Bomber didn't deign to lift the gates off or unload the logs or rolls of wire. He would invariably have a little friend with him, not always the same one, but always someone he could order about.

'Oy, Billy, get that wood chucked off down by t'woodshed. 'Urry up, will ta.'

Billy was of considerable age, had a nervous tic and would repeatedly grimace and swear while meekly carrying out whatever order Bomber had issued. All of Bomber's sidekicks appeared to have some kind of issues. You could guarantee Bomber would always turn up at the most inopportune moment, when you could really do without him, because although Bomber was lazy, he was certainly a good getter-up. He'd always appear here early on in the day, usually when we were very busy. While his sidekick did the grafting, Bomber would get himself comfortable at the kitchen table and make his requests.

'Where's Clyde?' He always called Clive this. ''Ave yer med 'im 'is breakfast? Mek us a brew an' a bacon sarnie.'

Gloria had him on a permanent diet and sitting on the front seat of the truck would be a salad bowl and a bag of fruit.

'Shall I mek a brew for Billy an' all?'

'Nope, nivver. He's fine.'

Bomber's sidekicks, although not exactly healthy-looking, were always of a more athletic build than he was, and after his death several people commented that Bomber's life expectancy would have been higher if he had got off his arse and done some of the work himself.

We bought things from him: we're always in

need of a gate somewhere, and we burn wood all the time, and he was cheap. He could turn up with literally anything, even sea coal and telegraph poles. It got to the point when he would just tip it off below the farmhouse without any form of consultation, which put us in a good position with regards to haggling because he couldn't be bothered to put it back on the truck.

His product list knew no bounds. He once sold us a case load of Hungarian wine, issuing the health warning, 'There's a babby in every bottle.'

He knew we kept black-and-white gypsy horses, so he offered to treat us to a guided tour of his own horses, probably with half a mind to sell us one. We thought this was a splendid idea; we really fancied a trip out to his home on a council estate near Durham and wanted to finally get a look at some of the legendary horses we'd heard so much about.

It was an interesting day out, to say the least. Off we went to Co. Durham with little in the way of directions; apparently all we had to do was ask anybody where Bomber lived and we would be pointed the right way. We rattled along in the Land Rover, having brought a horse trailer with us too. Bomber, I suspect, had talked 'Clyde' into the idea of buying me another horse, as a birthday present, if we saw one we liked.

As we entered the estate we felt like we were in a war zone. Half of the houses were boarded up, with metal shutters over the windows; even the local shop where I stopped to buy mints had a mesh grille and a serving hatch that customers spoke through. There was no browsing to be done in this establishment: you told the assistant what you wanted, she got it and after you'd paid it would be shoved through the hatch. There were transit vans, half-built vardos and wandering dogs and horses everywhere, some tied up, some roaming free. Bomber told us later that every so often the estate would be raided and the council and the RSPCA would round up the horses and take them away. Magically, most of the horses would have been spirited away before officialdom arrived. Last time it happened, he said, there was one horse they couldn't catch.

'If they can git hod o' that bugger they can 'ave it,' he said.

Everyone we passed eyed us with suspicion, even though we were in a beat-up Land Rover and horsebox. But the minute we asked for directions to Bomber's house, the suspicious scowls disappeared.

We drove slowly through groups of children playing in the road, and eventually pulled up outside a palatial-looking house with a large fountain on the front patio, a pair of stone Lurchers bordering the gateway, and the familiar flatbed truck parked on the pavement.

'That 'as to be Bomber's gaff,' I said.

He appeared at the door in his usual attire, vest and slippers, welcomed us, then yelled something unintelligible across the street and suddenly people appeared: a couple of blokes and some kids. He said to one of the kids with a mullet haircut, 'Ga an' fetch thi father.'

Having rounded up his cronies, Bomber set off in his truck with us following close behind. We drove through a maze of backstreets, past deserted industrial areas, wastelands with little bits of rough open land between derelict units that once upon a time provided jobs and wages for people. Eventually Bomber pulled up at a gate just beyond the units. It fronted a real garden of Eden, hidden away between the shabby concrete and brick buildings, and scrubby patches of land. This was a small stretch of proper countryside, a lush field.

We climbed the gate – for someone who made a living selling gates, this was a particularly bad example, rusting and broken, with what appeared to be a shelf from a fridge and part of a snapped advertising hoarding tied to one side. His retinue remained with the vehicles, listening to the radio and smoking while we strode out towards a line of trees, all the while Bomber giving us a running commentary:

'It's taken me a lifetime to amass these,' he said.

In the shadow of the trees was the most beautiful collection of coloured horses I'd ever seen. Stocky piebald mares and foals with flowing feather, their coats gleaming in the late summer sun, a world apart from the sad, broken-down nags that wandered the estate. Our eyes and mouths were open: this was truly a stunning collection of well-bred animals. Bomber was in his element as he detailed the breeding of his mares and how much time, money and devotion had gone into the accumulation of his outstanding herd.

He was in full flow when from the direction of the gate behind us we could hear the beginnings of a ruckus.

'What the f*** are yer doin' in ma f***ing field?' yelled a red-faced man, marching towards us purposefully, and not in an altogether friendly manner.

He was threatening to kill us, Bomber included, and there was a presence about him that made me think he might just do it. It turned out that it wasn't Bomber's field and they weren't Bomber's horses. The real owner was one of a family of brothers, very well-known breeders of gypsy horses.

Bomber never broke stroke, just said he was showing us the horses, and we might want to buy one. He was completely unfazed, simply saying he was doing the owner a favour, brokering a deal. In the end, after much bartering and discussion, we did fix on a horse to buy, a colt foal that we later called Monty. When the deal was done and a price agreed, Bomber shouted over to his lads.

'Cum on, get this 'oss catched and into t'box.'

I'd never seen anything like it. They surrounded the horse, and between them manhandled it towards the gate, then picked it up and put it in the trailer. Bomber wasn't the least bit embarrassed about his make-believe tales and we never mentioned it: he just seemed pleased we'd had a good day out and done a bit of business. We've often wondered since if he would have dared sell us one of those horses, and what the consequences would have been when their owner found out...

We kept the foal, Monty, as a stallion. We bred

from him, and for a while we would charge a stud fee and people would bring mares to him. We're aware with the horses, like the sheep, that we need to change the sire every so often, to prevent inbreeding, so we kept Monty, broke him to ride and drive, and then sold him when we were made an offer that we couldn't refuse. Every year he returns to Appleby Fair, pulling a vardo, and only last year I was shown pictures of the owner's granddaughter learning to drive him pulling a tub cart.

We liked Bomber's visits, he made us laugh and he told us tales. Sadly, he died of a heart attack a few years ago, and we only heard about it after his funeral. Apparently there was a big show of people at the funeral; he was a truly larger-than-life character and his coffin was carried by a horse-drawn hearse.

We owed him money when he died, £130. He'd brought us a couple of gates one day when we weren't around – and we knew he'd be back for it. We were really sad at the news of his death, but Clive couldn't resist a smile that he'd died before collecting his money.

'Just for yance, I've gotten one over on t'old bugger,' he said.

He didn't enjoy the feeling for long. A couple of weeks later we got a letter from Gloria. Apparently Bomber had a little black book where he kept a record of what was owed to him. Who'd have thought it? He didn't seem the type for keeping accounts. We sent her the cheque with a condolence card. We miss the old rogue.

We always reckon that being friends with Bomber was one of the reasons we didn't have any thieving from our yard. And the theory might be right because it wasn't until after his death that our quad bike was stolen.

Clive had been away all day tup crowning. The Swaledale Sheep Breeders Association, which has been going since 1919, was set up to maintain the breed, and set standards for what is a true Swaledale sheep. When it was formed, its aims, which remain the same today, were:

The encouragement of the breeding of Swaledale sheep and the maintenance of their purity.

The establishment and publication of a Flock Book [Clive's most treasured possessions] of recognized and pure-bred sires, and the annual registration of the pedigrees of such sires as are proved to the satisfaction of the Council or Management.

The investigation of doubtful and suspected pedigrees, and the general protection of the breed.

The holding of shows and sales, the obtaining of classes and giving of prizes at shows, and the appointment and recommendation of the judges.

So every year all the different tups that farmers have bred have to be inspected and approved as pure Swaledales. It's called 'tup crowning', and different members of the association are chosen to go round all the Swaledale breeders and 'crown', or approve, the tups. It's an honour to be chosen and Clive's been selected a few times.

It's quite an event round here. Every farmer whose tups have been crowned follows the crowner on to the next farm. It's very social, and everyone wants a good look at everyone else's animals. We're one of the last farms in the dale, so by the time they get here there's a whole motorcade of Land Rovers coming up our road, a real entourage of farmers following the crowner, coming for a sneak preview of the tups. There are certain traits that they are all looking for, apart from the obvious of four good legs, a pair of testicles and a good solid frame. It is the colour and texture of hair on the faces and legs of the tups that really matter; certain small deviations from the perfect ideal are forgivable, but never the shade of black. It has to be right. If someone says to you, 'That tup's face is the colour of Cherry Blossom shoe polish black, like shiny,' that's bad. If they say, 'That tup looks like a bloody great crow landed on it,' that's bad.

Or if they say: 'Ya tup was seriously off at black,' that's positively an insult.

What you want is matt black. Any woman who's tried to team a black dress with a separate black jacket knows that there are different shades of black: the Swaledale has to be the right matt shade. It's definitely Fifty Shades of Black round here, not grey...

If you go to the Swaledale tup sales or to shows then you will notice fully grown men apparently stroking the faces of the sheep. It is not that they are showing their softer side, but because they are feeling the hardness of the black hair; the harder the better. If you imagine a Brillo pad,

254

then that's what you want to feel.

'That's better than sex,' one Swaledale breeder muttered to me and Clive as he stroked the brow of a good tup. Fortunately, Clive bit his tongue.

One year when Clive was selected to do tup crowning he had to go to Derbyshire. Swaledales are bred in many different areas, not just Swaledale. I asked him, 'Does ta know where thoo's garn?'

'Aye, Derbyshire,' he said. 'It's just t'other side o' Skipton.'

Needless to say, it isn't, and he had to set off very early in the morning as he had a lot of farms to visit and plenty of tups to inspect. I gave him assurances that I could handle everything on the farm, and that as it was going to be late when he returned, I – helped by the children – would get everything done. We did too: we were very proud of ourselves. Everything was sorted, lamb hoppers filled, stock checked, dogs fed. When Clive got back at 9 p.m. there was nothing more to be done, so we had a cup of tea, a chat and then went to bed.

A storm had been forecast and it came sweeping in, hitting us at nightfall. Everything in the farmyard was banging and rattling, so it was a disturbed night, and somewhere in my half-asleep, half-awake state I remember seeing a flash of light across the bedroom window, but then drifted off again.

The next morning I was up with the lark and busy alongside Raven filling bags with cake to put in the hoppers to feed the lambs. It was a wet, horrible morning; the river was in full spate,

255

welling out and over its banks.

'Ga round and fetch us t'bike,' I said to Raven. It's easier to transport the feed by bike than carrying it.

'It's not there,' she said a few minutes later.

'Course it is,' I snapped impatiently. 'Don't be such a muppet.'

Off she went again and then came back.

'No, Mum, it's not there, come and look.'

Then I did that idiotic thing of looking everywhere for it even though I knew where I'd left it. I called Clive, who was having his breakfast. He came outside and he did exactly the same thing, refusing to believe it had gone until he had searched himself.

'Someone's nicked the bloody bike!'

We rang the police. The only evidence that we could find was a discarded rubber glove, which was turned inside out, and some horrible half-chewed plastic wrapping from one of those nasty cheap sausage treats for dogs which cost about 30p in a supermarket. The thieves had obviously lobbed one to Bill, who was dozing in his kennel in the yard, and should have at least barked, if not ripped their legs off, but he'd clearly been bought off. We weren't best pleased with him. We'd have hoped he would have held out for a better bung...

It was still throwing it down with rain, so any forensic traces the thieves had left were well washed away by the time the police arrived, later that morning. There was nothing they could do other than commiserate with us, and give me a number for victim support. I realized in the cold light of miserable day that the beam I had seen cross our window in the night was most likely the headlights of the thieves' vehicle: we sleep at the front of the house with our curtains open, and there is a moment when vehicles bump across the track by the ford that their headlights rake up across our window. The thieves must have quietly pushed the bike past the house and down over the bridge and loaded it into their van on the other side of the river.

In some ways I'm relieved I didn't wake up: a friend of ours, another farmer's wife, said when thieves came into their farmyard and stole their pickup, trailer and quad bike she was just glad her husband didn't realize what was happening or, 'Someone would 'ave been dead in t'yard; he'd 'ave shot the buggers.'

That's the way you have to look at it: it was only a bike, and Clive would have probably been attacked if he'd tried to stop them. Anyway, we were insured. Or so we thought...

We were certainly paying the premiums. But after a couple of hours searching for the papers, and talking to the insurance company, we realized we had actually been paying for our old bike: we'd never changed the policy over when we had part-exchanged it for a newer one. It was a blow, but we had no one to blame but ourselves. So that was a bad day at the office, and we were about £6,000 out of pocket for another quad. We also discovered, months later, when the first flush of summer grass came through, that the petrol strimmer had gone too: they must have noticed it sitting in the woodshed as they wheeled the bike away and made off with that as well. Worse things happen: nobody was hurt, nobody died.

11

Clive's Big Break

This is a tale of two tups and a stubborn man, my hubby Clive Owen, who turned down the chance to be a film star. And, much to my annoyance, proved to have made the right call.

One of our old yows, 'the crusties' as we call them, who we keep on because they are good breeders, had been scanned for triplets: the older they are the more likely they are to have multiple births. It's not good when they are having triplets, because it puts a lot of stress on their system carrying three lambs; far better that they have a big strong single lamb.

We kept her with the other crusties for the first four months, and then for the last month of her pregnancy we separated her and brought her into the end stable. The pressure on her was immense and we were very worried about her – she wasn't coping well at all. I fed her plenty of treacle, my panacea for all ills. I buy it in 1,000-litre drums and it provides a good energy boost, easy for yows like this one who had lost all her teeth. She was so enormously heavy with lambs that I had to help her to stand but I got her onto her feet every day and encouraged her to take some gentle exercise round the stable, as I know that once an animal becomes immobile it is pretty much doomed.

One morning I was up at 4 a.m., because it was lambing time, and as Clive had done the night shift it was my turn on the early shift. I went in to check on her. She was ready, starting to lamb. I shot back to the house and shook Clive.

'T'owd lass is on lambing,' I said quietly, trying not to wake the children.

He pulled on his wellies and leggings and came out to the stable. We knelt down with her and she gave birth to her first lamb, a decent-sized tup. Clive was beside himself. It was one helluva lamb. Next came a really good gimmer, fantastic. Clive was practically dancing round the stable, the good old girl had produced two wonderful lambs.

Finally the third one slipped out. It was a tiny tup, a good sort, but a midget. We thought he was dead, he lay so quiet. I broke the sack over his face and squeezed his nose to clear away the mucus. He moved his head fractionally and gave a small gasp. Clive shook his head as he rose to his feet.

'If thoo can mek that live, yer can 'ave it...' he said. He thought it was a goner.

I don't ever like to give up on an animal, not without a fight. So I took the tiny little fella away. Clive left one of the triplets with the old yow and found another to adopt the other one: she was far too old to rear two.

I wrapped the tiny one in a towel and put him

259

in the warming oven of our black range, which is a perfect temperature for a fragile newborn, and began gently heating some colostrum from the freezer.

He lived in the oven for a couple of days. I fed him frequently with little amounts, got him looking a bit stronger. But although he could now lift his head, he was still very small, too tiny to stand up. Then Clive said, 'I've brought a yow in who's lost 'er lamb in a gutter. She's a proper good mother. Do yer want 'er for t'lal' fella?'

It was important to adopt him on to a patient, good yow, because he was so small that one of the ratching, impatient yows would have just stomped him into the ground. But this was a sheep with a strong maternal instinct. We didn't bother skinning her own dead lamb and making him an overcoat from the skin because it would have been far too big, we just rubbed the dead lamb all over the little one, put him on the straw in a pen, and let her in with him. She was a marvel, taking to him straight away. He couldn't suckle because he couldn't stand up so it was a real labour of love, with me milking her and giving him the milk or picking him up and letting him suckle himself. But she did the loving: nuzzling him, treating him as though he was the most precious thing in the world. On finer days I'd carry him out into the garden so the yow could have a bite of grass and then carry him back to the pen at teatime with his mother following. She was an absolute star.

Gradually, over time, he gained more strength. I dosed him with vitamins and mineral drenches and when I had a quiet moment I would sit on the stone steps and give him my very own adapted-for-sheep version of a Reiki massage.

Then, one day, I went to the stable and he was standing up, albeit in a wobbly manner. I yelled for Clive to come and see.

'I've gotten a name for 'im, an' all,' I said. 'He's called Lazarus. After all, he almost rose from t'dead.'

'Well, I cannae believe it, I nivver woulda thought he'd mek it,' Clive said.

We didn't send Lazarus and his mother up to the moor like the other single lambs, because he was always small and had such a poor start in life. He needed as much chance as possible to catch up, so was kept in the greenest, grassiest fields we had. He did well and went from strength to strength but he was never going to be a big one: he was small but perfectly formed. I would tell Clive, 'They don't mek diamonds as big as bricks, thoo knows.'

He said size mattered.

The firstborn of the triplets was, in the mean-time, Clive's pride and joy, and he gave him a name to go with his hopes for him: Glory. He kept quiet about his prospective wonder sheep around the other farmers. You can set yourself up for a right fall if you think too much of a tup – everyone else will be looking for faults in it and pulling it to pieces. It's very competitive. We don't show sheep at the Tan Hill Show in May because it's too early in the season, it gives the other farmers a long time to debate what's up with it, why it's not a right 'un, why theirs is better. It is far safer to wait and show them at Muker Show, which comes in September, a lot closer to the back-end sales at Hawes in October.

To win at the Hawes sale, to be named as the overall champion, is what everyone wants. It's a once-in-a-lifetime achievement to win with a Swaledale in Swaledale country, and Clive was secretly very hopeful about Glory but there are many factors to contend with. What will the other competitors have? Who is judging?

A decision needed to be made about what was going to happen to Lazarus. I had high hopes for him too. He was a good example of his type; definitely on the small side, but maybe time and feed could remedy that. Clive decided we'd put him with the group he keeps each year as potential breeding tups, the tup hoggs. We start out with around thirty, and as the year wears on they get whittled down and sent to auction, so that by the time of the tup sales we have only about five left, the cream of the crop. So Lazarus went with them, down to the other farm for the winter.

Clive and his friend Steven, another Swaledale enthusiast, spend a lot of time looking at tups. They stand and study them for an absolute age, pondering, weighing up their pros and cons, consulting the breeding records and flock books, just watching and assessing them, hatching plans for how they are going to breed the perfect specimen.

They take the tup sales incredibly seriously, these men. I am not so much of a purist, and I can't show quite the same enthusiasm. I chose to be a shepherd because I wanted to tend sheep, any sheep. Whether it be a top-of-the-range show sheep or the humblest of fat lambs, I love them all.

Lazarus was still with the tups come springtime when they came back to Ravenseat, and although no decision had been made about his future I was holding on to my hopes.

It was at this time that Clive's big break in the movies came – and went. One day a man in a suit drove up and had a cream tea. As I've said, the people who call at Ravenseat tend to be dressed for walking or a day out in the countryside, so men in suits always make me nervous. This chap said he was a location scout, looking for an abandoned farmhouse to use as the setting for *Wuthering Heights* in a new film being made of the Emily Brontë book. I showed him the abandoned Close Hills farmhouse, which is on our land south of Ravenseat. It's not been lived in for over a century, but they built well in those days and it's still in remarkably good condition. Trouble was, it wasn't close enough to a road to get the equipment and the stars in, so that was that. (The farmhouse they eventually used for the film was Moor Close, at Thwaite, which had been empty since the 1970s. A famous naturalist, Cherry Kearton, was born there in 1871. He was a pioneering wildlife documentary maker, a forerunner to David Attenborough, who recently named him as a great influence.)

When Clive came home later that day I told him about the location scout and he said he had some news too: he'd been approached at the auction by a woman.

'Oh, yeah?'

'Nowt like that. She wants me t'be in a film.'

'Oh, yeah?'

'Nah, I knows how yer mind works, but she's mekkin' a proper arty film an' she wants me to be in't.'

He showed me her card, and it said she was the casting director. He'd given her his phone number, and that evening we got a call, asking if it was all right for Andrea Arnold, the director of the *Wuthering Heights* movie, to come and see us the following evening. She's an acclaimed director, but I'm afraid we are not movie buffs so the name meant nothing to us.

Andrea came to see us, and told us that she would like Clive to play the part of Joseph, the surly manservant at the farm where Heathcliff and Cathy grow up. He would need to get an Equity card, which they could arrange, and he would be paid the going rate as an actor. I was very excited, and even Clive was quite chuffed.

Everything was going beautifully, when Andrea said they were also looking for a child to play the young Hindley. She was sitting at the table staring out of the window and studying Miles intently. Miles, who was four at the time, was sitting on his own, playing with a stick in the dirt in the farmyard, muttering away to himself. Miles has got the sunniest smile in the world, but he's also at his happiest in his own company and is capable of giving you an incredibly dark look, which is exactly what she was looking for: a sullen, insular child. She asked if we would consider Miles being cast as Hindley. She said he would be perfect, and that he would need a chaperone. This was it: I could be the chaperone. Hollywood, here we come.

She got out her Filofax and as she looked through the dates she questioned Clive.

Was he going to give this film 100 per cent commitment?

'Not a problem.' He was going to be paid handsomely, after all.

Was he going to be OK with the violent scene? In the screenplay Clive's character, Joseph, has to horsewhip the young Heathcliff.

'Definitely not a problem.'

Was he going to be OK spending time in costume and wearing make-up?

'As long as it's tasteful, not like drag or anything.'

Was he all right for filming on these days? She handed him some dates on a piece of paper.

'I cannae do that day. That's tup sale day at Hawes tha' is.'

You could have cut through the atmosphere with a knife. Andrea was not used to offering someone a part in a movie only for them to tell her that they couldn't come on one of the days because they wanted to sell a sheep. I desperately tried to persuade him to reconsider. I told him not to worry, I could take Glory to the sales. But Clive shot me a look that said, *Are you kidding?*

He wasn't having it: this was the best tup he'd ever bred. The film director didn't understand, but Clive was adamant. I was furious with him: I didn't speak to him for the rest of the day, or the next. Not only was his film career over before it began, but without him helping out with the chaperoning, there was no way Miles could be in the film, either.

It was a rotten summer, it rained and rained. The film company turned the village of Thwaite, just along from us, into a mini-city with their Winnebagos and catering vans everywhere. The local cash and carry did great business, supplying them with all manner of exotic foods. Props were needed to set the scene, and Ian at the antique shop lent them various items to use in the farmhouse. Horses, cows and sheep were drafted in for filming and in one scene you see Heathcliff carrying a sheep across his shoulders that he later kills. That was one of our neighbour's very best gimmer hoggs.

Back at Ravenseat, the time had come to decide Lazarus's future. Clive broke the bad news to me.

'He's too low. Nae bugger'll want yan on short legs.'

That was it, game over.

Clive, knowing I was going to be terribly disappointed as I had become fond of him, came up with a plan so I could keep him. Lazarus was going to be vasectomized and then used as a teaser, putting him in with the yows to bring them into season before the actual breeding tup goes in with them.

I thought, *Oh well, at least I get t'keep 'im. He'll be t'bonniest teaser on the block.*

Luckily for Lazarus (and me), before he was

shipped off to the vets' for the snip, an old friend of ours, Ron Metcalfe, came to visit and to tell Clive and anyone who would listen where they were going wrong with their sheep. Ron was the doyen of Swaledale breeders: he'd won every prize going, broken records for the highest prices made for Swaledales. What he didn't know about the breed wasn't worth knowing. He was the man to ask about your sheep. He never minced his words. 'What the hell, it's off at black, it's snipey, it's nowt,' were some of the colourful terms he used, which basically meant back to the drawing board.

By the time he came up here to pass judgement on Glory his health was failing, he was in a wheelchair and had an oxygen cylinder with him: he died a year later. He could be a bit cantankerous, but he knew his stuff, better than anyone, and commanded respect from all around. It was coming up to tup-crowning time and Clive knew that a whole host of farmers would be following the crowners down our road pretty soon, so before they showed up he wanted Ron's full and frank opinion of Glory.

As it was, Ron was very taken with Glory, he really liked him. Then he said, 'Where's yer tup, Amanda?' He'd heard all about the lamb that couldn't stand who had gone on to make a miraculous recovery.

'Poor owd Lazarus. Clive says he's for the snip, he's gaan to be med into a teaser,' I said.

'Where's he at? Bring 'im here, let's 'ave a look.'

Off I went to the pens, returning with Lazarus. I held him by his horns, standing him up as

267

squarely as I could outside the kitchen door. Ron was sitting at the kitchen table having a cup of tea.

'Nay, thoo's gonna 'ave to let me 'ave a closer look-see.'

I dragged a reluctant Lazarus into the kitchen. Ron reached out and ran his fingers through the hair on his face and down his cheeks.

'He's got a good lug, I'll say.'

Praise indeed.

'He's a good sort.'

I knew that.

'Clive's right, he's pretty low but I's thinkin' he's a helluva tup, might even be better than Glory. You'd be mad t'mek him into a teaser.'

This was good news indeed. Nobody could ignore what Ron said.

'Ron says my tup, Lazarus, might just be better than your tup,' I crowed to Clive.

We were like kids in the playground. Clive took it in good part, but I don't think his faith in Glory wavered for an instant.

The trouble was, because we hadn't intended to have Lazarus crowned, he hadn't had the necessary blood test. I had to arrange all that hurriedly, so that when the crowners came his paperwork was in order (all pedigree Swaledales have to be tested for their susceptibility to a sheep disease called scrapie). His test results showed him to be an A, the best possible grade. Things were looking up for Lazarus.

So both Glory and Lazarus were put into the catalogue for the tup sale at Hawes. There was a lot of preparation to be done to get them both looking their best, using tweezers to remove any stray white hairs and to carefully tighten up the lines between the black and the white, a process known as tonsing. It takes a lot of patience, a decent pair of tweezers and excellent eyesight to become a good tonser. An undesirable side effect is that while the tups may look their very best, my eyebrows are neglected.

The pressure was really on. The years when Clive doesn't think so much of his tups are less stressful for me than when he's got some he really likes. Glory and Lazarus were under close surveillance, their every move monitored.

'Don't let them tups scrat against owt,' he'd say. It's the time of year when the sap is rising, hormones raging, and the tups would very much like to be doing anything other than sitting quietly in a pen waiting patiently to be showed. Their one aim seems to be to self-destruct before the big event.

Everything went well, the big day arrived and Lazarus and Glory set off for the show and sale at Hawes. Such was the worry about getting them there without any damage to their appearance that Clive risked a serious case of travel sickness by riding in the trailer with them, holding them steady. Only Glory was taken out to show as, no matter how good he was, Lazarus was always going to be too small. Clive, to our enormous delight, showed Glory and won! He was the champion, the highest accolade for a Swaledale breeder. It was a great moment.

Then it was time for Glory to go into the sale ring. I stood up the alley that approaches the

269

ring, craning my neck to see over the heads of the crowds, holding Lazarus, who was to be next into the ring. Clive was presented with his trophy and then Clocker, the auctioneer, set the bidding off at £1,000. A nod here and a wink there from prospective buyers, and the auction room fell silent as he reached £10,000.

'Are yer all done? I'm gonna sell 'im.'

He raised his gavel just as a flap of a catalogue at the far side of the ring set the bidding off again, this time in £2,000 increments. I couldn't believe my ears, up and up it went. The atmosphere was electric as the hammer finally went down at £28,000. Clive's face was blank, he was dumbfounded, in shock.

Glory left the ring through the wooden painted double gates opposite the rostrum, and as he left the drover swung the other gates open to let Lazarus in. It was my turn in the ring. The tup sale draws crowds for the sheer excitement, the sense of fortunes being made and lost, success walking hand in hand with disappointment. The place is packed with people, a sea of faces, but the moment you walk into the ring you don't see anyone, you focus only on the tup. Clocker introduced us, telling the assembled throng a little of Lazarus's background and his breeding, and set the bidding off at £500.

'He's on the market, full brother to the champion today.'

It was all over in a matter of moments: £6,000. I was astounded, and felt quite emotional. That frail scrap of a thing, who had such a struggle to live, had, against all the odds, triumphed.

Both Glory and Lazarus have gone on to be what is known as 'good getters', with Lazarus being the father of the 2012 champion tup lamb at the Kirkby Stephen tup sales. Hopefully one day their names may be as famous in Swaledale sheep-breeding circles as Viceroy, Winky, Commander, King Kong and White Heather, famous tups every Swaledale sheep-breeding enthusiast has heard about.

I'm not keen to admit it, but Clive made the right call when he chose going to the tup sales at Hawes with Glory over being a film star. We've watched the *Wuthering Heights* film on TV and it's very good, and so is the actor, Steve Evets, who plays Joseph. But I can't resist digging Clive in the ribs and reminding him, 'That could'a been thi...'

Winning with Glory was a great achievement, especially on our own patch where the competition is so fierce and everyone is vying for the top spot. My only tiny bit of disappointment is: how can Clive ever top that? He could do it again, but most folk only manage it once in a lifetime and, of course, he can never better it.

I've always liked the idea of having people to stay at Ravenseat. It seemed the ideal place to do bed and breakfast for walkers, or people who just want to visit the Dales for a night or two. But there was no room in the farmhouse, which we have filled with children. I thought about putting up yurts, but my feeling was that they just don't belong in this kind of landscape. They may look all right in a forest, but not on the moor.

271

I wanted something in keeping with what we did. The old shepherds round here didn't have shepherds' huts, but after the railways came the farmers used to buy old railway carriages to use as huts in the places where there were no barns, up on the moor. You can still see some dotted about the countryside. In the summer they would have been stuffed with hay so that in the winter the shepherd wouldn't have to carry it up to the sheep, a difficult job before quad bikes.

So I thought, *They look right.* Although they had not been part of the original landscape, they fitted in. It was a natural step from railway carriages to old-fashioned shepherds' huts with iron wheels.

I trawled the Internet looking for a wider one, because I wanted to have a bed sideways in it, with another pull-out bed underneath. I found a firm that would adapt one to how I wanted it, but they were at the other end of the country, in Somerset.

Clive was in the living room watching television.

'I've found a shepherd's hut to put in t'lal' garth near t'waterfall. I'm gonna get it.'

'Yes, dear.'

'If I buy it, will ta go an' fetch it?'

'Yes, dear.'

It must have been a really engrossing TV programme because he wasn't listening to me – always a good way to get an agreement out of a husband. So I bought it, then booked a night in a pub for Clive and his navigator friend when they set off with a triple-axle trailer on the back of the Land Rover. It was a seriously long haul, and he rang me when he finally arrived to say, 'Flipping heck, I'd nay idea 't'would be so heavy.'

It's built on a cast-iron chassis, and in order to get it on the trailer they had to take its wheels off. It weighs about three tons, and the tyres on the trailer went flat because of the weight.

'Ne'er mind, drive back real slow,' I said.

It was a monumental day when we finally moved the shepherd's hut into position a few months later and it was a little while after that Simon, the producer of a brand-new television series called *The Dales*, got in touch.

'We're making a television programme about life in the Yorkshire Dales, and we're looking for a family-run hill farm. Can we come and talk to you about it?' he asked.

It was all quite vague, but there was no harm in talking to him. Sure enough, Simon bowled up wanting to know what we do, how we do it and what happens at particular times of the year. We chatted and got on very well; he'd got a baby girl the same age as our Violet. Then he rang again, and this time he said he'd like to bring a film crew up and start filming us.

Of course, we had to think of things to do that would work on camera and interest the viewers. I mentioned to Simon that in and amongst the farming we were attempting to put together a shepherd's hut. He came up with the idea of filming us putting it together and furnishing it. The hut had been languishing for a while, other things taking precedence, and what I needed was

273

a kick up the backside to get me back on assembling it. They filmed us as we set about furnishing it. Interior design is not my forte and my intention was to make it as traditional as possible and keep the shepherding theme integral throughout. When the huts were in use at the end of the nineteenth century, there would have been a basic bed for a shepherd and, underneath that, a small pen for orphaned lambs. Although we were going for a bit more comfort, I definitely did not want the twee Cath Kidston look.

A wood-burning stove was installed with a tiny oven and hotplate, a bookcase full of shepherd's guides and flock books, a Mouseman milking stool, crooks and sticks and all manner of things that seemed to fit the bill. I am still adding bits and pieces to it, whenever I see something that looks right.

Viewers saw us putting up curtain rails, cast-iron ones shaped like shepherd's crooks, but what they didn't see was me working like mad the night before making curtains out of hessian material to resemble sacking. I commented on camera somewhat wryly that DIY was not our strongest point but there were one or two things that really had to be done correctly.

'They've got to be straight,' I said and Clive was nodding away in agreement. Then the drill bit fell out because I hadn't put it in properly. We looked pretty amateur and you could see the camera shaking as the cameraman was laughing so much. When I stood back to admire my handiwork, they definitely were *not* level…

Clive was filmed spending a night in there, to

test it out and see how good it would be for our guests. He had no complaints, he was quite happy – what was there not to like? Peace and quiet, books on sheep and, to top it all, a full English breakfast in the morning. In fact, in the second series of *The Dales* Ade Edmondson, who presents the programmes, stayed there. Many people didn't believe that he really stayed the night in the shepherd's hut, they thought it was set up just for the cameras, but they are wrong: he did stay the night and then shared his breakfast in the morning with Chalky the terrier.

Twice I've been filmed entering my scones at a local show, and twice I've been filmed losing. What would happen is that I'd take my time and bake a really good batch, and then we would get some cream-tea customers and I would serve the perfect scones to them. Then I'd hastily make some more for the show which, inevitably, would not be quite as perfect. Honestly, I'm not making excuses. Clive says my scones are renowned as the best locally, so he thinks it's amusing that I always lose. I actually market them now as non-prize winning scones.

When the first series was filmed Violet was a baby, and I was carrying her everywhere on my front in the papoose. One day, a friend rang up and told me they had just shown a clip of me serving cream teas with her on my front on *Loose Women*, the lunchtime programme. Apparently Ade was on, talking about *The Dales*, and a snippet of the programme was shown. The women presenters seemed to think there was something unusual about working while having a baby strapped to you. The truth is that serving cream teas is one of the easier jobs that I do while carrying a baby. It's second nature for me now.

They also filmed us taking the children camping. I bought a cheap tent on eBay; the instructions said it was easy for two capable adults to assemble due to its simple colour-coded poles. Two snags: the poles that came with it were not colour coded, and the 'two capable adults' were me and Clive.

The kids were really excited as we loaded up the car, and kept asking, 'Where are we going?'

Luckily, they weren't disappointed when we drove down to West End field, one of our fields at the far end of the farm: it was the thrill of sleeping out that was the attraction for them. We did about twenty trips back to the farmhouse for things we'd forgotten, and we couldn't find a pump that fitted the airbeds, so I was lightheaded after blowing them all up. After finally putting up the darn tent we did have a wonderful barbecue, but our sleep was disturbed by the terriers Pippen and Chalky trying to get into the tent with us, which was quite unnerving until we realized it was them. I can rough it with the best of 'em, but I'm not so sure that Clive enjoyed it much: he likes his home comforts. And what the kids didn't know was that the next morning was Tuesday, auction day, and a massive rush to get the trailer on, the lambs sorted, the licences filled in. So it was a very short holiday.

Every small segment about us on the programme takes hours to film. We don't mind, but it's a bit annoying that at the start of filming the

276

children are pristine, and by the time they finish they're covered in dirt, as usual. On the day they filmed Raven going to school they were here at 6 a.m. to record her doing her chores before school, and they were still here at 7 p.m. Admittedly, though, they do get their best footage when things are not going quite according to plan.

One bugbear for Clive is that when they film him they often do a cutaway to some sheep. But they're not necessarily his sheep. And sometimes they aren't even Swaledale sheep! He stands there shouting at the telly while I try and appease him by reminding him that only a very few people would be sheep-savvy enough to know the difference between a Dalesbred sheep and a Swaledale sheep.

After the first series it was odd to suddenly be recognized by strangers. This would frequently happen when I was picking up provisions in Hawes, which is a small, quaint market town. If people were coming on holiday to the Yorkshire Dales, then it was highly likely they had watched *The Dales,* and when they saw me in the street they would come up to say hello. I don't travel much – like the sheep, I'm hefted to Ravenseat – and when I do go to Hawes and Kirkby Stephen for auctions I know a lot of people anyway, so being approached by complete strangers took a bit of getting used to.

When we first filmed for *The Dales* we had no idea, of course, that it would be such a successful series, and neither did the production team. We've had a lot of fun making the programmes. They filmed us making a fifty-mile round trip to have my five-month scan when I was expecting my sixth baby, and they filmed us going to a photography exhibition of pictures by Stuart Howat, a friend of ours who had asked to do our portraits. They filmed Miles's first day at school, and Raven in her first riding competition at Reeth Show, with my horse Meg (where my scones lost out again...).

One programme showed me taking the children with me to an auction to sell the lambs, something I do regularly. The children are a familiar sight in the canteen at the auction at Hawes. At the Christmas poultry auction Miles put a bid in for a turkey by mistake. He was having some kind of heated debate with one of the other children and raised his arm to make a point. Raymond the auctioneer took this as a bid, said, 'Bid up yonder,' and banged his gavel down. Miles was rigid with fear and the other children suddenly became very silent.

I called out, 'Book it down to Ravenseat,' more to save face than anything else. I'm happy to buy an extra turkey if the price is right, then put it in the freezer and cook it at hay time or another busy period when I have a lot of people to feed.

Clive was quite worried about us looking rather amateurish on TV but I told him there was no need to stress about it as that was why people enjoyed watching the programme. Things don't always go right in life and the viewers at home could relate to just that.

The overriding feeling we had about *The Dales* was that it would be a lovely thing for the children to look back on in years to come. We've all

278

listened to tales of what things were like 'back in the day', and they would actually be able to see for themselves, for real.

We attract some interesting visitors to Ravenseat. We have occasional visits from a group of aviation historians who come here to look at the remains of a crashed World War Two Hurricane. One of these enthusiasts was called Dick Barton. If he had not handed me his card or told me his name I could still have guessed where his interests lay: he had the neatest handlebar moustache, a side parting, a yellow spotted cravat and a comb peeping from the top pocket of his blazer. He and his three fellow enthusiasts arrived on what can only be described as the day from hell. The rain was pouring and the sky was filled with dark clouds, so we agreed to help them out by taking them up to the crash site on the quad bike and trailer. We went as far as we could on the bike and then, due to the boggy terrain, the last leg of the journey was on foot. It was as we were crossing a particularly waterlogged area that we noticed one of Dick's friends was in some difficulty behind us. When we turned back to assist him we were astonished to discover that under his ankle-length trench coat he had two artificial legs, which had become detached and were firmly stuck in the mud. He was man-handled onto drier ground and the legs were extricated from the bog. They took some uprooting, but finally he and his legs were reunited.

He walked so well that we had not realized. Clive and I were thunderstruck, we just didn't know what to say. Then, sensing our surprise and guessing what we were thinking he (Douglas Bader) said, before anyone asked, 'No, a combine harvester, actually.'

The aviation enthusiasts aren't the only visitors we get with unusual hobbies. When we hosted a field trip for the North of England Pteridological Society (fern appreciation) we didn't think there would be a big turnout, but we were wrong. About thirty people turned up. There were even a few hangers-on, one being an entomologist who specialized in wood lice and a conchologist. I showed my ignorance by commenting that his medical career must be incredibly stressful; he looked at me with a certain amount of derision and told me that a conchologist is not a doctor but an expert in slugs and snails. Trying to redeem myself by saying something more appropriate, I came up with, 'It'll 'ave bin a crackin' year for t'slugs, what with all t'rain – that'll 'ave brought 'em out.'

He said flatly that the rain was good for common slugs, but not for the rare specimens he was seeking.

'Really? I didn't know that rare slugs existed.'

It turned out that he had a hit list of twenty slugs he wanted to see before he died and, unfortunately, it wasn't his day because I don't think he found any of them here.

One ecology expert who visits us occasionally always tells us, slightly disparagingly, that our newts are 'common' newts, our sandpipers are 'common' sandpipers and our shrews are 'common' shrews. Clive dared to suggest that perhaps his wife was also of the 'common' variety.

But the botanists and wild-flower experts never go away disappointed. At the far end of the Close Hills there is a ghyll with very steep, near-vertical sides and a river running through the bottom, making it virtually inaccessible to man or beast. You have to walk along the riverbed when it's dry to get down into it. As a result, animals don't often get in there and the plants have a chance to grow without any interference: there is a plant growing there that experts believed had died out in the Ice Age. This magical little place has now been designated a Site of Special Scientific Interest (SSSI), which makes it a magnet for the plant experts.

Another reason the ghyll has been left alone for centuries is that the local children never dared venture there: its nickname is Boggle Hole. A boggle is a ghost, and in the old days when the Ravenseat children were making their way back across the hills from school in Keld, they would hear the wind groaning and moaning down the ghyll, and hear the water tumbling and falling many feet below in the inky blackness. They were terrified, especially on dark winter evenings. They would run past as fast as they could; it was never a place to play and explore.

We've had one or two sheep crag-fast down there, which means they are stranded on a rocky ledge, unable to get back up or get back down. We leave them for a couple of days to see whether they extricate themselves and if they don't we call in the Swaledale Mountain Rescue: they like nothing better than a crag-fast sheep to practise on. And as if rescuing a sheep trapped halfway down a hundred-foot cliff isn't exciting enough, they usually defer the rescue until dark, to make it as difficult for themselves as possible.

We had a hogg stuck down there once, on a ledge that allowed it to move a few feet in each direction. We watched it for three days, hoping it would find a way out. It had some grass above it and below it, so it wasn't starving. In the end Clive's friend Alec decided he'd rescue it. Alec loves a challenge. If there's something you want doing, just tell Alec it's impossible, and the next thing you know, he'll have done it.

Anyway, Clive and another friend, Edwin, anchored a rope to a large rock and then lowered Alec down the cliff face. The health and safety people would have had a fit: Alec's only safety device was to pass the rope through his body-warmer, supposedly to prevent the rope from becoming detached. The children and I were on the other side of the ghyll, watching and shouting directions because Clive and Edwin couldn't see below them to judge where Alec was in relation to the hogg. We were pointing and calling out, 'Left a bit, right a bit...' and the damned sheep was moving away every time, dodging him. This went on for a very long time and eventually the sun began to set and we had to give up. We decided to call Mountain Rescue the next day, but when we went to look, the sheep had gone. We were convinced it had fallen to its death, there was such a huge drop below it. But a couple of weeks later, the hogg turned up in the field. It must have fallen but, miraculously, it was unharmed.

It's not just Boggle Hole that fascinates the botanists. Swaledale is famous for its wildflower meadows and in late June the upper dale is a glorious kaleidoscope of colour. Our traditional, natural ways of farming, which don't rely on chemical fertilizers, mean that the meadow flowers have survived. Ravenseat has many examples of rare types, with unusual varieties of marsh marigold, devil's bit, scabious, yellow rattle, saxifrage, globeflower, and many others. Not only is there an abundance of rare plants, but there is also a rich diversity of wildlife, including birds, hares, stoats, shrews, newts and bats. We have recently been visited by bat fanatics, who arrive at dusk armed with their sonic listening devices. They walk around the barns listening for the inaudible noises that bats make and unfortunately sometimes leave the gates open. Our two shorthorn cows, Felicity and Freda, escaped one night from their barn and sprinted around the hayfields before wandering back up into the farmyard and having a good scratch on the Land Rover. The car alarm went off, the horn beeping, hazard lights flashing. We sat bolt upright in bed and heard the sound of cows galloping past the bedroom window. Clive opened the window, bellowing into the night that Batman should, 'Bog off back to Gotham City.'

That wasn't the first time Clive has conducted operations from the bedroom window. There was once a very large brown rat who made his home in our rhubarb patch and would run along the garden wall and then bask in the sunshine, preening himself in full view of everyone. After several failed attempts at dispatching the rat, Clive announced that he was going to take him out once and for all by shooting him from a terrific vantage point, the bedroom window. Unfortunately, Clive is not a great marksman and after giving him both barrels the rat ambled off, completely unharmed. We were left to scrape up rhubarb shrapnel from the surrounding area. It did rid us of the rat, but only because Clive had destroyed his home.

Clive has a bit of history with rats. While we were living in the caravan, when the front of the house was off, someone else moved into the farmhouse... Roland! When they put the front wall back, Roland was trapped inside. I kept telling the builders there was something in there, but they took no notice. We called it a 'mouse' in front of the children, but we knew damned well it was a rat. We just didn't want them using that word at school.

It always woke up and started scratching around the house just as I was going to sleep. I sleep lightly because I'm always listening for the children. I'd be saying to Clive, 'Can yer 'ear it?'

'Shut up, will ta? I were nearly asleep...'

He's a bit deaf, sometimes selectively so, but he really genuinely couldn't hear the thing. I could hear it gnawing and could track its every move as it cavorted around the house. It went behind the skirting boards, along the beams and one night even played the piano, running over the keys. I could hear it going up and downstairs, leaping up each step with a jump. It caused serious ructions between me and Clive – we were both getting a lot of elbow, me to wake him and give him a running commentary on its movements, him to tell me to shut up. You can't rest while there's something like that in the house, and I'd lie awake just waiting to hear it.

Sometimes we'd be sitting in front of the fire in the evening and we'd see a shadow scuttling along, out of the corner of our eyes. We even ripped the skirting boards off, looking for its den. The few people we confided in all had different theories about how we should catch it, what we should bait the trap with: pork pie, cheese, chocolate, bacon rind, peanut butter. Nothing worked.

I attempted to hit it with a shovel on more than one occasion, but it always managed to dodge me.

'If you are going to hit a rat with a shovel you need the shovel up high to start with, otherwise by the time you lift it t'rat's long gone,' Clive told me helpfully. Like I would walk around with a shovel above my head just in case I spotted the damned thing.

One night I had lain awake in bed for long enough to know that Roland was in the sitting room. I could hear it and I thought if we could trap it in there sooner or later our paths would cross and that would be that. I woke a disgruntled Clive and we both crept down the stairs, me in my nightie and Clive in his pyjamas. Clive went in with a shovel, I went in with trepidation. Clive slammed the door behind us. Bad words were spoken, the air was blue. He was going to get this thing no matter what…

But rats can squeeze themselves into unbelievably small places. As Clive moved the sofa it shot out from underneath and went for the door, and we were amazed when it scrunched itself up and got out through the sliver of a crack underneath. I had no idea a rat could make itself so thin. More angry, bad words.

We decided it was time to call in the professionals and rang a pest control company. They sent out a representative.

'We're like the Mounties, we always get our man. I've got the deadliest rat poison ever. One grain of it can kill fifty people,' he said.

This sounded promising.

He put poison in the loft, at the back of the skirting board and in the airing cupboard. The next day we noticed that this highly deadly rat poison was dropping through the floorboards and into the kitchen. I couldn't have that so the bloody rat got another reprieve.

It was coming up to Christmas and the children each had an advent calendar, the ones with chocolate inside the little windows. I'd even bought one for Clive. The children were only on door number three when the rat found them, and we came down one morning to discover that Roland had broken through the silver foil and cardboard and eaten all of the chocolate. Every single bit. The calendars were thrown on the fire, and I needed to get replacements, but all the local shops had sold out, because it was already December. Then we went to Barnard Castle for a dental appointment, and there happens to be a high-class Belgian chocolate shop in the town. We tramped in, past all the beautiful boxes of truffles and violet creams, and there on the counter were some vastly over-priced chocolate advent calendars. Raven spotted them and said, 'We need those chocolate advent calendars because the rat has eaten ours.'

The Belgian man, whose English was not quite up to this, said, 'What? Your dad has eaten your chocolate?'

'No, the rat.'

'The cat?'

I hurriedly said yes, and shot a look at Raven to shut her up. Raven was old enough to know the 'mouse' was really a rat. I bought the calendars begrudgingly, and vowed that the rat had to die at all cost.

Finally, on Christmas Day, there was The Big Showdown In The Dairy: Clive Versus The Rat. An epic story, better than any of the repeated adventure films on TV that day.

It had already been one of those days. I had woken up to find that the kitchen was decidedly cold because we had somehow managed to run out of kerosene for the Aga. This is not good when you've got a large turkey to cook. I always buy outsize, mutant turkeys, thirty-six pounds or thereabouts, because they're cheap. I mean, who else would want to cook a turkey for about thirteen hours and have to mutilate it to fit it in the oven? Clive likes turkey and there are plenty of people to feed, so it all gets eaten up. Finally, after a bit of improvisation, I managed to get the turkey cooked in our other oven, put it on a very big platter and took it into the dairy to cool. As I was carrying the bird across to the stone shelf I felt something run up my thick woollen sock-clad leg. I didn't see it but I knew it was Roland. I faced a choice: I could have dropped the turkey and screamed blue murder, or I could carefully put the turkey down and then scream. I hadn't spent all that time cooking the enormous turkey to drop it, so I went for the second option.

Cue Clive, and the battle with the rat. I had the video camera to hand because it was Christmas Day, so instead of the usual ritual of the family opening presents under the tree I recorded a rather more exciting event.

'That's it. I know t'lal' bastard's in there. I'm not comin' out till I've got 'im.'

He shut himself in the dairy and jammed the bottom of the door so it couldn't escape. All we could hear was everything being tipped off the shelves; every bottle, every jar was moved. He even wrenched a very heavy filing cabinet out to look down the back. No rat.

I was getting a running commentary.

'Are you sure it were Roland, you dozy mare?'

'Course it was 'im, I didn't imagine it!'

Finally, all that was left to search was the giant chest freezer. He managed to pull it out. The rat wasn't behind it. He tipped it forward. The rat wasn't under it. Then he got a torch and looked through the mesh grille that covered the access hole to the motor. There it was, sitting as still as could be. He could just see the eyes glinting in the torchlight.

Clive couldn't get it, so he decided to see if he

could kill it with noxious fumes, spraying it to death with WD40, Impulse, anything we had in there. No effect at all. Then he had a brain-wave.

Clive's friend Steve had crafted us a pair of ornate sticks for our wedding, and for Christmas he had made the children some miniature shepherd's crooks. Clive got one of these crooks, the only thing he could find that was narrow enough to go through the mesh, and kebabbed the rat with it. Clive said proudly: 'I just let it 'ave one.'

His triumph, walking out of the dairy with his enemy defeated and speared on a stick, is all on film, the best Christmas video we have ever made.

I carry a camera with me wherever I go and sometimes get to record things happening that I would rather forget about, like the day the fire brigade was called to Ravenseat, when our precious hay went up in smoke.

Hay has to be stacked and stored properly (mewed), or you get problems, and we lost nearly half our crop through taking our eyes off what our helpers were doing. It was a Tuesday, market day, and I was just loading up the trailer with the lambs that were going to the auction when Clive came down the yard.

'The hay's on fire.'

'Are yer sure?'

'Yeah, ring the fire brigade.'

The hay had been mewed in the barn fifteen days earlier, and we knew it was steaming, which isn't unusual. Clive had asked one of the old-timers he knows who said, 'It'll steam for fifteen days and that'll be an end to it, hod thi nerve.'

He was one of those old boys who seemed to know about these things, so we marked it on the calendar and counted off the days. Well, he was certainly right. It did stop, but unfortunately the steam turned into smoke.

When Clive told me to call the fire brigade I was unsure as there was only the thinnest wisp of smoke coming from it, not much more than you get from a cigarette. I climbed up on top of it. It's always warm on top of the hay, and there will sometimes be fungus because of the warmth and damp. It's a place where the chickens like to lay their eggs. The kids like sitting up there too.

But I could smell it when I got up there: this was an acrid smell, definitely smoke, not steam. It was a thin plume, but it was still smoke. The first thing we did was to get the animals, lambs and horses, out of the adjoining barns and into the fields.

I rang the fire brigade under duress. I still wasn't sure, it didn't look dramatic enough. You think you need flames for the fire brigade, and I'd never had any experience of hay combusting. We began pulling the hay bales from the front face out, with the skid steer (a small machine with a loading shovel that we use for moving bales and mucking out the cows). As we dug into the haystack it became black and charred, and some of the bales we rescued were crisp and tinder-like. Towards the centre, everything was disintegrating. Of course, what we were doing, while salvaging as much hay as possible, was introducing oxygen and that's when the fire caught hold and we had real flames.

The fire brigade arrived, and we were trying to stop them dowsing everything; we still wanted to save as much hay as possible. One of the fire-fighters, a woman wearing breathing apparatus, rescued a chicken who was stoically refusing to leave the eggs she'd laid, even though they must have been hard-baked by then.

We lost about fifty tons of hay, which was half of that year's poor crop. In a good year we can harvest 300 tons. The bad weather was the cause of the hay combusting: we'd been rushing to get the hay in during a break in the weather, and the longest, wettest grass, from around the edge of the fields, which should have been loaded into the barn last, went in first. We'd had a contractor here baling and he'd made bigger bales than normal, as we'd thought this would speed up the process as we battled with the weather con-ditions. The bigger bales were more compacted, which meant they held the dampness more. Damp hay combusts more easily because it provides the right conditions for the growth of organisms that generate heat, and can increase hay temperatures by up to 150 degrees Fahren-heit. If it is loosely packed it can cool, and may turn brown or go mouldy, but it won't burn. We had the double whammy: tightly packed and damp. A catalogue of errors that cost us dear.

The fire was in our big, modern, middle barn, and luckily it didn't suffer any damage, apart from being blackened. If Clive hadn't spotted that small plume of smoke when he did then all of the farm buildings could have gone up. We were left with two big piles of ash that glowed red hot inside if you poked them. Even when the hay had finally burned away to nothing, the ground beneath held the heat for a long time afterwards.

For us, hay in the barn is like money in the bank. If we can fill our barns with hay, we can feed our animals in the winter. We grade the hay, and the poorer quality stuff is saved in case we have really bad weather. We call it 'storm hay'. We need as much hay as we can get, we can never have too much and can even store it until the following year, when we will call it 'over year' hay. The lovely flower-filled meadows that we mow make beautiful, sweet, herby hay, but the ground that we have to travel to mow is at best described as undulating, at worst downright dangerously steep.

When we had a farmers' visit from East Yorkshire, one of them asked, 'Where does ta mek thi hay?'

'Them's our hayfields, over there.'

'Oh, my God!'

They couldn't believe we had to contend with fields so bumpy and uneven. You need nerves of steel to drive a tractor around our hayfields – they don't lend themselves to the massive high-tech machines used in the lowlands. This farm is suited to the old, traditional methods. We still make the small conventional bales that need to be picked up and physically lifted onto the trailers and then stacked by hand in the barn. Some of the steepest banks are still raked off by hand. My record is accidentally tipping off a load of hay bales three times on the journey back to the barn: bad enough to load a trailer once, but three times is soul-destroying.

Over the past few years, the terrible weather has meant that it has not been possible to make as much hay as we'd like. We decided after a particularly bad year that we could no longer rely on using a contractor to make round bales of silage, which is grass preserved by being wrapped in plastic, and that we needed to invest in some new(ish) kit.

Clive's not into machinery, but I was on a mission, looking through the farming magazines for ads. There were three things on my wish list: a round baler, a rowing-up machine and a bale wrapper. Bearing in mind that I'm totally clueless when it comes to buying machinery, it seemed pointless going to view any of the advertised kit. I just put my faith in a man who sounded genuine, and luckily it paid off. When it all arrived in the yard Clive looked at it doubtfully, but it has proved to be worth its weight in gold as, when the rain clouds are gathering, we can rescue a field of grass by baling it up quickly and making silage.

We had a few teething problems in the first year of using our new equipment and we learned from experience that you should be very careful where you release the round bale from the machine. There was one very lucky walker who narrowly missed being taken out by a bale in a nasty *Raiders of the Lost Ark* moment. We watched, horrified, as a giant round bale rushed past him at high speed, smashed down the wall and finally came to rest in the river. The walker, meanwhile, carried on walking and was completely oblivious to his near-miss. It's not a good idea to get in the path of a half-ton round bale travelling at high speed.

The rough ground means our machines have a shorter than average life expectancy. I had to upgrade our mower recently because Clive was halfway through cutting the Seeds, our big field of grass which takes about thirteen hours to mow, when our old drum mower began to disintegrate.

Like a real trooper Clive kept mowing, even as more pieces fell off, until the inevitable happened and the mower snapped in half. He dragged it back into the yard and threw his hands in the air. Not a happy camper.

'How thi 'ell am I gonna get mi grass cut now?'

'Don't panic,' I said. 'Just don't panic. Ger'it on t'trailer an' I'll tek it an' see if I can ger'it welded.'

So I turned the 'Cream Tea' sign to closed and set off to see Metal Mickey, the mechanic we love because he can make do and mend.

I pulled into his yard at Reeth and shouted. His head appeared from underneath a JCB and he blinked, rubbing his eyes with his blackened hands. He got to his feet, wiped his hands on an oily rag, and came over to the trailer for a closer inspection.

'Can you mend this?' I asked him.

'When?'

'Like now.'

'Well, get it off t'trailer and I'll 'ave a look,' he said.

As he lifted it off, it fell apart completely. Mickey shook his head, all the while sucking air through his teeth. He liked a challenge, but this was a tough one. It wasn't looking good.

'If it were a 'orse, I'd shoot it,' he said.

Metal Mickey's yard is always full of second-hand machines, from forage harvesters through to ride-on mowers and everything in between. I asked him if he had a drum mower – they are bottom of the range, like really basic; good for bumpy ground, but nobody except a few hillbillies like us use them.

'Nope, nowt o' that. Tell yer wha' I do 'ave though.'

In the corner of the yard was a disc mower, a far more modern contraption. It was the only mower Mickey had. I'm thinking, *Clive's not going to like that.*

But what choice was there? The weather was good, dry and warm with just a gentle breeze, perfect for haymaking. We needed to keep mowing and I was never going to find another drum mower at short notice. Mickey gave me all the chat – one careful owner, you know the drill. I did what you do when you're buying a second-hand car: I walked around it, kicked it, pretended I knew what I was doing. But even I could tell from looking at it that it had seen a bit of action.

'Just cosmetic,' Mickey said.

'Stick it on the back of the trailer.'

'Are you sure?' Mickey knows Clive's reluctance to take on new stuff.

'I don't bloody know. But what choice is there?'

When I pulled into the farmyard, Reuben and Robert greeted me with sheer joy. Rubes loves anything mechanical. Robert was very pleased that I'd upgraded our ancient mower. Clive, needless to say, looked at it suspiciously.

I said, 'Everyone's using them, they're unbreakable.'

He gave a snort. He knows there's nothing that can't be broken on our fields.

'Look, I could understand you being annoyed wi' me if I came back with a designer handbag. You cannae possibly black me for buying a mower.'

I got the feeling that he almost wanted it to fail. But it worked well, and we cut all the grass with it.

I think it would be safe to say that where machinery or equipment is involved neither Clive nor I are well versed in their use or maintenance. When a piece of equipment leaves Ravenseat, the next destination is the scrapyard. We've had a succession of knackered trailers. I once drove over to Martin's in terrible weather with a trailer that had one locked wheel and was leaving a black smudge and a trail of smoke along the road behind us. I decided that the only remedy was to stop looking in the mirror and keep going. When I got to Martin's farmyard the previously round wheel was worn flat at the bottom and Martin, who had been watching my approach down Ash Fell, said, 'I thought it were a fly past by t'bloody Red Arrows.'

On another occasion I took a trailerload of lambs to the evening sale at Kirkby Stephen auction. I missed the ballot and was late through the ring so I called for fish and chips on the way home, rushing back at high speed before they got cold. Later that evening a friend rang and said, 'When I walked back through Kirkby tonight there was 'ell on. The glass window in t'news-agents' had been smashed, summat 'ad gone thra it, vandalism they said.'

The next morning when we went out into the farmyard we noticed that our livestock trailer now only had three wheels. We never did find that wheel – and if it was at the newsagents' then we certainly weren't going back to claim it.

The one piece of kit that we rely on most is our quad bike; we use it and abuse it. We feed sheep, we chase sheep, we carry sheep and carry food for sheep, not to mention carting posts and wire around the farm. We depend upon it. We also sometimes bog it, sink it, tip it and drown it. It has been fished out of the river upside down and on one occasion was even pulled from a bog with a pony. There's one thing that is for sure, I wouldn't like to be the buyer of a second-hand quad bike that had been at Ravenseat.

12

Free-range Children

Life at Ravenseat revolves round children and animals, a difficult combination at times. We are up at the crack of dawn every morning. Life here is about routine, and as long as the rhythm isn't disturbed then things run smoothly. Clive usually makes a start on the bullocking up, the feeding of the animals in the yard, but NEVER horses: they are my domain. I attempt to get school children into uniforms and breakfasted, babies fed and back to sleep and then, hopefully, children into waterproofs and off outside to do their jobs. They have responsibilities and I am a stickler for them not shirking their duties, come rain or shine.

Reuben revives the fire, emptying the ash from the grate and chopping his sticks for kindling, while Miles fills the coal buckets and the log box. Violet makes paper dogs by rolling up old newspapers, for the bottom of the grate underneath the kindling.

We have two flocks of chickens, an orderly managed flock in one of the outlying barns, and a maverick flock of about fifteen unruly chickens of dubious parentage. Some hens were here when I came, and sometimes we put eggs under a broody hen to hatch, leaving the offspring to join this rainbow family of chickens. They reject domestication and live semi-wild in and around the farmyard. Edith and Miles are on permanent egg duty; no chicken nest goes undetected. Every chicken is kept under close surveillance, and Edith is very accomplished at tracking down the secret nests. Miles is her accomplice; his job is to risk life and limb retrieving the eggs. The wearing of a hat is compulsory, used to throw over a protective chicken who does not wish to give up her eggs easily. While she is temporarily blind, Miles snatches the eggs from under her (leaving one, so that in theory she will come back to the same nest tomorrow), then whips the hat away and uses it to transport the eggs back home. This operation can be fraught with difficulties: sometimes eggs are dropped or sometimes a very, very old egg will find its way into the kitchen. The sulphurous fumes that you get from cracking an old egg are guaranteed to take away your appetite for an egg butty.

Raven makes a start on the horses, most of whom are over-wintered in stalls. The horses are tied, with a manger and hay rack in front of them, and then put into the yards during the day. The land at Ravenseat is so boggy that the horses would sink knee deep into the mire and suffer from mud fever if they were let loose in the fields. They are rugged up and led to water (despite the old adage, they do drink, but it can take a while) and then let into the yards for their daily exercise. There is a lot of the proverbial to shovel into the barrow, hay racks to be filled ready for night and the floor left clear of straw to dry. Raven usually has two horses out and their stables done by the time the school taxi arrives.

The daily chores change throughout the seasons, with more to do in the winter than in the summer. As soon as the weather improves the horses will go back out to the moor. We usually keep a couple of horses back at Ravenseat and tether them, moving them around every day and using them instead of a lawnmower. It also means they are to hand if anyone wishes to use them as a means of transport. Bait boxes and flasks of tea have all been delivered on horseback during hay time when other forms of transport are already deployed.

One beautiful summer morning, a school day, all was quiet at Ravenseat, far too quiet. There was not a sign of a child anywhere. The school taxi arrived in the yard, I was shouting frantically for the children and went apologetically to explain to the driver that he might be delayed due to absent schoolchildren.

'I 'avent a clue where they're at,' I said.

'I've just passed 'em,' he said. 'Coming past Black Howe on an 'orse. I turned 'em round.'

Sure enough, just coming into sight was Meg, plodding along with three children riding bareback, their only means of steering a halter tied into a loop. We waited patiently for them to return, not daring to shout to them to hurry up. They went to school that day with horse hairs on their uniforms and smelling distinctly equine.

It does not seem to matter how smartly I turn them out in the morning, somehow before the taxi arrives they always manage to look dishevelled. We often hand-rear calves and they tend to salivate at the prospect of their morning milk feed. School jumpers inevitably get smeared with milky slobber. Pigs exude a decidedly 'piggy' smell which seems to permeate clothing with remarkable ease. A favourite activity to pass the time before the school taxi arrives was pig riding: seeing how long they can stay on the back of a cavorting pig was, for a little while, a seriously competitive business. The Tamworth two, as we called the pigs we had at the time, took it all in good sport and almost seemed to relish flinging them off. I, on the other hand, was not too impressed, and was pleased when the pigs became

300

part of breakfast instead of a breakfast-time challenge.

There are many mornings when the school taxi has to wait at the other side of the packhorse bridge because it has been raining so heavily that there is too much water in the river for him to risk driving across. The children wait in the porch, standing on the stone shelves and peering through the tiny glass window until the taxi comes into view. They announce its arrival with shrieks, then, grabbing their school bags, dash down the track and over the bridge. Whatever the weather, they are accompanied by our two terriers Chalky and Pippen, whose loyalty to the children knows no bounds. Wherever the children go, they follow. If the children split up and go off in different directions, I often see Chalky and Pippen hesitate, consciously trying to decide who to follow.

When the temperatures plummet, travelling to and from Ravenseat becomes a big problem. Snow and ice bring things to a grinding halt. The road becomes treacherous and stops the school run. Deliveries by animal-feed wagons and fuel lorries and other necessities have to be carefully timed. They can leave their depots on a crisp, cold, bright winter morning in Leyburn only to find the road blocked with drifting snow and sub-zero arctic winds by the time they reach the turn to Ravenseat. We watch the forecast carefully and try to plan well ahead: a dairy full of food, a barn full of animal feed and plenty of coal are all that are needed to keep us and our animals happy. If the people and the animals are safe, and we are not lacking anything important, then the prospect of spending a couple of weeks snowed in is not such a bad one.

We err on the side of caution with regards to sending the children to school in the wintertime. There is little point in putting them in a taxi only to spend the day watching and fretting about them getting back. Besides, with satellite Internet they can do their homework online – unless, of course, the dish is plastered with snow and not working. This may not always be entirely due to the forces of nature, as I have now and again spotted the children using the satellite dish for snowball target practice.

On one occasion we were caught unawares by a bad storm. The children had left for school when the sky began to grey over. Flurries of flakes in the wind soon turned to heavy falling snow. I rang the school and in my very best respectable voice said, 'Hello, it's Raven an' Reuben's mother here, I was wondering what you were thinking with regards to weather?'

'Well, yes, it is beginning to snow here, just starting to stick,' said the school secretary.

'I think I need them back home if possible, it's not looking too clever here.'

'They were looking forward to show and tell,' she said.

'Well, if you wouldn't mind just showing them the door and telling them to get the school taxi to bring them home.'

I waited for half an hour before setting out on the quad bike to the road end to meet them, wearing a scarf pulled up over my nose, a balaclava and a hat. It was almost impossible to see where I was going and to not veer off the road onto the moor. Visibility was so poor I had to keep stopping to get my bearings and work out where I was. At last I reached the road end, and turned left down towards Keld. The taxi had stopped on Hoggarths Bridge and could go no further. The children zipped up their coats, put on the balaclavas that I had stuffed in my pocket before leaving (too embarrassing to wear them to school) and perched themselves behind me on the bike. They huddled in tightly, their faces pressed into my coat to shield them from the stinging, driving snow. There is a point when you become snow blind and everything is white. No matter how hard I scrunched my eyes up and tried to focus I could not make out where I was. I knew that the turn into Ravenseat was somewhere close but I couldn't find it. It was only when Raven began digging me in the ribs after spotting the telegraph pole that we realized I had driven right past. I turned round and back onto the Ravenseat road, but it struck me how easy it had been to get disorientated, making a situation like that downright dangerous.

The novelty of snow and ice can wear a little thin, and after the skiing (I bought skis on eBay and the children love skiing down the hills), sledging, snow angels and igloo building has been done, there are water troughs to defrost, doorways and gates to dig out and feed to distribute to the sheep outside. Ravenseat is exposed, there is little shelter from the driving snow, and the bitter wind blows the snow around leaving some places where the grass can still be seen and others where the drystone walls are completely covered. Eskimos may have fifty words for snow, but around here we have our own word to describe the snow being picked up and blown around: stowering.

It is vitally important that we get our sheep down from the moor and to safety. We gather them into the sheep pens or in-bye (enclosed meadows and pastures) where we can open up the barns for them. If they shelter at the wrong side of the wall in a storm they can soon be over-blown and buried under the snow. There are gutters and ghylls here that are notoriously dangerous, and I remember wading slowly along a wall, through snow up to my thighs, poking down into the snow with my crook trying to find three tup hoggs that were missing presumed buried. Bill, Clive's sheepdog, is terribly good at locating buried sheep but unfortunately gets overexcited in the process and will try to eat them if he finds them. They can survive many days under the snow but, really, it is avoidable if you are shepherding your sheep regularly, watching the weather and know where you have them.

During the bad storms of the winter of 2012/13, we brought all of our sheep down the evening before the worst snowfall, setting out as darkness fell and bringing them to safer ground. If we can keep travelling to our sheep on the quad bike to feed them with hay and cake and make sure that they have access to water, then they will take no harm. But if the snow is too deep for the bike we have to travel on foot, and have occasionally resorted to the traditional form of horse power.

One year our old neighbour Tot had just a handful of sheep in the Smithy Holme, the field next to ours. They were perfectly fine, having a barn in which to shelter, but were marooned there with nobody able to get through the snow drifts to feed them. He rang us fretting about them. Clive told him not to worry and that somehow we would get there with some hay. We got as far as Beck Stack on the bike and then we set off walking, taking it in turns to carry the hay bales. We took giant steps through the snow, sinking down above our knees with each stride, every so often sitting on the bales for a breather. When we finally reached the hungry sheep we tossed a few canches of hay into the hay racks in the barn, and then retraced our steps back to the bike and home.

Everything becomes so hungry at times like this, children and animals alike. We once had a bull in a loose box in the yard. Every morning I would break the ice and fill up his water bucket, fill his hay rack and leave him a scoop of cake, and every morning a rabbit would squeeze through a gap in the door and join him, nibbling the short pieces of hay that dropped to the floor under the rack. It looked extraordinary, such a big beast sharing his food with a little rabbit.

It is during these hungry times that I revel in cooking traditional foods for us all, heartwarming stews that I can put in the range and forget about all day until evening. I like to feel that we can be self-sufficient and make good use of everything available to us. Nothing goes to waste: there is a hierarchy of animals, from dogs through to pigs and chickens, waiting for any leftovers.

It is not only snow that wreaks havoc. The sub-zero temperatures can put a stop to our water supply when the pipes freeze. No water in the outside taps and water troughs is bad enough but no water in the farmhouse makes life very difficult. The laborious task of carrying bucket after bucket of water from the beck to fill kettles which in turn are used to try, usually unsuccessfully, to thaw out water pipes, is back-breaking and soul-destroying. It is surprising how much water a household uses, and after a week of washing clothes and hair in the sink with tepid water the beauty of the snow has long since worn thin. It takes many buckets of water to fill a cattle trough, then a cow turns round, lifts its tail and deposits a clap in the trough, and you have to start all over again. The joy that comes with a thaw is indescribable, the sheer luxury of turning on a tap or the flushing of a toilet.

Water isn't the only amenity that gives us problems: we have been blighted by power cuts. We are lucky to have mains electricity, but being at the end of the line means we are subject to both power surges and cuts. I can be sitting quietly, usually waiting for something crucial to finish cooking in the fan oven, and suddenly the lights will go brighter and brighter and then ... nothing, darkness. My heart sinks, along with the cake. Only quite recently we had almost three full days without electricity and decided that, apart from the problem of freezers defrosting, we would embrace the idea of being powerless. We cooked entirely on the black range, went to bed when it was dark and got up when it was light – exactly as our forebears must have done.

Despite the challenges we face at Ravenseat, I really love the farmhouse and it seems that other creatures sometimes feel the same way. It was during a prolonged bitterly cold spell of weather that we had a visit from an owl. Edith discovered him sitting on the mantelpiece in the little sitting room. He was covered in soot and had clearly come down the chimney and then taken fright and tried to escape by flying at the window. He had dusted the sofa with soot and covered the windowsill with crap. Now he was sitting there, watching us with wide eyes and a stupid, almost nonchalant, expression. The children were very excited, there was even talk of keeping him and training him Harry Potter-style. But his impressive talons soon made them change their minds. I armed myself with a towel, did a few circuits of the room until he made a mistake and got stuck behind the TV then managed to grab him and wrap him in the towel. We took him outside to have a closer look, Reuben armed with a bird book, but he was so sooty we couldn't be sure whether he was a tawny or a short-eared owl. We had a countdown, then launched him skywards, watching as he headed for Tan Hill and out of sight.

The next morning Edith excitedly came into the kitchen and announced, 'He's back.'

'Who's back, Ede?' I asked.

'Mr Owl,' she exclaimed.

'No way!'

'Come and look,' she said, tugging my sleeve.

I followed her through to the small sitting room, pushed open the door and there, sitting this time on the fireside companion, was an owl. *The* owl! The room was trashed – again. I had only just sorted out his previous night's dirty protest. Once again he was unceremoniously slung out, and this time told he was barred. And I thought owls were supposed to be wise...

Warm summer evenings persuade us to leave the windows open, which is an open invitation to other winged intruders. One night, all was quiet, the children sleeping soundly, then:

'Mam, mam, there's a bat in mi bedroom!' Raven shouted.

'Is there? I replied sleepily.

When I looked, there was indeed a small bat, circling the room.

'Can't you just ignore 'im? I'm sure he'll find 'is own way out,' I said.

'Nah, I can't sleep wiv 'im in mi room,' she said.

Downstairs I went. I'd seen the children playing with a fishing net and this seemed a likely tool for the job. Back in the bedroom the bat had a captive audience, all the children now hypnotized as it did ever-decreasing circles round the light bulb. I waited until the bat was heading round for another lap, then stuck the net in the air and bingo – I had him.

'Let's 'ave a closer look,' said Raven, screwing up her nose and inspecting the angry little creature in the bottom of the net.

'Do thi bite?' she said.

'Nooooooo,' I replied, thrusting my hand into the net to disentangle the bat. I cupped it gently in my hands and lifted it free. Then, as Raven admired its tiny little mousey body, it sunk needle-sharp teeth into my hand. It didn't let go, just hung on for all it was worth. It was only when I put my hand out of the bedroom window with the bat suspended from it by its teeth that it finally let go.

Not long after, I was in a particularly deep and delicious sleep when something disturbed me. As I lay, semi-conscious, something wafted past my face. I instinctively tried to brush it away but whatever it was had gone. A few seconds later something swept past my face again, so I reached for the light switch. Another bat. Round and round and round it went, I was mesmerized as it circled the room. Clive was awake by this time.

'Not another bat,' he said as it did another circuit. 'Maybe it thinks you're Meatloaf?'

'Thanks for that,' I said. 'Now thoo can blinkin' well sort it.'

'I'm just gonna tu'n t'light off, you know how t'song goes.'

I did know the words by Meatloaf, but Clive was wrong, because our Bat out of Hell was not gone before the morning sun. In the end Clive became so frustrated that he threatened to introduce it to another bat, a cricket bat, before finally conceding that he would have to go and find the fishing net again.

One day, while I was down at the picnic benches

309

serving a cream tea, I saw a family of ducks trooping up the yard. It was a glorious day and I talked to my customers for a little while, then returned to the house with an empty tray. When I reached the front door, I was met by a low-flying mallard, and as I came into the living room there was a scene of chaos. The mother duck had clearly decided to take a shortcut through the house and had encountered Edith, panicked and taken fright, leaving behind her family. There were ducklings everywhere, Edith frantically trying to gather them up into my washing basket. Once we reckoned we had them all, we deposited the washing basket full of ducklings in the garth and, sure enough, within a few minutes, mother duck had returned. Reunited.

Another morning I was standing at the kitchen sink staring wistfully out of the window, planning the endless list of jobs for the day, when I felt a draught of air behind me and caught a glance of what I thought was a bird swoop through the kitchen and into the hallway. Drying my hands, I set off after the uninvited visitor. Reaching the bedroom, I saw a sparrowhawk perched at the foot of the bed. It was only after the sparrowhawk had been caught and released that we discovered a blackbird quietly hiding on the windowsill behind the curtain. It had clearly come into the house in a panic, with the bird of prey in hot pursuit. It had a very lucky escape.

We've had a vole in residence for some time. It's known to the children as Slow Mouse, because it doesn't scamper about like a mouse but proceeds across the room at a stately pace. It always emerges and takes a leisurely amble around the living room when I have visitors. One morning Slow Mouse made a mistake and took a stroll into a discarded wellie. Spotting it out of the corner of my eye, I decided it was time it had a taste of the great outdoors. I quickly grabbed the wellie, folding over the top, and then deposited Slow Mouse in the little garth. Half an hour later he meandered his way back through the front porch and into the house again. I hadn't the heart to turf him out. The distance he'd travelled was about the equivalent of walking the Coast to Coast for his little mouse legs.

It is not just wild animals that appear unannounced at Ravenseat: we also get our fair share of domesticated animals turning up quite out of the blue. We have had dogs here that have clearly just been dumped out of cars. A dog running loose is the worst crime you can commit round here, it upsets everything – even the kindest, petted dog can turn into a sheep killer if it's left to roam free.

We had a border collie dumped on us, and I put signs up all over the place and rang round the local area but I guessed it wasn't a local dog: its eyes had the glassy look of a dog that has been kept in the dark, not let out. The search for the owner proved fruitless and reluctantly we had to ring the dog warden.

Our flock of chickens had an exotic addition a couple of years ago. I'm always shocked by the way people dump animals in the countryside but who would go for a nice ride out in the car and dump their chickens? In 2011, just approaching

Christmas, a small flock of fancy chickens – Silver Spangled Hamburgs, Golden Sebrights and an Old English Game cockerel – were dumped at the end of our road. They were obviously not used to living in the wild, and they sat in a small sad clump at the side of the road in the snow. The chap who drives the snowplough through the dale has to turn round at our road end, so each day he would stop there to eat his sandwiches and throw his crumbs to the hens. It was just going to be a matter of time before something ate them: they were such an easy target. So we decided we'd catch them, which wasn't difficult. We took some, and the others were re-homed with neighbours who already had hens.

Clive always had a small number of wild game hens living in the farmyard, but egg production was limited. I eventually put that right, on a scale that neither I nor Clive was expecting. Especially Clive. I was looking for about twenty hens and decided to get them from a poultry farm where they are kept in big barns. Every so often the barns have to be emptied, cleaned and disinfected before a new batch of hens goes in. I was given a telephone number to ring and said, 'I've been telled that yer 'ave some chickens tha' need new homes.'

'Aye, free to a good home.'

He seemed like a decent chap: he certainly appeared to care about the chickens and was very keen for people to take them – otherwise they would go for processing into pies, I guess. The first time I went I didn't know what to expect. I took a half-size trailer, and had visions of me and the children choosing the hens we wanted.

When I reached the farm I backed up to the chicken shed while the farmer directed me: 'Left a bit, come on, keep straight, whoa.'

I had literally just got out of the Land Rover when the barn doors swung open, the farmer dropped my trailer's ramp and then him and another lad armed with a big piece of cardboard shooed chickens from one end of the shed. They just swarmed into my trailer. There must have been about a hundred. I thought, *Lordy, I wasn't wantin' that many!* But I knew that if I chucked them out and said I didn't want them, they were destined to be pies.

So I smiled sweetly at the farmer, thanked him very much and took them. All the way back the children were chirping, 'What's Dad gonna say?'

I didn't need them to remind me that Clive wouldn't be best pleased. I got them back home and into a barn. To the children's delight they had even laid some eggs in the trailer on the way. They sat in the barn, stunned, half bald, with gormless expressions on their faces. I realized they were feeling the cold. They didn't have many feathers because they were used to living inside a nice big warm barn so I shut the door to keep the draught out. Here was me thinking I'd done them a favour by rescuing them, when at that moment they probably hated me for it.

But they came right. For a while they were not sure about how to behave, and seemed perplexed at the whole outdoor thing – how to scratch and take dust baths – but eventually they feathered up and became like normal farmyard hens, laying

313

eggs all over the place. I usually replenish my flock every year, but after that first sting I'm careful to say exactly how many I want.

We also have a peacock and a peahen; I like to think they give Ravenseat that stately home feel. They were given to us by someone whose neighbour didn't appreciate the raucous shrieking noise that they make. I agreed to take them but I couldn't imagine they would ever thrive here. I thought they were tropical birds and that the impressively long tail feathers would make the peacock an easy target for the sheepdogs. The reality is that he rules the roost. He is fearless and will stare out any dog, fixing him with his beady eyes until the dog backs down. I also discovered that peahens are terrible mothers: they sit tight on their eggs until the first one hatches, then they abandon the rest. We usually try to put the peahen eggs under a broody chicken, to get more hatched. Fortunately we have a friend who is a peacock enthusiast and is happy to buy the peachicks. I believe he has no near neighbours

It is amazing how quickly animals can adapt to their situation and the peacock has become quite predatory, hanging about the picnic benches, looking menacing, waiting for an opportune moment to get his beak into an unsuspecting walker's scone. In fact, the picnic benches are a prime location for scavenging: the children, the peacock and the terriers, Pippen and Chalky, are all wise to the fact that here there are rich pickings to be had.

Chalky and Pippen spend many happy hours loitering around the walkers. Chalky is nimble and her tactic for obtaining food relies on speed and a certain amount of brazen cheek. Pippen, on the other hand, plays the sympathy card and will develop an entirely fake limp and sorry expression. One day a rambler came up to the house cradling Pippen in his arms.

'What a sad-looking dog,' he said. 'Was she a rescue case, has she been abused?'

That's how good Pippen's act is.

Chalky can be fickle and it takes no encouragement at all for her to happily jump into any car. This was nearly her undoing recently. She likes to patrol our road on the lookout for road-kill, a squashed rabbit or the like. It seems that she jumped into the car of a day tripper who, instead of enquiring about her home in the vicinity of here or Keld or Thwaite or even Richmond, took her all the way to the kennels at Bedale, an hour and a half from here. Fortunately she is microchipped, so they rang me. I was not best pleased. Chalky had an overnight stay, which cost me £45, and I got a telling-off from a snotty kennel maid about letting my dog wander free without a collar.

Farm dogs never wear collars. The risk of them getting caught up in something, such as a wire fence, is too great. You'll never see a sheepdog with a collar. The only time they wear a collar is if they are tied up. Unfortunately, Chalky's a wanderer, especially when she's in season. When we had the party of bikers camping here she disappeared. I felt quite guilty because I'd had harsh words with her for sniffing around the barbecue food. She was last seen following some walkers, and was brought back two days later by our neighbour Susan. Goodness only knows where she had been during this time. It was only a few days later that she went AWOL again, returned this time by the postman, who'd picked her up down by the road end.

We don't have our dogs spayed or neutered. It takes something out of a sheepdog, they're never quite the same. Pippen is quite an old lady now, and she's never had a litter, so we suspect that she is a non-breeder. Anyway, to put a stop to Chalky's wanderlust Clive borrowed a Jack Russell dog, a smooth-coated, squat little chap called Spud, from his friend Lawrence, and all three dogs, Spud, Pippen and Chalky, had a bit of a love-in, a canine ménage à trois.

We've sometimes had cats appear from no-where, also seemingly just chucked out of a car. Sheep farmers aren't happy about cats, because there's the risk that they spread toxoplasmosis. We let them stay, but they never seem to last very long in this environment. We had a bonny little ginger cat here for a few months but one day we found it dead in the walk-through trough. We suspected that the tups at either side of the trough had taken a dislike to it and it stood no chance when they came together and squished it. Not nice, but it simply wasn't bred for life on a farm, and the blame lies with whoever dumped it.

Perhaps the weirdest thing we have ever had dumped was somebody's girlfriend. She seemed a nice enough lass, dressed in white pedal pushers and high heels. She tottered into our yard and said, 'Could you tell me where the nearest bus stop is, please?'

It emerged that she'd been out with her boyfriend, there had been a row, he'd ordered her to get out of the car, which she did in a huff, and he sped off, back down our road. I persuaded her to wait for him to return.

'Don't worry, he'll come back,' I reassured her.

I really thought he would. I made her a cup of tea and sat her down, and time ticked on. It began to get dark, and she was obviously very embarrassed. Of course, there are no buses, and a taxi from here to Hartlepool, where she came from, would have cost a fortune.

In the end, we drove her to Kirkby Stephen, which I think is the wrong direction for Hartlepool, but at least she would be able to get a bus to somewhere. It's not exactly a bustling metropolis, but she had more chance of getting home from there than from Ravenseat. I have no idea what happened to her, but something tells me that relationship was doomed.

I suppose what I am trying to say is that at Ravenseat you must expect the unexpected. You never know who, or indeed what, you are going to find. Aside from unexpected visitors, there are the animals that the children bring into the house...

One summer we were hand-rearing a calf, Toffee, and I came into the living room one day to find the children had brought her inside. She's completely tame and will gallop along behind them, and they were engrossed in filming her doing a variety of simple tricks and tackling an obstacle course made from pouffes and foot-stools. They were planning her future as a performing cow.

'If we teach 'er to play t'guitar we can go on *Britain's Got Talent*,' Raven said.

Miles said he felt the trumpet was more suited to her.

Another farmer had a spare calf so we brought it up here as a companion for Toffee, so now we've got Bubblegum as well. The children love them, but they have a completely pragmatic attitude to animals, and they know that when their calves grow up they may be sold on.

Little Joe is our Shetland pony and he too has been allowed into the house. During the summer holidays a new game was devised: whenever the doorbell rang Little Joe would be ridden down the passageway and into the porch and the door answered by a small person on horseback. They were delighted with the reaction of the visitors, which was one of complete disbelief as Little Joe trotted off up the yard and then back again, waiting for the next unsuspecting arrival. The children like to shock visitors and I suppose I should be a little bit more of a disciplinarian. I'm not house proud though: as long as everyone is fed, warm and happy, then that will do. One of them did tramp a peacock poop in the other day, and was ordered out smartish, but on the whole life's too short to worry about such things.

13

Sidney in the Snow

Baby number six, Sidney, was due at Christmas 2011, but as usual he came early, a month before my due date. By this time Rav was ten and a half, Reubs was eight, Miles was five and a half, Edith was three and Vi was eighteen months – a great spread of ages.

It was quite lucky Sidney was early, because I was worrying about the snow coming and stopping us getting to the hospital.

As usual, life was hectic, what with all the back-end sales and tupping time. I'm usually too busy to notice the baby kicking; the only time I feel it is when I'm lying quiet in bed at night. My babies have a tendency to lie sideways so I don't feel them moving much anyway, but even I had noticed that for a couple of days the baby had been very quiet. I told Clive about it.

'Does ta want mi to tek thi to t'hospital?' he said.

'Nay, if summat's up, they can't do owt.'

I put it to the back of my mind and thought about getting on with what needed doing; we'd brought the horses in because winter was fast approaching, so I had three stables to muck out that morning. I also had a small group of James Herriot fans coming for afternoon tea and a tour of the farm. It's funny when they come: Clive and I slip into the roles, talking the parts as if we were out of the TV drama, without any pre-arrangement. It just seems to happen naturally, and then, of course, we egg each other on.

'It's a bit of a rum do...' he'll say.

'Veterinary's comin'...' I'll say.

'Eeeee, it's a plain owd day,' he'll add.

I have to go out of the room to stop myself laughing sometimes. Anyway, they were on their way, so what does any good Daleswoman do for visitors? I got down on my hands and knees and scrubbed the flagstones with caustic soda. They come up gleaming, but it's probably not a good idea when you're eight months pregnant.

Just before the tourists arrived, my friends Rachel and Elenor (the daughter and widow of the late Jimmy Alderson) called in to pick up some eggs. They could see I was having a frantic morning.

'How yer keepin'?'

'I'm fine, but the baby's not been moving.'

Elenor, a former midwife, said this might be a sign that the baby would soon be arriving.

As they left, the James Herriot fans arrived and I served them tea and scones while Clive chatted away with his OTT Yorkshire accent. Just as I was pouring the tea, one of them asked me, in a long American drawl, 'When's the baby due?'

'A'fore day's owt,' I said. I don't know why I said it.

They drunk up their tea sharpish. They weren't going to be hanging around for me going into labour.

'You've seen 'em off proper this time,' said Clive as we stood in the yard waving goodbye. 'Yer not *really* gonna 'ave t'babby this afternoon, is ta?'

'I bloody well think I might!'

Clive sprung into action and rang for an ambulance there and then.

The rule is that you have to stay on the line until the ambulance gets there, so Clive was twining (moaning) to the operator.

'This call's gonna cost mi a fortune,' he said.

'Could you tell me where your wife is now?' asked the operator.

'She's gone for a bucket o' coal,' said Clive.

It was the same old situation, the operator thinking I was gripped with labour pains, while I wasn't having any contractions at all. I felt fine but I knew what was going to happen.

I stuffed a few bits and pieces into a bag, had a shower and changed my clothes. Clive had become bored with talking to the operator, so put the phone on the dresser in the shower room, and I could hear a little voice now and again: 'Are you all right? Anybody there?'

I was busy manoeuvring myself into a decent dress and applying waterproof mascara and lipstick – I wasn't intending to look too rough when I got to hospital – so I kept shouting back, 'I'm fine!'

The paramedic arrived and after a quick check over established that – true to form – there was not a right lot going on, so as his medical skills were not required for the moment he went to chat with Clive.

Then the ambulance came, by which time

Clive had summoned the children and they were sitting in a long line on the sofa. 'Are yer havin' t'baby?' they wanted to know.

'I reckon so,' I said, smiling. 'Now thoo be good for thi father, I won't be away long.'

I set off in the ambulance, but we didn't get very far, not even as far as Reeth. I was sitting quietly, with my bag on my knee, watching out of the window as we followed the winding road down Swaledale. We were only half an hour into our journey, just coming into Low Row, when I had that familiar heavy feeling and I knew the baby was coming. The ambulance man banged on the window for the driver to stop. I clambered onto the bed, and before the paramedic who had been following us could get out of his car and get to the ambulance, I'd had Sidney. He was wrapped in a towel and handed to me, still attached. It wasn't the most comfortable position, neither sitting up nor lying down, one hand gripping the bedrail, the other arm jammed between the side of the bed and the ambulance wall. It was virtually impossible to get Sidney plugged in for a feed, and eventually I gave up trying and concentrated on keeping him warm, not dropping him or rolling off the bed. It was a relief when we pulled up at the front of the Friarage. I was trolleyed through the front foyer and up to the maternity ward. As I was being wheeled along I overheard someone say, 'Oh, look, it's that lady off t'*Dales*, ooh, look, she's got a baby!'

I didn't think I was looking too ropy, but I was slightly embarrassed by the umbilical cord that was on top of the pink waffle blanket between me and the baby.

The baby weighed in at six pounds, a good weight for a baby four weeks early. I wasn't the least bit fazed by his early arrival: after coping with a tiny one ten weeks premature, like Reuben, I didn't expect any problems.

We decided to call him Sidney, because it's a lovely old-fashioned name that's easily shortened, and the shepherd who features prominently in the book *Hill Shepherd*, and who is now a friend, is called Sidney Reynoldson. For a middle name we added Ingram, after the retired clergyman, Ingram Cleasby, who had visited us.

Sidney was a bit cold after the journey to hospital and was whisked off to the special care baby unit to be warmed up and checked over. I stayed in with him that night, trying to get feeding established. Clive and the other five children came to fetch me the next day. I had been given my discharge paperwork and was waiting patiently for him on the SCBU when I heard the buzzer ring and saw my nearest and dearest coming into the super-sterile area. Clive didn't look too bad but the children were looking pretty dire, their appearance at odds with their careful application of the antiseptic germ-killing cleanser. Clive was carrying Violet as she was wearing only one welly and a sock that looked as if it had been worn around the farmyard; Reuben was in his boiler suit with the usual oil stains; and Miles, although wearing a pair of wellies, had darts of rough muck stuck to the bottom of both. Raven and Edith had clearly been doing something with the horses and were dressed accordingly in wellies and cream jodhpurs – well, they had once been cream. This is how they dress on the farm, but I was mortified at how unhygienic they looked in this spotlessly clean, sterile environment. I was keen to get out of there before we were accused of contaminating the place.

I had a few problems feeding Sidney when we got home, he wanted to sleep, not suckle. I messed on, trying to get him going, but it was a struggle: his weight dropped to five pounds and I was told that if he lost any more then he would have to go back to hospital. The weather was getting worse and snow was falling, but I knew I had to take him to the surgery at Hawes to get him weighed. We set off, Edith and Violet with me, and drove the Land Rover over the Buttertubs Pass to Hawes. The road was passable as the snowplough had been over earlier and although the fresh snow was sticking I could drive it cautiously.

At the surgery I was watching through the window, fidgeting nervously as I saw the snow gently settling on the rooftops. The children played happily with the toys in reception, while other patients cooed over baby Sidney. The midwife was worried about him as he hadn't gained any weight since his last appointment, so she rang the hospital for advice. They decided that Sidney needed to be bottle-fed a milk supplement, but there wasn't any at the surgery so I needed to take the prescription to the chemist in the town. Off we went, accompanied by the midwife. Time was ticking, the snow was getting heavier, I was starting to get a bit nervous and it didn't help when folks kept saying, 'What's thoo doin' over 'ere? You've nivver come over t'Tubs, 'ave yet?'

Finally we had everything, and I could set off back, promising the midwife that I'd speak to her the next day about the feeding.

As we followed the road up and out of Hawes, the snow began to get deeper, and as I climbed on to Stags Fell it became difficult to see where I was going. There were no signs of any other vehicle tracks and the snow was drifting quite badly. I was crawling along, with visibility so poor that my nose was pressed up to the windscreen in an effort to see where the road was. The snow was at least a foot deep. We were travelling all right, except that I couldn't see the road. I wasn't looking forward to the descent into Swaledale, with its precipitous drop of hundreds of feet from the road edge and only a wire rope barrier between us and oblivion. I saw in my mirror another Land Rover approaching from behind so I decided I would pull over and let it take the lead. It pulled alongside me and stopped: it was a local lad attempting to get over to Reeth.

'I'm gonna go an' tek a look, you follow me.'

I was happy with that. The snow was getting deeper and deeper and as he reached the summit I saw his brake lights come on. I stopped and he reversed back alongside me.

'I's not goin' down there, I's turnin' round,' he said.

I sat there for a little while, wondering what to do. There's no phone signal in these parts, and there was no alternative route home for me. I was just weighing up my options when, in my rear-view mirror, I saw the flashing lights of a snow-plough, closely followed by a digger and a police four-by-four. They told me I had nowt to worry about and that they'd have me back home in no time, and for me to just sit quiet while they dug a road through. We listened to *Greatest Hits of the 80s* twice through, ate a whole family pack of crisps, and were just about to start on our supply of chocolate when we were waved through. The convoy continued down into Swaledale and we had a police escort to Keld, then finally, hours late, we got back to Ravenseat. I was sure Clive would be beside himself with worry as we were so late back but he'd been so busy with his sheep that he'd lost track of time. I like to think that he would have noticed if I'd still been missing at teatime.

Taking care of a big family isn't difficult, it's mainly a question of routine and preparation. The children help out a lot, and they learn to be independent very quickly. They're all different, not at all like peas in a pod, and we certainly don't have favourites. Clive says, 'I reckon to favour t'one that needs it most at that time. If one is lacking in confidence, or 'avin' a crisis 'bout school or summat, I try to favour that particular child until it's better. There's usually one that's poorly or summat, one that needs a lal' bit more care.'

Raven is a very confident young lady. One minute she will be taking charge, cooking and helping out with the little ones, and the next minute she will be playing with toys. I liken her to

Saffy from *Absolutely Fabulous*: she's the sensible one in this family. She's very organized. If I say to her, "Ave yer done yer homework, Rav?' she shoots me a look and says, 'Of course, I did it in my break time.' And she's telling the truth, she did! She works hard at school and gets good grades. She has it in her mind that she'd like to be a vet – she has certainly had plenty of practical hands-on experience. All of the children help out at lambing time but I particularly remember Raven helping me with a yow that was having difficulties. The yow was just a shearling and had been scanned for a single lamb. She had been on lambing for a while and so I had a feel to see what was going on. She didn't seem to have opened up enough to get the lamb out. I decided I would give her a bit more time. I made myself a cup of tea and then went back for a look at her. She was laid out and straining away but there was still no room for me to get my hand in to help her out. Raven appeared.

'I's gaan to get the pickup and tek her to t' vet,' I said.

'Can I 'ave a go?' she asked.

'If yer want.'

Within half an hour, Raven had lambed her. Gently and quietly, she had lain against her, her eyes screwed tightly shut, while she worked away. She felt the unborn lamb and slowly managed to get it into position: her smaller hands and her patience saved the day. That kind of job is not for the faint-hearted, and sometimes a life can depend on whether you are prepared to get your hands dirty. She'll never get experience like that from textbooks.

Reuben's the mechanic, the engineer in the family. He loves machines, and at bedtime spends hours drawing up detailed plans of new inventions, which he will try to realize in the workshop the next day. We're usually quite impressed with whatever wacky device he creates, whether it's a snowplough for the quad bike made from an old table, or a slurry tanker made from hay-rack wheels and a forty-five-gallon drum. But our admiration soon turns into frustration when we find he has used all our screws, nails and electrical tape for his contraption. There is also the contentious issue of the number of punctures acquired by vehicles at Ravenseat: a flat tyre on the quad bike due to a roofing nail from his home-made trailer; a flat tyre on the wheelbarrow caused by a screw off his handcrafted snowplough; and, worst of all, two flat tyres on the school taxi. I did wonder whether this was a case of deliberate sabotage: I wouldn't put it past him to have made a stinger in the hope of getting a day off school.

Clive took Reuben to a machinery sale at Carlisle, along with Clive's pal Alec. Apparently they were 'just going for a look', but I know that if they take the trailer they are plotting something, and I was right, as Reubs bought himself a 'spares or repair' ride-on lawnmower. He had been saving his pocket money from helping out with the cream teas and when added to some birthday money he had a total of £70. The children are all very good at saving their pocket money as they don't go anywhere to spend it. We go to the shops in town usually once a year,

328

during the summer holidays, to get new school uniforms, but everything else can be bought locally or ordered over the Internet. The grand sum of £58 was paid for the lawnmower and it was brought back to Ravenseat in the trailer.

They got home late afternoon, and all that evening Reubs tried to get it going, charging the battery, fiddling about doing other bits and pieces. He is pretty much on his own when it comes to anything mechanical, as Clive is useless at that sort of thing. I had to drag him away from it and he went to bed very disappointed. I was away early the next morning to pick up some shopping and when I got back to the farm Reubs was brimming with excitement. He'd found and cleaned a corroded lead from the battery, and now the lawnmower was running. He was ecstatic, but if I'd ever had a notion that Ravenseat was going to have finely manicured lawns, I was sadly mistaken. The mower is used for haymaking on a miniature scale, with Reubs mowing round the field edges and wall backs, anywhere that the tractor can't get, and Miles strawing it out and getting it to dry with a device Reubs made and mounted on the back of a go-kart. Edith then rakes it into piles and finally ties it into small bales to put into the barn for winter.

The funny thing was that no sooner had Clive and Reubs left for the sale where they bought the mower than some scrap lads appeared in the yard.

'Is Clive about?'

'Nope, but I've got some scrap for yer,' I said, secretly pleased that he wasn't around. Both Clive and Reuben have an aversion to parting with anything so I took advantage of their absence to get rid of all the broken gear they had bought the previous year at the sale.

Reubs is the scruffiest little beggar you've ever met, which is a great contrast with Miles, who is incredibly tidy and fanatical about cleanliness. He folds his school uniform neatly when he gets home from school and I never have to nag him to clean his teeth or have a shower. He is definitely a farmer at heart; he loves helping out around the farm, feeding the animals and digging. He hates school, partly because prior to school he went everywhere with Clive, never saying a right lot, just watching and helping when needed: that's what he likes. One bitterly cold day when there was snow on the ground we went up to Black Howe, as a gap had come down in the wall adjoining our neighbour's land. Miles was really poorly that day, so I suggested we stay at home and keep warm by the fire (maybe because I fancied this) but Miles was having none of it. I dressed him up warmly, an all-in-one waterproof suit over a fleecy onesie, and off we went. He sat for a little while, watching intently, then curled up into a ball and fell asleep at the back of the wall, the snow gently settling on him. I don't think he would have fallen asleep if he'd been cold and unhappy, although I admit I felt his cheek once or twice to make sure he was OK.

Miles is very keen on sheep and has already got his own small flock, some Texdale (Swaledale crossed with Texel) gimmer lambs that were late born. They go up to the moor with the other sheep, and they go away for the winter. He will breed off them in future years. While they were in the Close Hills, Miles was shepherding them and helping us out with their everyday care. There's one that appears to be blind in one eye, and he reckons she really likes him, because she lets him grab hold of her without a struggle.

'Look, she's standin', waitin' for mi,' he says.

'No, Miles, it's because she can't see you...'

He's very good with the sheep, and I have high hopes that he will become a good stockman. That's what shepherding is about, knowing your animals and having an empathy with them.

Edith's a feisty little thing, a tomboy who has no fear of mucking in with the bigger ones. Her tumbling curls and doe eyes mean that she can flutter her eyelashes and get people fawning over her.

Violet can be a bit more delicate than the others, not as tough. She has a tendency to ail and I suspect her thumb-sucking has something to do with it: not a good combination, farming and thumb-sucking. She will grow out of it in time, but we're a bit more protective of her, particularly Clive.

She has a striking likeness to Raven in her younger days, and also takes after Rav in her love of horses. Her potty training involved bribery: for every poop she did in the toilet she would get a ride on a horse. She soon got wise to it, and was managing at least three trips to the loo every day. I had to have the horse on standby in the garth, ready to saddle up every time the eagle landed.

Sidney loves being outside, getting dirty, and

being involved in everything that's going on. He will turn out whatever the weather. He has a fixation on a different toy each day, and the anointed favourite has to go everywhere with him. It's stressful when it gets lost, especially as there are so many places it could have been dropped: on the moor when feeding sheep, up the cow-house when forking hay across for them, any number of places. Every night the special toy goes to bed with Sidney, which is OK if it's a small model cow, but a different matter when it was a mini wheelbarrow which had been pushed around the farmyard all day filled with horse dumps. It needed a thorough clean before it was allowed in the house.

The children have all learned to dress themselves very quickly. It's first up, best dressed, as they used to say. The sooner you can learn to put wellies on round here, the better. We've got at least fifteen pairs, all different sizes and colours, and it's a miracle if the kids have matching pairs, and even more amazing if they are on the right feet. I recently bought Edith a new pair from the agricultural suppliers near the auction mart. When she got home she replaced her one leaking welly with one of the new ones and put the other new one back in the box for when it's needed. I get a lot of our clothes from charity shops, but it's amazing how much stuff is given to us. Neighbours and friends give us the things their children have outgrown, and we have a couple of ladies who make it their mission in life to knit for us: they obviously spent a whole winter knitting away, because they produced a huge bag of eleven jumpers and cardigans for the children. We don't mind what garish colours they are: when it's cold they get worn. The children, including the boys, wear tights, long johns, balaclavas, whatever it takes to keep frostbite and chilblains at bay.

People can get quite proprietorial about us: one woman turned up and said she hadn't seen me on TV in the cardigan she had knitted for me. And here's me yearning for Louboutins and Jimmy Choos, not woollies and wellies! But it's very kind of people, and we get some lovely things. As Clive says, 'We must somehow look like needy cases, that's why people give us tons of stuff.'

One reason we may look like we got dressed in the dark is that I more or less let the children choose what they want to wear when we are at home. We have been given frilly dresses for the little girls, real princess-style party clothes. My attitude is that if that's what they want to wear, let them get on with it. I could put it all away in drawers, but that would mean it would never be worn. If Edith wants to wear a spangly, diamanté-studded Lycra dress, and Vi wants to look like a meringue, why not? All worn, of course, with the de rigueur wellies. If the weather is grim, we simply pull on the waterproofs over the top. But if the sun is shining, and they are playing around the farmyard all day, why not wear tutus and frilly skirts?

I've got pictures of Raven when she was just a dot feeding the cows while dressed as a fairy, complete with wings. I don't bother about clothes getting dirty or even the children getting dirty: it all washes off. On a bad day I can change their clothes three times before the day is out. When Sidney was learning to walk he was magnetically drawn to the puddle of black ooze that forms around the bottom of the midden. He would totter towards it and happily sit in it. I would change him into fresh clothes, then he would do it again...

In the summer, on really hot days, they can plunge into the river and get the worst of the muck off, and have a good time doing it. I have sometimes resorted to washing the muck-plastered clothes in the river in an attempt to not break the washing machine again. I have a troubled relationship with the washing-machine repair man who, on various occasions, has extracted penknives, screws, nails and even once a dead moudie (mole) from the internal workings of my washer. I remember clearly his disdain as he dangled the disgusting, wet, grey furball from his fingers while I identified the corpse. Moles are tactile and the children sometimes put a dead one in their pocket just so they can stroke the beautifully soft, velvety coat.

There is one item of clothing that has never seen the inside of the washing machine and that is my favourite lambing coat, specially adapted, with one sleeve removed. I have had it for years, since long before I came to Ravenseat. It's made from felt and has a number of patches and darns holding it together. Clive hates this coat and has threatened on more than one occasion to throw it on the fire. It reached a point where it smelt so fusty that I decided it needed a freshen-up and, after emptying the pockets of baler twine, a penknife and a dog whistle, I put it in the river, weighted down with some rocks, and left it for a couple of days. When I retrieved it I was surprised to find that it had been chewed by something. The other arm was quite raggedy now and the bottom of it had been half eaten. Clive was pleased.

'It'll 'ave to go now,' he said smugly.

I wasn't going to be parted from it that easily. A few repairs and I still have it. Other coats come and go, but that one has outlived them all. Clive still hates it.

All our clothes get spoilt because of the work we do and the outdoor life we lead. The pet lambs chewed a hole in my dress while I was teaching the little ones to suckle. It takes only one encounter with a barbed-wire fence and that's the backside of your leggings gone. Zips don't work long when there is mud embedded in them, and hats and gloves have a tendency to be thrown down in the fields, only to be found months later when we accidentally mow them or bale them. Nothing ever goes back to the charity shop: once we've finished with it then it truly is wrecked.

I have some nice things, but eventually I decided that, like the children's clothes, there was no point in keeping them for best. Unless they are totally unsuitable, I may as well wear them around the farm. There are many days during the winter months when I see no one apart from the

335

family, and I don't suppose it matters whether I brush my hair or put on lipstick. But it's not about looking good for other people, it's about self-confidence. I am determined not to go to seed just yet.

I even got us some brand-new waterproofs when I won a competition in the *Farmers Guardian*. Well, I didn't actually *win* it, sadly, although that's what the girl said when she phoned me. I was so excited: first prize was a tractor... Then she broke the news that I'd won the second prize, which was a hundred pounds' worth of waterproofs. We did get an all-expenses trip to a farm equipment show at Earls Court in London, where we were presented with our prize. I stood there clutching the green Flexothane clothes, trying not to look too obviously envious of the chap beaming as he sat on his brand spanking new tractor. Once the presentation of the waterproofs was over we sloped off and enjoyed a day out in London.

We did get invited to another awards event, the Yorkshire Awards, with the producer and some of the crew from *The Dales,* and on that occasion I managed to conjure up an evening gown for the princely sum of £5...

When the barns around Ravenseat are being repaired we have to clear out the contents before work can commence. Some of them are full of junk – rusting bits of machinery, old feed sacks, kists (storage bins) and the like. But one was full of cardboard boxes, tea chests and wicker baskets.

Clive and the gamekeeper, who was helping

out, lit a big bonfire, and the gamekeeper started throwing some of the boxes and their contents onto it. I walked across to have a look and started poking around inside them.

'Whoa, don't throw any more of these on t'fire till I've looked in 'em,' I said.

'There's nowt, just material, blankets, and t'mice 'ave been at 'em,' Clive replied.

There were old papers, bolts of fabric and net, blankets and clothes. Some of it had rotted where water from the leaking roof had leached through the boxes and this was beyond saving, but there was a whole cache of what looked like vintage clothing which was beautifully preserved.

I hope we haven't burnt owt good, I thought, looking at the parched remains of boxes already crackling merrily on the fire. I stuffed what I wanted into bin bags and carried them back to the farmhouse, and there I carefully went through my hoard, which included delicately embroidered tiny cotton nightdresses, lace baby bonnets and small crocheted baby jackets in pastel colours. I love them: the nightdresses are so much better for babies in hot weather than the modern babygros, and I have used them for the younger children. I wanted to save the blankets, some of which were woven from lambswool and were so fine and delicate, almost gauze-like, but sadly moths had got into them and I reluctantly had to throw them all away.

There was also a fringed flapper-style shift dress from the 1920s and three black taffeta and damask Victorian skirts, one with a bustle and lead weights in the hem to make it hang well. I assumed, because of the colour, that they were mourning clothes.

There were even some leather and suede lederhosen. It's one thing putting the babies into the nighties and bonnets, but I think the children would ring the NSPCC if I tried to make them wear lederhosen. There was a collection of old gas masks, obviously from the Second World War, including an all-in-one baby gas mask, which would cover the whole child. They are stamped with PROPERTY OF THE MINISTRY OF WAR: TO BE RETURNED AFTER THE WAR.

A prize find was a wooden chest full of ancient cure-alls: pink pig powders, black drink and Osmond's Patent Yow Dose 'for gaseous bloat', 'garget' and 'dropsy'. It harked back to the times when people would doctor their own animals, though I don't imagine these remedies were used with any success. Clive told me that he remembered as a child an old farmer dosing a very sick yow with an old-fashioned elixir, claiming it was such good stuff that 'he could almost see it working'. The yow was, of course, wholly dead directly.

So when we were invited to the Yorkshire Awards I needed to lose the wellies and morph into the epitome of elegance for one night only. As I drove through Kirkby on my way back from Sandwath I spotted a boned bodice on the dummy in a Barnardo's charity shop window. I did an emergency stop and parted with £5 for it. All I needed was a skirt. I remembered my treasure trove, and dug out the mourning skirts. The one with the bustle was a no-no – if there's one thing I didn't need, it was a bigger backside –

but there was one that I fitted into quite nicely. The fact that it had a train meant it didn't matter that I was taller than the diminutive Victorian lady who first wore it. All I needed to do was breathe in a little and invest in some industrial strength hooks and eyes and stitch them in: I didn't want any wardrobe malfunctions.

The event was held in Leeds. After hiring a tuxedo suit for Clive and borrowing some shoes, we set off for the champagne reception. I couldn't wait, it was a chance to let my hair down and really enjoy the fabulous meal and entertainment that was laid on: there were going to be acrobats, a live band and a free bar. We went into the ballroom and waited to be directed to our table.

'Oh, you can sit wherever you like,' said the waitress to the assembled throng. 'Apart from you,' she added, looking at me. She led me to a table at the front of the stage where there was my name on the place setting. I was starting to feel a bit nervous.

'Why can everyone else sit wherever they like an' I've gotta sit 'ere?' I said.

'Oh, the presenter wants to come and talk to you as part of the evening's entertainment,' she said, smiling.

I couldn't settle, knowing that I was going to be projected on to the big screen at the back of the stage. I didn't want my face to be red and my words incoherent through wine. I was on tenterhooks the whole evening, until finally, nearly at the end, I was pounced upon. Once the live interview was over I'm ashamed to admit I let myself go. I went round the tables collecting the golden balloons adorning them to take home for the kids, lost a shoe, drank too much and was quite ill when we got back to the hotel. I suppose you can take the girl out of Huddersfield but you can't take Huddersfield out of the girl.

The next morning at the railway station, feeling quite the worse for wear and carrying half a dozen oversized helium balloons, I was approached by a train guard who tried, unsuccessfully, to confiscate them.

'There is a risk that you may cause a short circuit if you let go of them, there's about fifty million volts up there,' he said, gesturing towards the station roof.

'I've carried 'em this far, I's not partin' wiv 'em now.'

And I didn't, despite his protests. The children loved them.

The person who really deserved an award that night was my friend Helen, who babysat all six of the children.

The children technically all have speech problems: their pronunciation is a bit slurred, and when they go to school they are inevitably assigned a speech therapist. They have their own language, and they can understand each other and we can understand them. It's just a question of tuning in. When Edith was interviewed on *The Dales*, they subtitled what she said, in case viewers couldn't understand her, which made us laugh. I'm going to keep a speech therapist in work for the next few years. I believe that if they were left to get on with it, their speech would come right in time. I had a letter from school about Miles's speech, asking me to practise saying 'p' and 'f' with him. He says them the wrong way round: 'I want to be a parmer,' he says.

'I can't see what all the puss is about,' says Clive.

When the teachers send letters home, they Sellotape them to the front of the children's school jumpers: they know that's the only way we will get to see them. There's such a rush when they arrive home, dumping their school bags, pulling on their overalls and heading for the hills. I don't believe that school is the be all and end all. The children learn many things at home: common sense, to be polite and respectful, and plenty of the basics like mathematics, reading and writing, which are better learned if applied to real-life situations. Going to the auction teaches them to count, recording pedigrees and filling in entry forms covers the reading and writing, and as for physical fitness, there's nothing quite like chasing sheep about to get you fit.

In the winter, when the nights are drawing in, they watch the television for an hour after tea, but in the summer it never goes on at all, unless there is something special on that we want to watch. They read a lot of books. Raven reads about horses, Reuben about tractors, and Miles likes dinosaurs. They make their own amusement and games. Recently I saw Reuben pretending to auction off all the farm equipment to his siblings. He was really giving it some: 'Who'll gimme a hundred pounds for this tractor? Fifty pounds? Where d'ya wanna be?' Then he went up in increments. What better way to learn arithmetic?

They have a collection of toy farmyard animals and it always amuses me to watch them farming in a realistic, true-to-life manner.

'Knacker wagon's comin' for that yow, it's died,' says Miles, pushing a toy lorry towards an upturned toy sheep. 'I don't knaw what ailed 'er.'

'Scannin' man's comin',' says Raven. 'This un's 'avin' three,' as she puts a tiny felt-tip-pen mark on the toy yow's back.

Then the gelding and dehorning of the toy cows is done with the hot fire poker.

They grow up understanding the facts of life, because they see animals reproducing all around them. The other day Edith came in shouting that the stallion had grown an extra leg. I just said, 'No, that means he wants to get into the field with the mares. And we don't want him to do that or they'd be having baby horses.'

'I'd like a baby horse.'

'Well, Josie's 'avin' one, isn't she? What do we call a baby horse?'

'A foal.'

They see new life, and they also see death. Edith very much wanted two pigs and so for Christmas we got her the two Tamworths, Dandelion and Burdock. We were all fond of them, but when Easter came she accompanied me and the pigs to the abattoir, accepting that we got them back as chops and sausages. If we're having a leg of pork from the freezer there will be a big discussion about whether it's from Dandelion or Burdock. When we had Gloucester Old Spots it was obvious which of them was on your plate as you could still see the coloured patches on the larger joints of meat. People may be horrified to think that we could look after, nurture and rear a lamb, calf or pig and then eat it, but I honestly don't see it like that. If you are a meat eater then you should take great pride and be wholly confident that the animal you are about to eat led a healthy and happy life. What better way to be sure than to have looked after it yourself?

They've got a good work ethic, our children. I think Clive and I between us have taught them that you don't get owt for nowt, you have to put the effort in if you want something. When they grow up they may move away from here completely, or they may want to stay. I just try to make sure they can all turn their hands to whatever job needs doing – the boys will bake and Raven will drive the tractor. If nothing else, Ravenseat teaches you to become more self-sufficient and able to deal with whatever situation life throws at you. Nothing must faze you. It's not just about physical strength, it's about mental strength and a willingness to have a go at anything, whether that be plumbing or building or maybe struggling with the forces of nature and trying to save the life of an animal. What could be more exciting and exhilarating for a child?

A walker passing through Ravenseat once said, 'You can't keep these children cooped up here, this isn't the real world.'

I was indignant, because this is a very real world – maybe not the same as everybody else's, but just as real. I get my fair share of people who feel they can tell me what I should be doing for my children, and it bothered me for a while. But now I think they are having a good childhood, it's just different. My great hope is that they will look back on their childhood as a happy time. It's just a different, more old-fashioned way to raise children.

Raven's taxi arrives at 7.10 a.m. to get her to the school in Richmond. It can be particularly tough during the winter when she leaves for school in the dark and returns in the dark. Raven actually had a place at a state boarding school in Keswick, as a weekly boarder. We took her to look round, she had an interview with the headmaster, and she was offered a place. At first she wanted to go, but I let her have two weeks to think about it, and during this time she changed her mind.

'I'd really miss mi 'orse,' she said. No mention of her nearest and dearest...

I would have missed her terribly if she'd have gone, but she does now have to cope with a ten-hour day, from leaving home to getting back at 5.10 p.m. If she ever complains about me digging her out of bed at six o'clock on a cold winter's morning I remind her that she could have stayed in bed until 8 a.m. at boarding school.

Reuben, Miles and Edith leave an hour later. Reuben splits his time between both Reeth and Gunnerside schools. Miles and Edith are at Gunnerside and each is taught in a classroom on their own as there are no other children of their age group at that school. There was talk at one stage of sending all the children to Reeth but this didn't make sense to me, nearly two hours of

344

travelling every day for the little ones and driving right past a school. No way. I threatened to home school them, and a lady from the County Council education service came from Northallerton to see me. She was supposed to be here mid morning but it was after midday when she arrived.

'Sorry I'm late, I can't believe what that road's like,' she said.

'Exactly,' I said. 'Now do you understand the problem?'

So she went away and sorted it.

One of our biggest nightmares is when they have to do things after school, or even sometimes when they are asked to arrive early to go to a swimming lesson in Richmond. It's a logistical nightmare, impossible to co-ordinate. It certainly acts as a deterrent for the children when it comes to after-school detentions, just the thought of how unhappy we'd be having to drive nearly sixty miles to rescue someone who wasn't on the school bus. We had a letter the other year saying that 'due to climate change we are encouraging the children not to send Christmas cards this year'. I wanted to write back and say:

'Don't you think that owing to climate change it would be sensible to make sure they all finish school at the same time? That would save a lot of unnecessary driving around, which must be more damaging to the planet than Christmas cards.'

I can see many more battles ahead as the younger children start their schooling.

14

Annas Makes Seven

The kitchen table was laden with food, there were people everywhere. Some had brought their own deckchairs and picnics, some were dressed in their Sunday best and others had turned up in overalls and wellies. Random walkers were passing through – and stayed. There were people from as far away as South Africa whose names I don't know and who I will probably never see again, but for just a short while we all gathered together in celebration.

The occasion was a mass christening for the children. I had asked Caroline, our local vicar, if it was possible to have the children christened in an informal way, perhaps in Whitsundale Beck at Ravenseat, and she'd agreed.

It was the summer of 2012, and for no particular reason we felt it was the right time, and the right thing to do. I made it an open invitation, Caroline put a notice in the parish magazine, and I put the word out down the dale that there was to be a relaxed, informal do at the farm. I spent a couple of days preparing food, baking a ham, making pastries and biscuits and, of course, baking a christening cake of epic proportions. I wasn't the only person slaving over a hot oven though: many people had baked and cooked and brought their home-made creations with them, so there was a magnificent spread.

We pictured the sun shining and everyone sitting in the grass on the riverbank while the children waded into the river, but, of course, it rained, so all thoughts of al fresco dining evaporated and we decamped to the house. The ceremony was performed in the ford, upstream from the packhorse bridge. Caroline donned her cassock and wellies and one by one the children were doused in the beck water. The smaller ones were quite reluctant to participate in proceedings and Clive had a firm grip on Miles, who had half a notion to do a runner when Caroline loomed large with a jug full of icy-cold, peat-stained river-water.

We specifically asked that there should be no christening presents for the children. We don't believe in presents for their own sake: not because I'm particularly miserly but I believe that a well-thought-out gift at the right time is much more sensible. Of course, at Christmas the children get presents, but not enormous amounts. We try to think of exactly what they want, a practical present, whether it be a couple of pigs for Edith, a bicycle for Reuben or a saddle for Raven. They have a little gift in their stockings to open when they wake up, but for us Christmas Day is like any other: the animals need feeding before anything else. Present opening might not start until lunchtime.

The one thing the children enjoy more than anything is the dash at midnight on Christmas

Eve across to the stables to see whether the horses are bowing down in reverence to He who was born in a stable. I admit that one year I put the children to bed and then altered the clock, bringing it forward to get them up to look. So far we have only managed to catch Meg and Little Joe kneeling (and that was probably because they are slow at getting to their feet, as they are getting on and a little arthritic).

I always make a cake for the children's birthdays, although perhaps not on exactly the right day. When they are too young to know the dates of their birthdays, we may postpone the special day until we've finished lambing, clipping or whatever is happening. They don't know the difference, they still feel special for a day. Again, they get presents but sometimes these are amalgamated into one big shared present, say a go-kart or even a pony. Raven is old enough to know her own birthday, of course, and it falls right in the middle of lambing time, which is a nightmare. My good friend Rachel always brings birthday presents for the children – she remembers their birthdays better than I do. I say to her, 'Quick, let me 'ide it. We're not doin' the birthday till next week, when things will be calmer.'

It's not a question of getting our priorities wrong, it simply means that a nicer day is had if we are not so madly busy.

As for Clive, the best present I've ever got him was a cattle crush. It may not sound so exciting, but it was a present that was long overdue as the old cattle crush was not in good shape. A crush is a metal contraption that the cow walks into, then you trap its head, a gate closes behind it and it's held in position while you give it an injection, a wormer dose or put an ear tag in, in other words whatever you need to do to it that it would probably not let you do if it wasn't restrained.

We had the world's worst crush, it had probably been used to restrain prehistoric oxen. Honestly, it was an antique. There was no solid floor in it, the cow would run into it and stand quiet for a moment and then run off, wearing the crush like some sort of medieval instrument of torture. Watching a demented cow running around a farmyard trying to shake off a crush would be funny if you weren't the one who had to catch and calm the animal. So coming up to Christmas a few years ago I went online and bought Clive a state-of-the-art cattle crush. It's wonderful: the cow walks in and traps its own head, and you can keep well out of the way. It means that handling the younger, wilder cattle is much safer for us, and them.

Clive's also had a quad-bike trailer and a space heater for presents: a bit tricky wrapping them up, but if it's the thought that counts I was certainly thinking about what would make his (and my) life easier and better.

He's just the same, he buys me practical presents like a wheelbarrow. One year I got a foal. Now he reckons he's cracked the whole present thing: he bought me a vintage charm bracelet, and every birthday or Christmas he just has to buy another charm.

For some inexplicable reason, our neighbours

and friends thought the christening was symbolic: they believed it meant that our family at Ravenseat was complete and that Sidney was the last of the line. We never actually said that, nor did we think it. But it was generally assumed that my child-bearing had reached an end.

They were wrong, because within a couple of months of the christening, number seven was on the way.

In the meantime, there was the usual round of problems to deal with, the worst being a real scare over Violet. I'd noticed that she was off colour, a bit poorly, but thought she was maybe just starting with a cold. It was Mother's Day 2013, a beautiful, cold, bright day, and snow was falling softly. Violet stayed very quiet by my side all day and had a nap on the sofa mid afternoon while the others went out to build snowmen. Sadly, Clive's mother had died a few days earlier, and I was busy baking a very big fruit cake for her funeral so I was in the kitchen for much of the day.

It wasn't until about 7 p.m., as Clive was getting Violet ready for bed, that he saw her feet had swollen to almost twice their normal size and were purple, and she had a dark purple rash all over her lower body. He was horrified and shouted for me to come and take a look. I took her temperature and she had a fever. Nothing was said, but we both thought the same thing: it looked like meningitis.

We both panicked, and I rang the out-of-hours doctor service immediately. The doctor went through a set of questions with me, including asking me whether the rash disappeared when I rolled a glass over it. It didn't. This is the classic test for meningitis, and a bad sign.

I was told an ambulance and paramedic were on the way. I told the ambulance service that they wouldn't get up our road in the snow, and we had the usual argument about it, them asking for a postcode and me telling them that although the road wasn't blocked with snow it wasn't passable without a four-wheel drive. Finally they agreed I should meet the ambulance at Keld.

Clive was trying hard not to let the other children see how worried he was, but there was no fooling them: some were crying, while Sidney just looked confused. I wrapped Violet in a duvet and laid her across the front bench seat of the Land Rover, grabbed some money and a phone, and set off as fast as I dared. Our timings were perfect: as I reached Keld, the ambulance rounded the corner. I carried Vi across the road and laid her on the stretcher.

While they made her comfortable, the paramedic gave her a strong dose of antibiotics. It was now a full-scale emergency, and they decided that as a police helicopter was already in the area they would airlift her to James Cooke Hospital in Middlesbrough.

'Where's the nearest flat field with no power lines?' one of them asked.

'Thwaite,' I said, knowing that the air ambulance had recently landed there.

'You know you won't be able to come on the helicopter, don't you?'

Because I was clearly pregnant it was against

the rules for me to be taken with her on the heli-copter, something about air pressure making it dangerous. I wasn't happy, but I wasn't going to kick up a fuss if it meant getting Violet the urgent treatment that she needed.

We set off for Thwaite, downhill for a couple of miles, and then we stopped, the lights of a heli-copter hovering above. The crew were on their radios talking to the pilot. It was clear the weather was causing problems. The powdery snow on the ground was being picked up in a vortex, whirling around and hampering his vision. This, coupled with the total blackness, meant that landing was impossible, it was just too dangerous. Instead we were going to the Friarage at Northallerton by road. Violet was restless and tried to pull at the drip line in the back of her hand while I was being very sick in the back of the ambulance. I'm not normally travel sick but the speed we were travel-ling meant that the vehicle was swaying from side to side. When we finally pulled up at A & E we were told there was no paediatric cover, so the ambulance had to carry on to Middlesbrough.

It was 11 p.m. when we finally reached the hospital. More antibiotics were given and blood samples were taken. The general consensus was that it wasn't meningitis, she wasn't really ill enough. But they had to err on the side of caution until they were sure. The medics suspected it was HSP (Henloch-Schonlein Purpura), a rare chil-dren's illness, which starts with similar symptoms to meningitis but is not usually as serious. It causes vasculitis, the inflammation of blood vessels, which is what results in the purple rash.

It's most common in children, but occasionally occurs in adults and it can, in some cases, cause serious joint inflammation and damage to kidneys. Violet was lucky not to have it this badly.

The following morning we were given the news that Violet did indeed have HSP, and I needed to keep a close eye on her and check her urine regularly to make sure she hadn't got kidney damage, but there was no need to stay in hospital. I rang Clive to tell him the good news and set off on the epic journey home. Clive set about finding a babysitter and agreed to meet me at Richmond.

It was snowing in Middlesbrough, and we didn't have coats, so I wrapped Violet in the Postman Pat duvet and carried her in my arms as by now she only had one shoe: she must have lost the other en route to the hospital. We caught a bus to the centre of Middlesbrough, then another bus to Northallerton, and then another one to Richmond, where we sat on the steps under the clock in the town square. Any passers-by would have thought we were down on our luck: a pregnant woman with a one-shoed child wrapped in a duvet. I'm surprised people weren't throwing me their change. Luckily, we didn't have long to wait before Clive showed up.

I cannot express the elation I felt as we drove back over our cattle grid and looked down on to Ravenseat. The sun was setting, the snow so white and perfect and undisturbed: Ravenseat was as I had left it nearly twenty-four hours before. It seemed like nothing had happened. Violet was going to be fine, and in that single moment I felt so fortunate to live in such a timeless and beautiful place.

The feeling of calm and reflection didn't last long. After getting everyone settled down and the little ones to bed, I went into the kitchen to inspect the fruit cake that I had left cooling on a rack the previous day. I lifted the foil off tentatively, and underneath was my perfectly risen super-size cake. I guessed that as it looked so good it would taste pretty fine, so I was feeling pleased with myself. But as I turned the cake round I realized that it must taste incredibly good, because someone had found it irresistible. Not only had they tried it, but they had eaten a substantial lump, and then tried to cover their tracks by putting the crusty top bit back. Nobody knew who the culprit was, nobody owned up. I was faced with a dilemma: start again or try to rescue it. I didn't fancy the first option, it was a miracle that I'd managed to bake the darn thing in the first place. I decided that copious icing was the answer, so I trowelled it on and finished it off by sticking a large flower on the top. Clive went off to the funeral with strict instructions about where to cut into it, and no one was any the wiser.

Violet recovered well, and there have been no after-effects, thankfully. So many of my children have had to go to hospital for one thing or another, but I guess that's just family life. When Raven was eight she had to spend a week in the Friarage with psoriasis, having special emollient baths and dressings. I went every other day to spend time with her, and when she was discharged I had to take her back twice a week for light treatment. The treatment took one and a half minutes under a high-powered UV light, and the drive each way was two hours. She was treated for three months, and her skin cleared up beautifully, so it was worth it. She hasn't had it since.

Sometimes, no matter how hard I try to be well organized, I still make mistakes, and I did so one evening when I had an appointment at the doctor's surgery over at Hawes. I set off and was about a mile from home when I casually glanced at the fuel gauge on the Land Rover: it was hovering at just above empty. Most of the gauges on the dashboard gave up the ghost years ago, so I never really pay attention to them. I'm quite used to not knowing how far I've been or how fast I'm going. After all, you're never going to break the speed limit in a Land Rover.

Never mind, I thought. *There's a garage at Hawes, I'll get diesel there.*

I was running late and wanted to avoid the wrath of the doctor, so went to the surgery before the garage. Then, when I went to fill up, I discovered the garage had closed early. That happens round here: on dark, cold winter afternoons, if there's no trade, businesses shut up shop early.

Cursing, I set off back, out of Hawes, and was climbing uphill onto Stags Fell when the fuel warning light came on. I wasn't sure that I was going to be able to travel the thirteen miles or so back to Ravenseat, and I didn't relish the thought of walking. Then I cast my mind back to my contract shepherding days, when I was often short of cash and to save fuel I would freewheel

355

from the top of Orton Scar down into Crosby Ravensworth. All I needed to do was round the corner at the top of Banty Hill and then it was all downhill into Thwaite – that would get me a bit closer to home. I knocked the Land Rover out of gear and flicked the ignition off. The engine died, the instrument panel dimmed, as did the road in front of me as the headlights went off. I was still OK: I could pick out the road with the sidelights. I was halfway down the hill, at a point where the gradient becomes a lot steeper, when I put my foot on the brake. Nothing, not a flicker. I didn't have long before a very tight bend at the bottom so I made a grab for the ignition to get the engine back on. It refused to fire up. I pulled at the wheel to get myself better lined up to take the corner but it was nearly impossible to steer. I was panicking, thinking I was staring death in the face, careering downhill at speed with no brakes and dodgy steering, thinking about the wall and then the drop at the side of the road, thinking about my unborn baby, thinking about Clive, and all the children, really convinced that it was curtains.

My brain was racing to think of ways I could safely stop the runaway Land Rover. What would happen if I pulled the handbrake on, would the wheels lock up? It was just before the bottom corner that the engine fired and I got the Land Rover round the bend, albeit faster than usual. I can't put my relief into words. I crawled home after that, not my usual confident self. As for the diesel: I probably had enough anyway, as the gauge on the Land Rover is very crude. But it would have been better, by far, to have been stranded with an empty tank than to have risked that awful, death-defying drive. That's one thing I will never do again.

Annas was born a couple of weeks early, on 3 July 2013. I'd gone after tea to collect our stray sheep. Our neighbour Raymond had been gathering the moor, and he'd left the strays in the pens at Beck Meetings. By going later it meant that the other farmers had been and collected their strays, and ours were the only ones left, so I simply had to back the trailer up, open the door and shoo them in.

I brought them back and put them in the garth, and Clive and I decided we'd clip them the next day. We hadn't really made a start on clipping, as the weather had been awful, and the sheep are better with their wool on in bad conditions. I got the children into bed, and then went to bed myself about 10 p.m., but I couldn't settle. I felt quite restless, I tossed and turned and then got up. Everything was deathly quiet, everyone apart from me was fast asleep. I was looking for a sign that labour was about to start, but there was none. I got back into bed, my hands on my belly, trying to feel the baby.

Is the baby moving? I wondered. I remembered from having Sidney that when they go quiet it can mean they are ready to come. Then, just after midnight, I woke Clive.

'I think it's time to go,' I said.

'Right, I'll mek tea, thoo ring for t'ambulance,' he said.

He was very calm, he's used to it by now. On the

phone I had to answer the usual questions about how far apart my contractions were coming:

'I'm not actually having contractions.'

'Well, you're not in labour until contractions start.'

'Trust me on this one.' Then I asked, 'What'd 'appen if I just stayed 'ere and had t'baby? I's likely gonna 'ave it afore I get to t'hospital anyways.'

Clive was nodding, bless him. He's always been quite happy to wave me off in an ambulance, but he was quite prepared for me to stay home. After all, it would save him a trip to pick me up...

'No, the ambulance will come for you. We can't send a midwife, you've got to come to hospital,' she said. 'Now stay on the line.'

I can't talk for forty minutes to someone I know, let alone to someone I haven't a clue about. I handed the phone to Clive and went to get myself ready.

'Don't let your wife out of your sight, make sure she's lying down and you have lots of clean towels,' the woman said.

'She's gone to put some washing on and she's searching for her lipstick,' Clive said.

The ambulance control woman asked him if he was worried about me having the baby before they got to me.

'Nope, I's a farmer,' he said. I was proud of him.

Meanwhile, the children slept soundly through, unawares. All that fresh air means that they sleep very deeply.

It was the local ambulance that arrived forty minutes later, and I was escorted to my seat by

Steve again, who had been with me for Reuben and Edith. His heart must have sunk when he heard the address he was heading for.

'What's your baby count so far, how many have you delivered?' I asked.

'Five, but two were born before I got there,' he said. So one of those was Reuben, and one of those he delivered was Edith. He was expecting the worst.

'We're not gonna get there, are we?' he said.

'Nay, I don't think so.'

We headed off into the dark and the mist. It was a new ambulance driver, who was a bit unsure of our road. I could tell where we were each time we hit a cattle grid, but by the second one, just past our road end, I said to Steve, 'I think I need to lie down.'

He told the driver to slow down. We got as far as Keld, about three miles from home, and then had to make an emergency stop, as the baby was coming. In the dark I had no idea where we were, but we had actually pulled up outside Hope House, my friend Elenor's house. The next day when I spoke to her she said, 'Fancy, being woken up in the early hours by the blue lights of an ambulance outside my window.'

So when this baby is bigger, I won't have far to take her to show her the spot where she was born. I've taken both Edith and Sidney back to see the lay-bys where they came into this world. I suspect that plenty of babies are made in lay-bys, but not many actually arrive in them. When I visit the registrar to register the children's births I have to take a road atlas so that the correct road

359

number can be put on the birth certificate.

Annas was an easy birth. There were no contractions, my waters broke and seconds later there was a baby, a little girl. As usual, I had no idea until the birth whether it would be a boy or a girl. There was no nursery to paint in either blue or pink, no new clothes required, other than a packet of nappies. I had everything I needed: girl or boy, it just didn't matter.

The journey wasn't the most comfortable and I was glad when we arrived at the hospital, me now with a seven-pound baby girl and a serious crick in my neck from lying in such an awkward position, once again trying not to drop the baby or roll off the bed. I suppose that in the scheme of things I don't come off too badly if the only after-effect of giving birth is a cricked neck.

They wheeled me up to the labour ward and the midwife greeted me: 'You again.'

It was the same midwife who had delivered Violet, which was good because I felt vindicated: she knew I was telling the truth about the rapid delivery, not just being blasé about it. I stayed at the Friarage for the compulsory six hours and by this time Clive had recruited my friend Rachel to look after the other children. I do wish they would let me stay at home, it would make so much more sense and save everyone a lot of trouble.

Of course, the question I am always asked is: 'Will there be any more?' I'm not ruling it out and I'm not ruling it in. I was only thirty-eight when Annas was born and I don't feel so long in the tooth yet. When people ask I just say, 'Farmers, they don't like running things geld,' or

'There's ten seats in t'Land Rover,' or 'Bloody bad TV reception.'

Clive says, 'I only 'ave to pass 'er on't stairs an' she's in t'family way.'

People sometimes suggest that having so many children limits what we can do in life. They point out that we can't go to the pub or on holiday, but we are genuinely not bothered about doing these things anyway. We get such pleasure out of the children and take a pride in bringing them up in a free and natural way. We believe that you can do anything if you want it enough.

We chose the name Annas because it's a very traditional name that is unusual nowadays. Annas was one of the five Whitehead children (a sister to Jennie) who were born at the other farmhouse, just behind ours, so there is a link with Ravenseat. We've given her the middle name Patricia, after Clive's mother.

It was the early hours of a Wednesday morning when she was born, and we were anxious to start clipping. I took the Thursday and Friday off as maternity leave, and on the Saturday I clipped the stray sheep. I reasoned that the post-natal exercise sheet that I was given with recommendations for exercises for new mothers showed pretty similar moves to those I make clipping sheep: stretching and bending, with some fancy footwork for good measure.

Clive was marking the sheep up after their fleeces were off, because they lose their flock mark with their woolly coats. He was also dosing them and mothering them up again, matching the right yow with the right lamb, which is trickier than it sounds because the yows lose some of their familiar smell when their fleeces come off. The New Zealand shearing gangs I worked with when I was contract shepherding used to ridicule the farmers helping the yows to find their lambs: 'Aww, mate, if it don't know its bloody lamb by now...'

But they do need a bit of time to get themselves mothered back up. It's a real waste if a yow goes back to the moor without her lamb, because although it will live, it will not thrive without its mother's milk. All our sheep are precious, every one of them counts, and that's part of the reason why we prefer to clip our own sheep rather than bring in a shearing gang. Having hold of every single yow means that we get a chance for a full inspection, checking if she's healthy and if we like her. It's no good clipping a yow and then turning her away with a lame foot. It's also a good opportunity for Clive to spot any with show potential. Plus, of course, we don't get a huge clipping bill (it's cheaper if the wife does it) and you can clip them in smaller lots which, in itself, prevents mis-mothering.

I couldn't wait to start clipping the sheep, it's one of my favourite times of the year. I like to wear shearing jeans that protect my legs from the sheeps' horns, but three days after giving birth, they wouldn't fasten up. I used the farmer's friend, baler twine, to keep them up, and each day I clipped I could fasten up another button. It really is a brilliant workout.

The children love helping out by rolling the fleeces and squashing them down into the large wool sheets. They bounce and jump up and down to get them compacted, and in the process they become very dirty and greasy. The lanolin in the wool is so good for the skin that by the time we have finished with our sheep, our hands and feet are super soft. The bigger children sew up the sheets with a packing needle using blanket stitch, the sheets are then stacked and used as trampolines, picnic tables or a cosy nest for a small baby. It takes us a fortnight to gather up all of our sheep and clip them, and on the last gather recently we came across a yow that had lambed that day. Reuben carried the newborn lamb home, while its anxious mother followed on behind. We sometimes get a few late-born lambs on the moor; their mothers were marked as geld, with a red stripe put over their rump, because at scanning time they were in the very earliest stage of pregnancy, which didn't show up on the scanning man's ultrasound. Their lambs are known as 'white lambs', not because they are white but because they are unmarked. A bit of detective work is sometimes needed to find their mothers.

And when finally the supposedly last sheep is clipped (we still have the odd woolled yow turning up for weeks afterwards) I bake a shearing cake, a traditional celebratory spiced cake heralding the end of another important time in the farming diary, another annual ritual that we have observed. The rhythm of farming life is the rhythm we live by, and we are probably far more aware of the turn of the seasons than most.

I don't want to look too far into the future. I enjoy what we have, here and now. I think the children will find it very hard to move away from this place. Like me, and the sheep, they are hefted to Ravenseat. Of course, I will encourage all of them in any future plans they may make, and if that involves them moving away, that's how it will be.

As for Ravenseat, standing still and peaceful, four-square to the wind, it remains as isolated as ever, a timeless place, unchanged in centuries, a testament to those who have gone before us, its wildness and austere appearance such a contrast to my measured, suburban formative years. We never forget, me and Clive, how lucky we are to be custodians of this unique and special place.

I could never have imagined that I, the town girl who was engrossed by the James Herriot television series, who was transfixed by the evocative photographs in *Hill Shepherd,* would one day live and work in the very places in which those images were captured. My dream to become a hill shepherd was realized the day that fate brought me to Ravenseat.

Acknowledgements

With thanks to Ingrid Connell, Jean Ritchie, Ben Mason, Jo Cantello, Mark Robinson, Simon Paintin, Ernest and Doreen Whitehead, Rachel Hall, Elenor Alderson, Jenny Harker, Steven Raine and Colin Martin.

The publishers hope that this book has given you enjoyable reading. Large Print Books are especially designed to be as easy to see and hold as possible. If you wish a complete list of our books please ask at your local library or write directly to:

Magna Large Print Books
Magna House, Long Preston,
Skipton, North Yorkshire.
BD23 4ND

This Large Print Book for the partially sighted, who cannot read normal print, is published under the auspices of

THE ULVERSCROFT FOUNDATION

THE ULVERSCROFT FOUNDATION

... we hope that you have enjoyed this Large Print Book. Please think for a moment about those people who have worse eyesight problems than you ... and are unable to even read or enjoy Large Print, without great difficulty.

You can help them by sending a donation, large or small to:

**The Ulverscroft Foundation,
1, The Green, Bradgate Road,
Anstey, Leicestershire, LE7 7FU,
England.**
or request a copy of our brochure for more details.

The Foundation will use all your help to assist those people who are handicapped by various sight problems and need special attention.

Thank you very much for your help.